BISHOP GEORGE

Man of Two Worlds

To Donald,
with whom I shared the experience
of Papua New Guinea.

BISHOP GEORGE

Man of Two Worlds

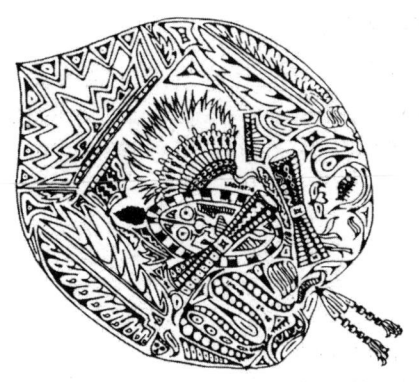

by
Elin Johnston

First published 2003

National Library of Australia Cataloguing-in-Publication data

Johnston, Elin.
  Bishop George : man of two worlds.

  Bibliography.
  Includes index.
  ISBN 0 9581202 3 4.

  1. Ambo, George, 1922- . 2. Anglican Church of Papua New Guinea - Bishops - Biography. 3. Anglican Church of Papua New Guinea - History. 4. Missions - Papua New Guinea - History. I. Title.

  283.953

Design, typesetting and publication by
Robjon Partners, 22 Lockwood Street, Point Lonsdale, Victoria 3225

Printed in Melbourne by Currency Communications Australia Pty Ltd

Also by Elin Johnston
  Dodoima – Tales of Oro (ISBN 0 646 25304 2),
  published and distributed by the author, 1995

Bishop George Man of Two Worlds is distributed by the author,
  Elin Johnston,
  PO Box 114,
  Point Lonsdale, Victoria, Australia 3225.
  Telephone: +61-3-5258-2139, +61-3-9690-0549
  Fax: +61-3-5258-3994   E-mail: dnejohnston@a1.com.au

Contents

Foreword

It was Bishop Philip Strong 'of New Guinea' who had the clear inspiration from God to nominate George Ambo in 1960 to be an assisting bishop — the first national-born bishop in Papua New Guinea.

It was Bishop Strong who, 10 years before, had nominated myself to be the first-ever assisting bishop.

In this welcome biography of 'Bishop George', Elin Johnston — than whom no biographer has ever researched more thoroughly — describes the Philip/George relationship as one of father to son. She adds, George's relationship with me was, rather, brother to brother. And so George himself and I have — I think — always seen it. And so, in my own book *Modawa* — at present vying with Elin's to win the race to publication! — I have seen and described it.

I have been happy to have the opportunity — in *Modawa* and in having been invited to write this Foreword — to give testimony to what this spiritually-powerful and yet deeply-humble man has meant, not only to myself but to the Church and Nation of Papua New Guinea and the Church at large.

It requires of a Papua New Guinean a high degree of commitment to Christ to defy some of the demands of the 'wantok system'. There were, I fear, among George's fellow Papua New Guinea priests some who — because he was not a traditional 'wantok' — at first refused to acknowledge him as a bishop (though his own humility duly won his way). But he had already faced and solved this problem when he forbade some Gona wantoks at Dogura who were planning to bring to the wharf for his formal arrival as bishop, a traditional gift of pigs, etc. which would identify him with them and exclude him from others. He broke custom by forbidding the gifts.

Furthermore, George has presented to his people, always and everywhere, total absence of the fear which characterises Papua New Guinea traditional beliefs in the power of sorcery and evil. If anybody ever gave full and literal obedience to our Lord's Command 'Fear not', it is George.

An Australian priest who was George's Archdeacon at Popondota told me of an occasion when he and several thousand people gathered outside the Provincial Court House on the occasion of a trial for serious crime. Everybody seemed to be at everyone else's throat, and the noise was deafening. Into the crowd strode Bishop George with such majestic mien and certainty of purpose that the whole mob was reduced to silence; and in the silence the voice of God's authority spoke so firmly and convincingly that no more talk, let alone argument, was required. The Australian said to me that he had never more convincingly felt that shiver down the spine that greatness, of whatever kind, produces in us. It might have been, once again, our Lord and the woman taken in adultery.

We have had, amongst us, an inspired prophet, a great priest, a spiritual titan. And so we thank God for such privilege and blessing, and we thank Elin for favouring us with the story.

Read it, and inwardly digest it.

+David Hand,

Bishop David Hand, KBE, MA, ThD
First Archbishop of the Anglican Church of Papua New Guinea

Acknowledgments

This book could not have been written without the contribution of many people. Their voices speak through interviews, so generously granted, creating a vivid picture of the life and background of a remarkable person. As well, I have been lent much material for research. I am deeply indebted to so many people for so many things, and want to express my heartfelt thanks to all.

First of all, I must thank Bishop George himself. With firm handwriting on countless foolscap pages, he has written most openly of his life. Gaps have been filled by the numerous interviews which I recorded with him at Popondetta. These sources form the framework for my biography.

Also I thank Ms Helen Ambo for her willingness to pass messages between her father and myself. She, and her brother, Mr Oliver Ambo, have supplied much information for which I am grateful.

In 1998 Bishop Denys Ririka provided accommodation for me and my husband Donald at Newton Theological College, enabling me to record many interviews. He gave me helpful information about traditional customs and village life. I greatly appreciate the assistance given to us by him, his wife, Leslie, and our former 'Old Boys' from Martyrs' School studying Theology at Newton College.

I an indebted to Bishop Roger Jupp who, in 2002, as Principal of Newton Theological College, gave Bishop George and us accommodation at the College when I was recording the last interviews. I am thankful for his support in many other ways.

Throughout the writing of this book, Dr David Wetherell has made constructive comments on all my drafts and lent me much useful material for research. His interest and encouragement gave me great confidence. I give him my warmest thanks.

Bishop David Hand kindly agreed to the request of Bishop George that he write the Foreword for this book. Furthermore, he allowed me to use his material concerning Bishop George from *Modawa*, Bishop David's autobiography. He has given interviews and answered numerous questions. I thank him.

I am indebted to Mr Stephen Tago, former Minister for Defence, the Rev'd Lancelot Sangitari and Mr Arthur Jawodimbari, author and former Secretary of the Department of Oro Province, for helpful interviews.

Dr Blanche Biggs generously made available for me the personal correspondence between her and Canon Oliver Brady, Bishop George's mentor. As well, I thank her for the loan of diary notes, articles and photograph.

Bishop Oliver Heyward gave me much information about his uncle, Canon Oliver Brady, and entrusted me with the Brady-Biggs letters, placed in his guardianship by Dr Biggs. I greatly appreciate his help.

I am grateful to Mrs Patricia Hyde, daughter of the late Mrs Mavis Burke (née Eather), Bishop George's first white teacher. She kindly lent me her mother's collection of diaries, letters and papers from her time at Gona Mission.

The Rev'd Richard Bowie provided much material relating to the origins of the clans in the Buna area and the life of Fr James Benson. My thanks to him and to Mr Howard Benson, nephew of Fr James Benson, for the loan of letters and photographs.

I owe gratitude to Mrs Ray Kendall who generously allowed me to use the *Personal Memoirs* and slides of her late husband, Bishop Henry Kendall.

The late Canon David Durie lent me his collection of *Komboro*, the magazine of St Aidan's Teacher Training College. I am grateful for his help and the insight I gained into the life of the College.

Miss Elsie Manley provided extracts from Bishop Philip Strong's diaries and willingly answered many questions. I thank her.

I am grateful to Sr Jean Henderson, the Rev'd Charles Helms, the late Fr Graham Stout, Mr Martin Gardham and his wife Aileen, for interviews and other help.

Archdeacon Martin Chittleborough and his wife, Anne, have entrusted me with much valuable material dating from their time at Agenehambo. I thank them warmly, also for their hospitality and interviews.

The Rev'd John Wardman generously provided slides and photos of the Gona Mission as well as much useful information. My thanks for his generosity.

I think gratefully of the late Miss Nancy White who gave me a copy of her complete manuscript, which was later published in abbreviated form as *Sharing the Climb*. It was useful for my research. I also acknowledge her gift of letters and photos.

My thanks also to Bishop Bevan Meredith and the Rev'd Tom Williams for interviews and other assistance.

Many other ex-missionaries, both in the UK and in Australia, have contributed to this book in various ways. I am especially indebted to Canon Edward Kelly and his wife, Ruth; the Rev'd Douglas Jones and Mrs Caroline Jones; Canon Peter Robin; Mrs Chris Luxton, the General Secretary of the PNG Church Partnership; and the Rev'd Michael and Mrs Forrest. 'Thank you' to them all.

The decorative designs were drawn by students at Martyrs' School in the years 1986–1990. I am grateful to be able to enhance the value of my book by including these designs which so clearly witness to the artistic ability of many young Papuans.

The maps relevant to my story have been drawn and generously donated by Mr Ian Heyward, cartographer at the Australian National University, Canberra.

My thanks also to John Bedggood who, as editor, has worked meticulously and conscientiously with the layout of this book.

Finally, my warmest thanks to my husband, Donald, who untiringly has given me advice and encouragement. English is not my first language, so his support has been invaluable.

Elin Johnston

Introduction

To my great surprise, Bishop George Ambo asked me if I would write his biography. Though overawed, I felt honoured and happy to be trusted with such an important task.

My association with him stretches back a considerable time. We first met in the early 1970s, when I began visiting Papua with groups of Australian school students led by my husband. Later, in the 1980s, Bishop George specially requested that we come to work for the Church in Papua New Guinea, and so he was responsible for one of the most enriching experiences of my life.

It has always been a joy to be with him, when he called on us at meetings of the Board of Governors at Martyrs' School, of which he was the Chairman, or at his office in Popondetta when we sought his advice. To us, as to so many expatriates and Papua New Guineans, he has been a wise counsellor and a very special friend.

For the Anglican Church in Papua New Guinea he has been a remarkable leader. His breadth of personality is mirrored in his breadth of experience. A transitional man, his life stretches from the end of the Stone Age, through the Colonial Period and into the modern Technological Era. Spending his childhood in a traditional village, he absorbed the spiritual qualities of his people and grew up with their ancient customs. As a boy he heard the tribal stories from his grandfather, a warrior and a cannibal. He worked to buy a steel axe from the nearby mission to replace the stone tool which his father was using to hollow out a tree for his canoe.

As a Bishop he attended three Lambeth Conferences, a worldwide meeting held every tenth year in England for Anglican Bishops. As well he travelled to many other countries and was given an audience by the Pope. Later he entertained Queen Elizabeth II at Popondetta. Much he experienced was far removed from his village roots.

Although a product of the Christian Mission, he freed himself from his colonial upbringing, retaining his Papuan identity. Rather than accepting an imported Church, he brought joy to the worship with the beat of drums and traditional dancing, and so made it belong to his own people.

His story shows his courage and perseverance, especially in face of opposition. He is a man of deep spiritual strength and integrity, widely acknowledged by all who meet him. His words are by many taken for truth. With his sympathy for people and innate understanding of human nature, he has touched many a human heart. Yet, upon meeting Bishop George, it is not his greatness which is the most noticeable feature — what strikes one first is his warmth and humility.

It is a privilege to write his story.

Elin Johnston
Point Lonsdale 2002

Bishop George tells of his life in a taped interview at Oro Guest House, Popondetta
(Photograph by Elin Johnston)

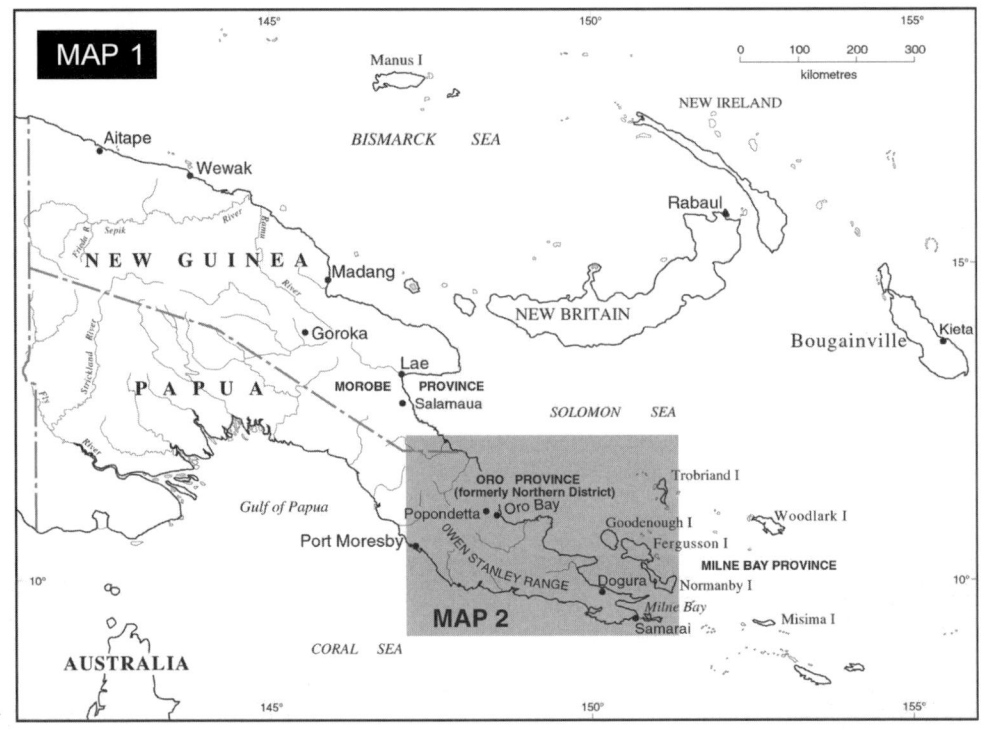

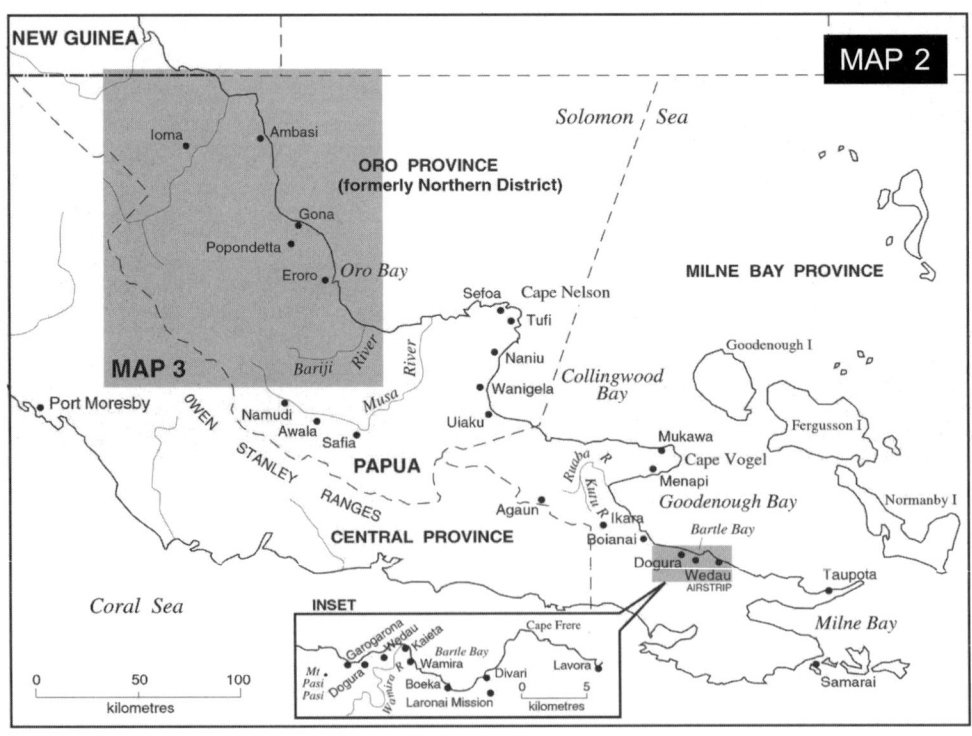

xii

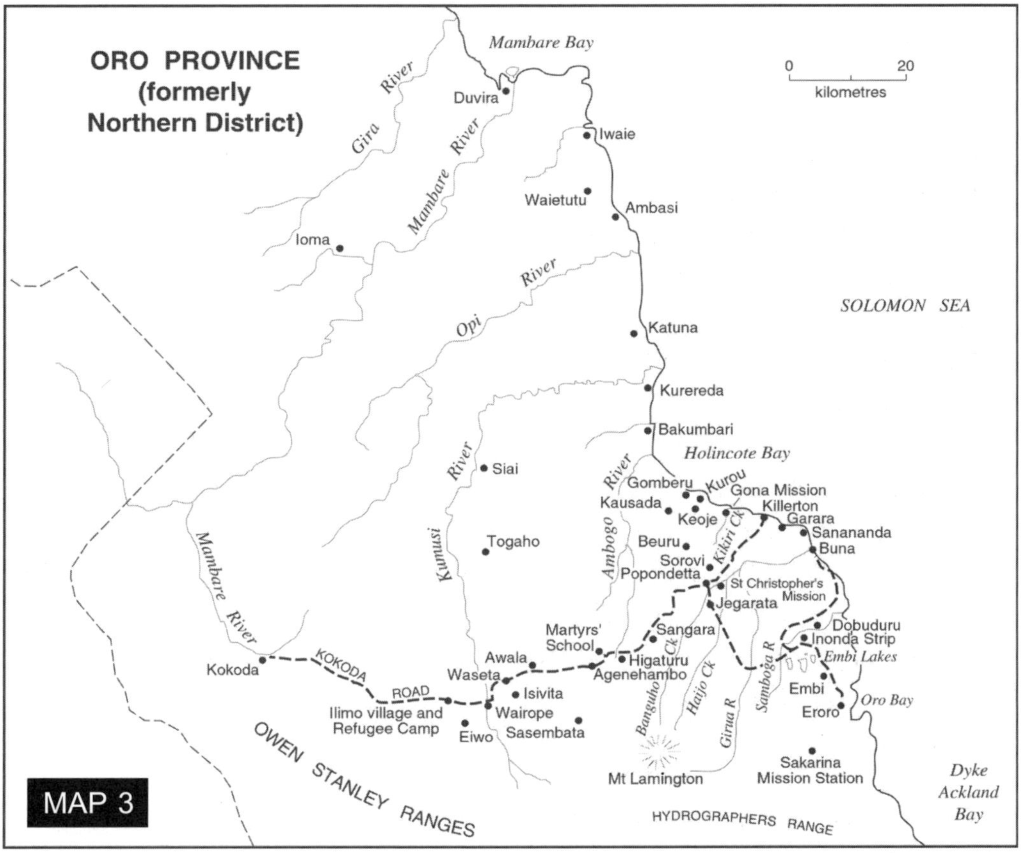

ORO PROVINCE (formerly Northern District)

Mambare Bay

0   20
kilometres

Gira River

Duvira

Mambare River

Iwaie

Waietutu

Ambasi

Ioma

Opi River

SOLOMON SEA

Katuna

Kurereda

Bakumbari

River

Siai

Holincote Bay

Ambogo River

Gomberu   Kurou

Kausada   Gona Mission
Keoje   Killerton
   Garara

Kumusi River

Togaho

Beuru   Sananananda
Sorovi   Buna
Popondetta

Kikiri Ck

St Christopher's Mission
Jegarata

Mambare River

Martyrs' School

Sangara

Dobuduru
Inonda Strip
Embi Lakes

Kokoda

KOKODA

Awala
Waseta   Higaturu
Agenehambo

Banguho Ck

Hajo Ck

Samboga R

Embi
Eroro

Oro Bay

ROAD

Ilimo village and
Refugee Camp

Isivita
Wairope
Eiwo   Sasembata

Girua R

Sakarina
Mission Station

*Dyke
Ackland
Bay*

Mt Lamington

OWEN STANLEY RANGES

HYDROGRAPHERS RANGE

MAP 3

Maps by Ian Heyward, cartographer at the
Australian National University, Canberra

Photographs

Photographs

Bishop George, first Papua New Guinean Bishop, with
Fr Peter Rautamara, first Papua New Guinean Priest, at
Dogura 1960.
(Photograph courtesy of Bishop David Hand)

CHAPTER 1

'Kikiri and Gatara' — An Ancient Myth

There was joyful celebration at the Mission Station at Gona on the north coast of Papua. With drums and dancing, the people were welcoming back their beloved priest, Fr James Benson. This was on Boxing Day, 1946, a year after peace had come to the land. Having miraculously survived the war in Japanese prisons, he had returned to his faithful flock. For weeks, villagers in the district had been practising their traditional dances in preparation for the great occasion. Day and night from secluded places in the jungle the beat of distant drumming had drifted through the air.[1]

Fr Benson wrote about this Boxing Day, that from early morning different groups of dancers had appeared simultaneously on the large playing field by Kikiri Creek. Moving in different rhythms to the beats of their drums, the colourful performers sang and danced the ancestral story of their clans. With faces brightly painted and bodies wrapped in bark-cloth, *tapa*, the dancers carried on their heads spectacular feathered headdresses, gently moving in time with the dance. As each group finished, another would appear on the field, taking its place — in and out, an endless stream of sound and movement.

A young teacher with the mission, together with his senior students, was to dance and mime the ancient story of 'Kikiri and Gatara'. The legend was well known by the local people. Long, long ago, Kikiri, the evil witch, had lured the young men of the Bapa, Yega and Jajora tribes to their deaths. Finally, she was killed by Gatara, the strong and faultless hero. Her evil spirit was believed to live on in the creek which flowed through the station and bore her name of Kikiri. Her tale, passed on by mouth from father to son through generations, has become part of the history of Gona.

The climax of the day arrived. All the groups withdrew from the large dancing-ground. A hush of silence lay over the crowds of spectators, excited in anticipation of the performance of 'Kikiri and Gatara'. All eyes were turned towards the mouth of Kikiri Creek. Low, threatening drumbeats were heard in the distance, as a dark shape emerged out of the tall *kunai* grass on the bank. Looking around carefully, the sinister figure came forward, hesitantly, hiding now and then behind bushes and clumps of grass.

Reaching the dance-ground, Kikiri, the witch, approaches a small hut. To the rhythm of drums, she fetches a broom from inside the house. While sweeping around the hut, she pauses and listens several times, her eyes peering into the distance where a group of weary warriors has appeared.

Only Gatara, the magnificent dancer and leader of the group, shows strength and vigour, as they approach. His headdress of glowing bird-of-paradise feathers tosses backwards and forwards, as the slim, strong figure gracefully advances. Beating his drum in perfect time, he leads the weary fighters past the witch's house.

But Kikiri draws them back towards her. Her evil powers make the men, one by one, break out of the ranks and collapse by the house. To the hushed murmur of drums, they fall into a deep sleep. Stooping down to the right then to the left, the witch plucks out the eyes of the sleeping men and puts them in her string bag.

Only Gatara has not succumbed to her spell. With force, shown by his vigorous dancing, he confronts the witch, overcomes and kills her. Taking her bag, he gracefully puts back the eyes into the sockets on the blind faces. His men arise. Together they rejoice in a wonderful dance of victory to the wild applause of the crowds.

'Such is the story of the triumph of good over evil; of light over darkness,' wrote Fr Benson, when he later described the dance, '...the age-long story of man; going back to the dawn of human consciousness...' This Gatara was the best portrayer of that story and the finest Gatara Fr Benson had ever seen.

This Gatara was George Ambo—the future Archbishop of Papua New Guinea.

Traditional dancer of the Ewa-ge people. With face painted and body wrapped in *tapa* (bark-cloth), he wears a headdress made of bird-of-paradise feathers and beaks of hornbill.
Ewa (sea) *ge* (word) was George Ambo's native language.
(Photograph courtesy of Bob Hay)

Traditional dancing in Oro Province, formerly Northern District
(Photographs: Elin Johnston)

CHAPTER 2

Childhood in the Village

Sir George Ambo, KBE, who rose to the highest position as Archbishop of Papua New Guinea, came from a small, traditional village near Gona. Born at Kurou on 25 November 1922, he was given the names Ambo Arukaba after his father's father. Later, as a schoolboy, he was baptised George and was thereafter known as George Ambo. [2]

For generations, his ancestors had been warrior-chiefs who led their people in tribal fighting (see Appendix 1). Bishop George speaks of them:

> Our earliest ancestors were Toumo and Waragi. These are the names of two wild orchids which are the plant emblem or totem of my people. But our great-great-grandfathers, Gaume and Ginjari, were considered to be the real founders of my Somboba Clan. They were the first to hand down our oral clan history. In their time, our ancestors migrated to the sea.

Ironically, according to Bishop George, who became the first of his Papuan flock, the name 'Ambo' means 'the last'. The origin of the name goes back a long time. As he recalls,

> there were six brothers, brave and savage fighters, who used to lead their people in wars. They were all my ancestors. Often they won the battle but if they had to flee, the six brothers would go to the back of the line of their fleeing men. Forming the rearguard like a shield, they protected their warriors from the pursuing foe. When all had reached the safety of the beach, the brothers arriving at the end, the people would shout, 'The Ambos (the last ones) are coming! The Ambos are home!' They were all thankful for the Ambos who cared so much for their men.

George's grandfather, Arukaba, an elder of the Somboba Clan, was also a famous warrior-chief. Together with his wife, Iaoko, and their family, they came to live at Kurou Village, from where most of their children were married. There the old chief died, a heathen. 'My grandfather, Arukaba, was a cannibal,' said Bishop George, who still remembered some of the stories the old man had told him. As a boy, how amazed he had been to hear that the palm of the hand was the tastiest part to eat! Little did the wrinkled warrior know that the small grandson before him was to become the chief spiritual leader of the Anglican Church in Papua New Guinea.

From Kurou village a short track leads to the sea. From there is a wide view of the beach which sweeps towards the north-west, past Bakumbari village, as far as the distant Kumusi River. There, at the river mouth, before the turn of the century, white people had established a trade store. That was where the generation of the Ambo grandfather had made their first contact with white man.[3]

In the 1890s, in the upper regions of the Kumusi and other northern rivers, a frantic search for gold had begun. Supplies of food and equipment for the white miners were transported from the trade store upstream in whaleboats and canoes. Bishop George talks of his immediate ancestors:

> My grandfather's people paddled those whaleboats up the Kumusi River. The white men gave out beads, tobacco, knives and other things to those natives who worked as labourers. My father was just called Ambo. Most of his life he was a heathen, although he lived like a Christian. He gave all his children to the Anglican Church.

Ambo's two sons, Simon Peter and George himself, became Anglican priests. Five of his seven daughters married teacher-evangelists working for the Anglican Mission, while two daughters died from sickness. After the war, when he was an older man, George's father was baptised John Oliver.

According to Fr James Benson, the missionary priest at Gona, George's father was a highly respected man of considerable influence in his district. Although rather small of stature, he held the title of *Ya Bajari*, 'Master of Dance', leading the dancing in his Somboba Clan.[4] From his forefathers he had inherited the skills of performing the ancient stories of the tribe in music and dance, and he travelled widely to pass on the old traditions.

Traditional dancing was an art form, passed on for generations by specially trained and initiated people like the Ambos. They guarded their secrets with care. Away from the village, in the deep parts of the jungle, the dancers would erect a hidden enclosure, surrounded by a high screen of plaited leaves. There, to the muted beats of drums, the Master would teach the secret steps. 'Dancing was in the blood of my forefathers,' said Bishop George. 'They were all the same — Masters of Dance.'

By a cruel and ironical twist of fate, his father was forced to give up dancing. As an older man, he was stricken by the dreaded sickness of elephantiasis. His legs and lower part of his body became swollen and weak. Bishop George recalls,

> We had no medicine in those days. He still managed to struggle to his food garden with his two big legs, and he could make *sago* and go fishing. But he had to give up dancing. He taught us to dance by words. His legs were never cured.

Ironically, later in life, as will be revealed in the story, Bishop George was also prevented from performing the ancestral dances of his people, although he, too, was a leader of traditional dancing.

The young Ambo Arukaba (later George) grew up in a traditional village home. He recalled how their small hut was set on hardwood posts, a metre or so above the ground. 'We collected *sago* leaves for our houses, which were used for roofs, and their stems for floorboards. The rafters were made from the hard mangroves.' A rickety ladder led to the verandah, where the family, at the end of the day, caught the cooling north-easterly breeze from the sea. There, sitting on mats on the floor, the father taught the children the stories of the clan, while Emboia, their mother, cooked the meal in a clay pot on the fire. George Ambo continues:

> My home was very simple. We did not have many possessions, only a wooden box containing some ornaments made from seashells and pig tusks, some woven bracelets and feather headdresses. There was no furniture in the rooms and we slept on *pandanus* mats on the floor. Under the floor were stored spears for fishing or wild-pig hunting, as well as stone axes and knives for work in the food gardens.

As a small baby, George would have spent the day rocking gently in a string bag hung from the rafters in the ceiling (see photograph, page 11).

His parents had never learnt to read or write. His mother had been amongst the first students when a small village school was established nearby. There she learnt to sing some English hymns, but her education was broken off by the war. At home, the family spoke *Ewa-ge*, the language of the sea-people. George describes his family life.

> I grew up with *Ewa-ge*. English was my second language, which I learnt at school. It was always a worry to me. Through my life, I felt my English was not good.
>
> My place was very beautiful, set amongst coconut palms and sweetly scented frangipani flowers. The huts, with croton hedges in red and orange, stood clean and tidy in their neatly swept grounds, their verandahs decorated with hibiscus and purple bougainvillea. The administrators at Buna, the nearby Australian Government Station, were keen on flowers. Sometimes, having provided the flowers, the government would present a shield to the most beautiful village. The people used to compete for the first or second shields, trying to keep their homes and village pretty. My own village won the shield twice.
>
> Our home was almost on the beach where my elder brother, Simon Peter, taught me to catch fish. He made me go out with the village community when they went fishing. Sometimes, we would walk to the Government Station at Buna to barter for fishhooks. We depended on fish and vegetables from our gardens but we always had more than enough to eat. There was never any shortage of food. When we were big, we had our own fish-nets with which we used to catch four or five hundred fish in one go and have a wonderful day.

From an early age, the young George was taught to work in the garden.

My father and my brother made me dig the soil with a digging stick or weed the *taro*, because one day I would be married and then I would have to produce food for my family. When they were clearing land for a new garden, they would mark my plot and give me *taro*-tops to plant. For other seedlings I had to look myself.

Later, at mission school, the young George's garden skills proved very useful. The students had to bring offerings from their own gardens. Every Monday, George would give bananas or *taro* or some other vegetables.

We were not allowed to bring food from our parents' garden, but we had to grow it ourselves and so earn our fees by offering a gift to God. We had to practise developing ourselves to learn all the skills in the village such as garden work, fishing and hunting of pig or wild boar. Oh, my brother was a good hunter! In the night, when he was going out to spear a pig, I had to come and watch, holding a lamp. We had to become good at all these things, in order to lift up the family name. If we didn't share generously of whatever we caught, or if we couldn't do this or that, we would not be allowed to undergo initiation. My father was very important to me and taught me many things in the customary way. I had to honour the elders, the chiefs, the spirits and the sorcerers. If I did not obey them, my father believed I would be killed.

From an early age, George learnt to be loyal to the clan. Whatever happened to it, he would have to take part. Full participation in the affairs of the community, loyalty, obedience and self-discipline were expected from the start. These concepts, learnt in childhood, were to remain with him into his future life for the Church.

The young Ambo Arukaba was thankful for his father's teaching. Being of a loving and passionate nature, he was keen to lift up the name of his clan amongst other clans and to show his capability and devotion to everything in the village. With strong ambitions for achieving excellence in whatever he was doing, he was, in his own words, aiming for the top. Initially, being slight of build like his father, he came last in the children's dancing group and in sports. 'I was the last man but became the first man,' he said with a smile.

Before I started school, I became the leader of the dance. As small boys we tried to practise ourselves in the moonlight on the beach, when we had been watching our brothers dancing. Sometimes, the young single men would come and join us and teach us. I remember giving our first show for our fathers and mothers. Decorated with leaves and beating sticks together, we danced for them all.

Soon the young Ambo became one of the leaders.

Four boys had to be in the centre of the group and two girls outside when we danced. The four boys were the best dancers, and I was chosen to be one of them.

8

At an early age, he also became a very good sportsman. Practising hard in football and cricket, he soon played so well that, in spite of his small size, he was chosen to join the village football team. The Australian Government at Buna encouraged the playing of games in the villages. Regularly, officials would present a shield to the best football team, and cricket bats to the best players.

Bishop Ambo recalls the times when he and his brother were amongst the victors:

> Cricket is in my blood. Nowadays, my grandsons form themselves
> into teams and play against other groups. They play my old sport.
> It's in the blood.

While George still lived at home with his parents, tragedy struck the family. His mother, Emboia, died while trying to deliver her last baby. For some time before her death, she had wished to become a Christian. She had been training for Baptism and Confirmation at the newly-established All Souls' Mission Station at Gona, but was only a catechumen when she died. 'It was very sad. We were left motherless and my father never married again.'

A short time before his mother died, when George was about twelve years old, the time came for his initiation. By then, he had completed his first year at the mission school. Long before the ceremony, when he and other Somboba boys were going to be initiated, their families started preparing for the important occasion. They bred pigs and grew *taro* and other vegetables for the feast. A special house was built, in which the initiates stayed for some time in seclusion. Bishop George remembers this time:

> I was at school when our mothers started getting ready for the
> initiation. Then, in the holidays, while we were staying for some
> time in isolation in the hut, my father and other elders taught us
> the rules of the community.[5]

During the period of preparation for initiation, the physical, mental and spiritual strength of a young man had to be tested. His self-sufficiency had to be proved. Bishop George remembers how he had to make a canoe by cutting down a rain tree and hollowing out the trunk with a stone adze. He must show his father he was capable of such physically demanding tasks, as well as producing food to sustain a family.

'During drought and famine time, we had to go to the swamp and make *sago*,' he recalled. '*Sago* was always available when all other food crops failed.' He had to use all his strength cutting down the *sago* palm, pounding up the fibre and washing out the starch from the trunk. The method of the whole procedure had to be carefully thought out, according to strict rules. Before the sun set, he proudly carried home the *sago*. 'He is a man! He is a man!' the people shouted. They knew he was then capable of producing food for a family and therefore ready for initiation and marriage.

But first and foremost, the spirituality of the young initiates had to be developed and tested.[6] They learnt about the spirits of the ancestors, still

9

believed to be present and watching over their people in the living world, and about the spirits, said to be inhabiting the trees, rocks, lakes and rivers of their land. They learnt about the places where the forefathers used to meet their friends from other villages, exchanging pots of salt water or smoked fish for betel nut, and where their spirits were still believed to haunt the sacred sites. In the special hut, the young men learnt to commune with the spirits.

On the day of the ceremony, the initiates were decorated with ornaments, face-paint and feathered headdresses. As Bishop George recalled,

> Early in the morning, my mother and the other mothers caught the pigs which they had bred. Their legs tied to poles, the pigs were lined up in rows in front of the steps of a high platform, specially erected for the occasion. Then, stepping over the pigs we initiates walked up on to the platform. Above all the people, we solemnly promised to keep the rules of the community such as never to let down the name of the clan, to respect and honour the old people, and to share with them the food which we produced. We promised to stand up to temptations, not to muck around with girls, to be strong, show self-control and respect for ourselves. We promised never to run away from tribal fighting but to go through it and, if bleeding, to cause great pain and bleeding to the enemy. Then we walked down, stepping over the pigs, which were thrown up on the platform where they were killed. The people ate them at the following feast.

The climax was the moment when the initiates received the special shell, symbolising their full membership of the clan. The shell, decorated with the yellow and brown stems of the two wild orchids, *toumo* and *waragi*, was presented by the chief. Bishop George recalled how, to the shouts of the crowd, he was brought to the chief.

> He tied the shell to my arm, just above the elbow. In a mystical way, I was believed to become one with the name and the spirit of our earliest Somboba ancestors. They had the names of the orchids — they were also *Toumo* and *Waragi*, and the orchids are the totem of our clan.

Through the many years, Bishop George has carefully kept his initiation shell (see photographs, page 12). It has never lost its importance for him. Even in retirement, he keeps the names of the orchids, *toumo* and *waragi*, as part of his address. He still remembers the feeling of pride when, as a young initiate, he received the shell with the plant totem. It symbolised the acceptance of his manhood by the community.

> I felt proud to have full membership of my clan, with full rights of ownership to my land — proud to know that I have the right to say what I want to say, and to do what I want to do amongst the members of my Somboba Clan and the two clans which are related to ours, those of Bougaundi and Dunemba.

As a small baby, George would have spent much of the day gently rocking in a *bilum-bag* hung from the rafters in the ceiling or a tree in the garden. (Photograph: Elin Johnston)

Bishop George with his Initiation Shell tied to his
elbow, at Newton College, Popondetta

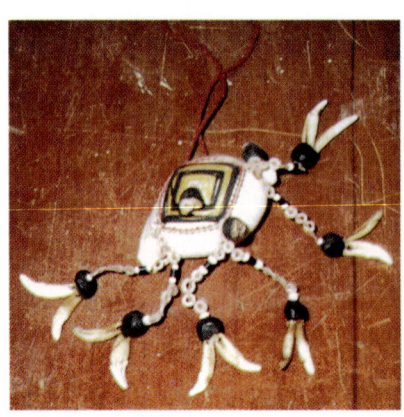

The Initiation Shell decorated
with a woven pattern of the
yellow and brown stems of two
orchids, *Toumo* and *Waragi*, the
totem of his Somboba Clan

(Photographs: Elin Johnston)

12

After his initiation, when the young George began the second year at school, the spiritual, moral and physical powers, as well as his leadership qualities, were already part of his character for the Christian Mission to build on. The foundation for his future development had been laid in his childhood in the village.

CHAPTER THREE

Mission School at Gona

Although there were many fears in his childhood—such as the fear of sickness, spirits and sorcery—life for the young George was largely free and full of interest. He did not want to go to school. Some years before, his elder brother Simon Peter had become a mission boarder at the school at Gona. Under the guidance and care of the missionaries he saw the value of education and encouraged his younger brother to come to school. But George refused![7]

An incident occurred which changed the direction of his life, however.

> One day, a large shoal of fish came along the shore. All the people were going out on the reefs to fish. My dancing mate, Laban [later Fr Laban Seia of Gona], and I were tempted to go too but had no lines and hooks. Carrying a big bunch of bananas and some oranges from our gardens, we set off to the mission station to trade our fruit for fishhooks. As we stood in front of the mission house, the white teacher noticed us two bush children with long hair, earrings, necklaces, armlets and a *bo*—strip of *tapa* (bark) cloth round the waist. She came running downstairs and asked, 'You fine looking young boys, are you school children?' 'No, sister, we are bush-children,' we replied. 'Which is your village?' she asked. 'What are the names of your fathers and mothers? Who is your Village Councillor? Your Village Constable?' Finally, taking our names, she sternly warned, 'If you don't come to school on Monday, your fathers will go to gaol for three months at Buna!' That was the way they used to do it. Tears falling from our eyes, we cut our long hair, broke the earrings and removed the beads from our necks. We started school the next day.

This was in the year 1934, when George was twelve years old. Two years before, the first white teacher had arrived at the station. Bishop George describes those days:

> Sister Miss Ves Ves, we used to call her. She was in charge of the school when I started. She loved music and taught us some English songs and hymns. My first teacher was Michael Aguru, my elder brother Simon Peter's schoolmate. I became so interested in school and asked many questions, so after one year I was transferred to another teacher, Nathaniel Iaura. He came from Iaudari near Ioma, on the Mambare River. He was a kind old man who could read and write.

In that class, George befriended a boy, Alban Jaipoba, from the old Gona Village (now called Kausada), who became his closest friend and his future brother-in-law.

In the second year at school, George experienced the deep sorrow of losing his mother. Emboia died in childbirth. Some of the Somboba relatives, who in the past had settled at Garara (now Killerton), a coastal village east of Gona, came across to Kurou Village to fetch the body and carry it back for burial in the ancestral land. George's father, together with the young George and some of his daughters, were to stay the next three years with the relatives at Garara to be close to Emboia's grave. According to custom, the spouse of a deceased person was confined to the house for a year or more of mourning. Bishop George remembers,

> So our father was kept in the hut for a year, until the food garden was ready with enough food for the death-feast. Our elder sister, Susanna, helped look after us children while we stayed at Garara.[8]

This was a hard time for the young Ambo family. Again in Bishop George's words,

> After my mother's death, we got into trouble. We were not healthy children, We didn't eat much and became very thin. We had no comb and scissors, so our hair was very long and untidy.[9] We used to cut our hair roughly with broken glass from a bottle.

Every morning, very early, George and two sisters would walk the long way on the beach across to the school at Gona. One day, the teacher didn't like the way they looked and told them that their hair and their clothes were too dirty and untidy for school.

> The teacher-in-charge, Godfrey Dabadaba, gave us six cuts each over the hands. My hands were bleeding. He told us to go and wash ourselves and to cut our hair. My sister washed my wounded hands and I was wondering what to do. How could we cut our hair and clean ourselves up? Crying, we went home. We felt we had nobody to tell about our problem.
>
> That night, God sent an angel to my father in his dream. The angel said that a coin was lying in the sand at the foot of a particular coconut tree by the sea. In the morning, our father told us his dream and to go and look for the coin.
>
> As we were walking back to school, we found a one-shilling piece amongst the rubbish washed up by the sea. It was covered in rust and dirt. 'After rubbing it hard with sand, it became a silver colour, and we bought a pair of scissors at the trade store with that money.'

Then, George set about making combs of bamboo for his sisters and himself. From that time, the children were able to keep their hair tidy. 'We believed that the coin had been given to us by our dead mother,' said Bishop George. As an older man, he believed several miracles had happened in his life. Looking back on this incident, he realised this was the first miracle which had occurred to show him the way to share his problems with Jesus.

In that same year after his mother's death, the young George was baptised with other boys and girls by Fr Clement Wadidika, the Papuan priest in charge of All Souls' Station at Gona.[10] 'We were baptised in Kikiri Creek, and we used to call that small stretch of water the Jordan,' wrote Bishop George. Before the baptism, the waters of the creek were blessed by the priest. Then the candidates, forming a queue, walked one by one into the water for baptism and on to the small bush church for quiet prayer. 'The reverence of these people and the dignity of the older men were something that had to be seen to be believed,' wrote an observer.[11] When all were baptised, the new Christians were received into the Church.

For George it was a deeply moving occasion and, unbeknown to him, the first significant step along the way to his life's work. Later in the year, he was confirmed by Bishop Henry Newton, third Anglican Bishop of New Guinea. It was a big occasion and lasted from early morning till late at night. Three to four hundred candidates were confirmed.

Bishop Henry Newton, who had ordained Fr Clement Wadidika, the Papuan priest at Gona, had later been very critical of him. The Bishop disliked his attitude to the local people's traditional customs. He had reprimanded him for not allowing them to wear traditional mourning garments during the period of mourning for their dead. Bishop Newton had told Fr Wadidika that 'the Mission had no claim on the heathen to give up their customs'.[12] From the earliest times of the Mission in Papua New Guinea, there had been great differences in the attitudes of some missionaries to traditional customs. Later, Bishop George himself was to feel deeply the force of this tension in his life and work.

About the time his mother died, a white teacher arrived at the school. Initially sent to Wanigela, a mission station further down the coast towards the south-east, Mavis Eather found the move to Gona a frightening experience. She wrote, 'I was just scared out of my wits'. Having become used to the Wanigela people who spoke 'a very gracious language', she found the coastal people further north very different, 'full of vitality and speaking a very staccato language with all speed possible'. After hiding in her flat for three days or so, she finally plucked up enough courage to face the students of the school.

Bishop George well remembers the arrival of the new white teacher:

> She came, but she remained in her house for several days. When at last she went to the school and saw the young boys, including myself, she took all the children to her heart.[13]

The Mission Station was spread out over two large areas, separated by Kikiri Creek. On either side, according to her description, the swampy land, thick with huge trees and tropical vegetation, had been cleared. Being a single, white woman, she had to live separately from the main station. She was asked to share with the white nurse, Sister Arliss, a house which was close to the hospital on the north-western bank. It was not easy for the young white teacher to reach the school and church on the other side of the creek. Every day, she had to cross on a plank bridge and walk about ten minutes in the hot sun. 'My clothes were wet with perspiration during the morning,' she wrote, 'and horribly uncomfortable'. But a cool breeze which usually arose about 1.00pm gave some relief. The sense of being isolated in her house, removed from her school and church, would have added to her general feeling that the end of the world had come. But her conviction that God had called her to do His work in this way, and that she was 'but the channel used by His Holy Spirit' carried her through this initial stage of despair.

When Miss Eather arrived, Nathaniel Iaura was in charge of the school. According to her, he was a wise old man with great dignity, highly respected by the people. He was well informed about the Christian religion, but knew less about the teaching of reading and writing. Only one teacher, Godfrey Dabadaba, had any training behind him, having reached Grade 3 standard. In his conscientious way, he was a great help to Mavis Eather, the only white teacher in the school.[14]

Although she was also assisted by two retired missionaries from the Solomon Islands living in Gona Village, Harry and Albert, Miss Eather was initially worried about the shortage of staff. The school had by then nearly two hundred children on its rolls. According to her, the work seemed almost beyond her and she was desperate to know how to make headway.

After some time an incident occurred which was to lighten the burden of difficulties for Miss Eather. By her own account, she was walking on the beach thinking about her problems with staff, when two young men came up to her and said, 'Sister, we want to be teachers!' A little bewildered at their generally untidy appearance and mouths red from chewing betel nut, she allowed them to start as station workers. Both men, Ambrose Burogu and Albert Maclaren Ririka, were from Gona Village (now Kausada). They had had some training, Ambrose at St Paul's School, Dogura, the headquarters of the Anglican Mission, and Albert with Fr Harold Thompson, the white priest who had left Gona some years before.[15]

(Both Ambrose and Albert were to become outstanding leaders within the Anglican Mission in the Northern District. It was a great loss for the Church when Ambrose, eventually a teacher at Sangara Station, died in the Mt Lamington eruption. Albert was ordained with George and served as a priest for many years. In 1941, when both Ambrose and Albert had gone to St Aidan's College near Dogura for training as teacher-evangelists, George took over Ambrose's position as — untrained — head teacher at All Souls' School.)

These two young villagers provided immense support for the white teacher. Later she wrote,

> Ambrose became my houseboy, and Albert worked generally on
> the station. I owe so much to Ambrose who became my interpreter
> and taught me so much about his people.

17

Eventually they were both taken on as pupil teachers. She wrote,

> Ambrose was overjoyed, and gave himself entirely to the teaching, and has absorbed my methods and everything I could give him. Albert…is the stronger character, and has done good work in the kindergarten school, his gentleness and love for the little children outstanding. He is rather artistic and…together we make all the charts and teaching aids used in the school.

During this early period of difficulties with shortage of staff, a firm friendship was formed between the young pupil George and his new teacher. When she arrived, he and his friend Alban Jaipoba were in Grade 3, which became Miss Eather's own special class. 'At that time, my desire for education was growing stronger and stronger.' Recalling his school days, he emphasised how lucky he and his classmates had been, to have had Miss Eather during the formative years in Grades 3, 4 and 5. She was a devoted and committed lady missionary. 'She became my second mother,' said Bishop George.[16] With her teaching and Christian way of life, she set an example which was to remain a lasting inspiration for George.

Mavis Eather had high expectations for her pupils. She encouraged them to work hard, not only in class with academic subjects but also outside on the station. For her they cleaned the grounds, cut the grass and, most importantly, grew the food. Bishop George recalls how they had to cultivate many varieties of vegetables in the gardens, planting beans, peanuts, cabbages, tomatoes, shallots and many other kinds. Perhaps this was the time when George learnt the importance of humble tasks, a lesson which, as the story will show, he still remembered as Archbishop of Papua New Guinea.

Miss Eather also inspired her children's awareness of beauty and spirituality. She made them grow different kinds of flowers for the altar in the small bush church, for their classrooms, and to take to their homes. Above all, she taught them some of the main texts in the Bible, leading them towards a life of beauty, goodness and prayer. Bishop George never forgot some simple tenets of her Christian teaching. As he recalled them,

> 1. Jesus, the Son of God, went about doing good. 2. Let others see that Jesus Christ is in you. 3. Pray Hard. Work hard. Play Hard.

Simple lessons, which remained with him throughout his life and which he was to imprint on the minds of his own children.

Mavis Eather had many interests and imparted these to her students. Although an Anglican, she had studied music during her last three years of school at a Roman Catholic convent. This resulted in a great love of music and a widening of her religious outlook. Hope of gaining unity within the Christian Church was always close to her heart. Later, after a time of studying the piano in Sydney, she decided to join the Mission.[17]

Mavis Eather had no formal teacher training but had educated herself in many areas. In order to gain some teaching experience before going to the mission field, she opened a little school on a property in the area of her childhood in New South Wales. Going round the farms she picked up the children, driving them to school with her horse and sulky. After the lessons, she would deliver them home again. She had a strong personality, a musician's sensitivity, an artist's appreciation of beauty, as well as abilities to paint and sew. Having read extensively, she became a mature woman with the ability to teach in a simple and inspiring way which her children and her Papuan staff could understand.

Being taught by such a person, George was given a unique opportunity for development and for acquiring knowledge at a school considered one of the best in the Mission.

An inspector who visited the station in 1939 and 1940 witnessed in his reports to the personality and capability of Miss Eather:

> School work is made enjoyable for teachers and pupils. A constant appeal is made to the curiosity and interest of pupils. The atmosphere is bright and cheerful. Singing is sweet and tuneful, of good quality. A fine display of articles in arts and crafts, each child showing one. The school is outstanding in the work achieved and in its outlook.[18]

In George's early training, the influence of Miss Eather helped build the foundation for his future attitude to his work, to the Christian Church and to the white race.

The young George was an exceptional student. Miss Eather soon noticed his keenness and ability to learn. 'A highly intelligent lad,' she wrote, '...beautifully healthy...hair always neatly clipped, a smiling face—one that could break into a hearty laugh at any time'.

Not just in class was George a special boy.[19] Being anxious to become a mission boarder and live at the station and to learn all he could, he followed Miss Eather around when she was working outside after school. As he later said with a twinkle in his eye,

> When she was watering her flowers or when she was trying to wash her dog, I offered to do it for her. In this way, she took special notice of me. She talked to me and shared ideas with me—about loving each other and growing up as brothers and sisters, and about sharing. I was greatly influenced by her, by the things she told me.[20]

Thinking that George and his classmate, Alban, might some day become pupil teachers and work for the Mission, Miss Eather interviewed them after school one day, asking them to become 'mission boys'. That meant living on the station as boarders and, under the care and guidance of the missionaries, participating closely in the life and teaching of the school and the Anglican Church. For George it was a turning point in his life. No longer living in the village, he transferred the concepts of obedience, duty, honesty and loyalty, learnt in childhood, to his new master—the Church. Above all, the spirituality, which had always been deeply rooted in his land and which had permeated his early life, now broke out into flowering in the new and fertile soil.

Miss Eather had introduced new ideas concerning the care of the boarders and the general outside management of the station. It was to be run on the teamwork principle. All jobs were shared on the basis of a monthly roster, so that each boy would have a change of tasks. The main job was to cut back the tall *kunai* grass to keep the playing fields in good order and to discourage snakes from coming near the school. The children arrived on the station at 6.00am, ready to cut the grass with their long knives. The day-children also brought their breakfast, which, according to Miss Eather, consisted of a small *taro* or a small lump of stodgy *sago* wrapped in a banana leaf. After a wash in Kikiri Creek, they were ready for school at 9.00am. Much supervision was needed, but the teachers felt that good, moral teaching was carried out through this teamwork.

Although Miss Eather received loyal support from her staff, she still needed more help. She was thankful when Cecil Uiari, a Gona man with some training at Dogura, joined the staff. He had married George's sister, Rachel, and they both came to live on the station. Soon afterwards, George brought his elder brother, Simon Peter, to see Miss Eather who was glad to accept him. He offered to teach in the mornings, but had to live in the village to care for his wife Jennifer and their family. George and Simon Peter had a younger sister, Iako, later baptised Anita Joy after Miss Eather's sister. Anita Joy offered to help with the housework. Of these new arrangements, Miss Eather wrote,

> We became very much a family. I can't speak too highly of these young people and their influence for good amongst their friends and neighbours, always thoughtfulness for me.[21]

With so many of his family members involved in the station, it was natural for George to spend much time around Miss Eather's house, wanting to help and to learn whatever he could. He tried especially hard to speak English, but always found it difficult, as he would right through his life. 'Oh, Sister, my lips are too heavy!' he complained.

Mavis Eather went on to write,

> With his eyes twinkling, his smile radiating warmth and joy, George was loved by all. I can't ever remember him showing malice or ordinary bad temper but if he thought a person wrongly judged, he would be most indignant and forthright in speaking his mind.

The innate understanding of what is right and wrong and the courage and strength of character to stand up for his beliefs, are characteristics of his personality which have never left him.

CHAPTER 4

George Ambo and James Benson at Gona

In 1937, Fr James Benson, a priest originally from England, came to take charge of the mission station at Gona. From the start, he loved the place and its people, and wrote:

> Imagine a tropical Sydney Gardens set above a lovely sweep of grey sand and blue water with coral islands to the east, and a reef running out to the west; imagine a creek spanned by a log bridge cutting the gardens in two, with a cluster of houses on either bank; and there is the setting of Gona'.[22]

Fr James Benson
(Photograph courtesy of
Howard Benson)

In that beautiful and tranquil area, he began a ministry which was to form the most significant part of his life's work. It left a deep imprint upon the future development of the Anglican Church in Papua New Guinea. This is most clearly shown by the fact that more Papuan men from Gona have been trained as teacher-evangelists than from any other Anglican mission districts. Giving their lives for service in the Church, they have been amongst its finest men.[23]

The local people soon discerned in their new priest a sympathy and intuitive understanding, which drew them to his church. Only few of them had been baptised since the establishment of the Gona Mission in the late 1920s.[24] Under Fr Benson's influence, however, the number of villagers receiving instruction in the Christian faith greatly increased. Although he could not talk with them in their own language, they sensed that he loved them and they took him to their hearts.

As Bishop Philip Strong (Bishop of the Diocese of New Guinea) wrote,

> Over and over again on my visits to Gona in the prewar years, I felt there to be at Gona a wonderful atmosphere, and I used to marvel at the way that James Benson had with the people and the simple and direct manner in which he imparted to them the Gospel and spiritual truth and in a way they could so fully understand.

At the impressionable age of fifteen, George was absorbing all the new experiences of a mission boy. It was for him a time of considerable bewilderment, as he tried to sort out his values. He compared Fr Benson's teaching with the traditional teaching of his childhood. He had believed in many gods or spirits — gods of the sky and sea, of trees, rivers and mountains. Worship of them had been part of his existence. The strength of his people had depended on the goodwill of their gods and of their ancestor spirits, whose bones were lying in their land. Prayers and food were offered to placate these spirits. At mission school he was taught that there was one God only — a God of love, all-embracing and all-forgiving, who through His Holy Spirit strengthened those who received Him in their hearts. He pondered on the meaning of the worship in the church, of making the sign of the cross before kneeling down, the meaning of the Ten Commandments, the Lord's Prayer and the Bible passages, all of which had to be learnt by heart. 'I reflected upon these things,' said Bishop George. 'I was trying to put them together and make a meaningful picture in my mind. Which way would I go? How would I try to live my life? How could I become a leader of my people?'[25]

Before long, George and Fr Benson became friends. 'They were men with similar characteristics,' wrote Mavis Eather, 'men with souls full of love and joy, in whom there was no guile. In Fr Benson's heart, George became his adopted son. They loved each other and there was a wonderful bond between them'.[26] Wholeheartedly, the young student dedicated himself to the life of the station with cheerfulness and zest. 'I tried to be a good mission boy,' said Bishop George with a smile. [27] In the classroom he worked as hard as he could and was one of the brightest students. On the sportsfield he joined the football team. Although he was small, he played so well that they always chose him for the team. Soon it was noticed that his dancing was better than that of the other boys, so he became leader of dancing. His early training in the village in sport and dancing proved very valuable in his new life. So did the concepts of obedience and loyalty, first to family and clan, now to Church and school.

George tried his hardest to keep the rules for the mission boarders, although his obedience often caused him to be unpopular. He recalled, for example, how at night time the boys would sneak out of the dormitory to go fishing or to be with the village girls. Only he and Arnold, a cousin, always chose to stay behind. When asked by the prefects where the other boys were, George would reply that he didn't know. 'I told a lie,' he said. His sense of right and wrong was wonderfully strong, but so was his loyalty to his friends! One time, Miss Eather came into the dormitory with the students' monthly pay of fourpence. She told them they wouldn't get their money if they left their beds at night or went home for weekends. 'You must stay on the station,' she said. 'Only George and Arnold will get their pay and they will go home for the weekend.' In this way, she created a bad feeling towards the two of them amongst the other students.

The fact that George always had the courage to stand up for what he believed to be right made him unpopular with the boys and also with some of the girls who were growing up.

> They knew what kind of man I was. A very hard man who never
> went near the girls. I just walked on, walked past them! My father
> had told me never to 'muck around' with girls.

Knowing they could always rely on him, Miss Eather and Fr Benson often took George along as interpreter when visiting the villages. This made some of the older mission boys and teachers very jealous. George remembered how he used to feel sad at the antagonism caused by the attention he received from the expatriate staff. Thinking back on his school days, he thanked God for letting all these things happen to him to teach him about human nature, especially about jealousy which he would often encounter in his future life.

At that time he struggled to balance and compare the things he was taught in church and school with his early experience as a Papuan boy in the village. Out of his reflections came an awareness of what it meant to be a Papuan living a Christian life. Often admonished by his white teachers never to imitate white men but always be himself and be proud of his Papuan background, George took special note of Fr Benson's interest in his people's traditions.

> Fr Benson introduced the drum into our church service. Not
> knowing the language he couldn't compose hymns, but he used
> conch-shells and drums with the English hymns.

George still remembers how Fr Benson taught the people to beat the drum as they sang *Onward Christian Soldiers*. 'He had a wonderful understanding of our culture.' [28]

Generally speaking, the Anglican missionaries in Papua New Guinea were not anxious to disturb the traditional customs. Being on the whole conservative rather than of revolutionary mind, they had been shaped by the Anglo-Catholic Revival in England. These missionaries tried to retain many of the valuable features of traditional Papuan society. Some workers in the mission field of a more radical disposition, however, seeing the old customs as a hindrance to westernisation, had tried to destroy them. In most Anglican districts, such destruction of the culture did not take place. Generally, the people were left to live their traditional lives in the villages, to dance, marry or mourn their dead in the customary way. They were not put into Western clothes; the men were not forced to give up wearing the *bo* (a narrow strip of bark cloth around the waist), nor were women forced to wear dresses. Most Anglican missionaries were concerned to promote the spiritual values which they had found already existed in the Papuan villages—values such as 'fellowship, brotherhood and spiritual mystery…' which were often lacking in their own materialistic, self-centred western society. [29]

Before arriving at Gona, Fr Benson himself had felt the need for fellowship and brotherhood. This he had found with the Community of Ascension at Goulburn, New South Wales, of which he was a member for seven years. Having experienced a deep personal tragedy, he had been greatly strengthened by the religious life of the Community. To understand Fr Benson's appreciation of the spiritual qualities of Papuan life and his influence upon George, we must consider something of his background which had been marked by such great suffering.

An Englishman from Yorkshire, he had come to Australia and studied theology at St John's College, Armidale, New South Wales. Shortly after his ordination in 1916, he had married Bertha Weston. Together they had a few happy years as missionaries in Papua, but were forced to return to Australia owing to the illness of a child. It was during his time as rector of a parish on the South Coast of New South Wales that tragedy struck. Late at night, after a family holiday in Sydney, he was driving south towards their home with his wife and young children. As he approached the jetty to catch the punt which crossed Batemans Bay, he mistook a red warning light for the light of the ferry and drove straight into the rushing waters. The only one awake, he alone was able to scramble out. He himself prepared the cement for the family grave and erected the wooden cross with his own hands. Shortly after the loss of his dearest ones, he wrote,

> I, James Benson, in the Presence of God, and of the Holy Angels…believing that such is God's Will and Purpose, do hereby promise to spend my whole life in poverty, celibacy and obedience to the Community of Ascension…[30]

These promises he kept for the rest of his life, except that the promise of obedience was transferred to the Bishop of Papua New Guinea. At Gona he created a community which became his family.

During his last few years with the Community of Ascension, Fr Benson felt a strong desire to return to Papua. At Gona, his love for the people and their way of life gradually made them aware of the value of their own culture. As Mavis Eather recalled,

> Fr Benson has just painted a banner for us, very beautiful indeed. He has taken a Papuan Madonna, with the child supported in a string bag. The background is sky, sea, a sandy beach—a quiet village house with a pathway leading from it. The borders are dark jungle trees, vines etc—with bits of Papuan life here and there, such as a *cuscus*, and bird of paradise. A crown of glory throws its light onto the Madonna, who is walking from the light into the dark jungle places.

The people, George Ambo amongst them, were 'tremendously impressed' by the ideas expressed in that beautiful banner.[31]

These early impressions of Fr Benson's attempts to introduce features of Papuan culture into the church at Gona were to remain with George. He remembers the traditional dancing at the station at festival times, so greatly encouraged by Fr Benson. These memories would be significant in George's future work for an indigenous church. Miss Eather's description of such an occasion gives a vivid picture of the mingling of mission and village ways. On Christmas Day, 1938, when George was in Grade IV, there was great celebration. After the Services of Matins and Holy Communion, the children's service was held at the school. They sang carols and received small Christmas bags.

Miss Eather wrote,

> Lovely gifts had been sent me this year...small knives, mouth organs, fishhooks and pencil cases...and the children received a few boiled sweets and a few beads. Everyone was very happy... The rest of the day was to be spent dancing on the mission grounds. About midday, the dancers were ready and waiting for us, so we took our seats under the shade of a tree, Fr Benson, Miss May Hayman [the newly arrived Nursing Sister, later to be a Martyr] and I.

Imagine the mission boys, with George standing out most prominently amongst them, dancing gracefully on to the grass *deba-deba* (playing field). Together with village dancers, they wore with great dignity their colourful feathered headdresses, as they stepped around in perfect rhythm to the regular beat of their drums.

Miss Eather continued:

> The dances were splendid. Most of the villages put on an excellent show, [with] individual styles of headdress and individual dances. Wholeheartedly and joyfully, the dancing continued for the rest of the day. By evening, as the sun was sinking into the western sea, all the tired people, led by Fr Benson, knelt together on the grass *deba-deba* for Evensong. The words of *Now the darkness deepens* were very appropriate and the tired voices gave of their best.[32]

When the time came for Fr Benson to go on furlough, Fr Oliver Brady, an Australian priest, temporarily took his place. Fr Brady was a deeply spiritual man who also made a significant mark on the religious life of the station. Every day he took the services in the church and went into the school to take religious instruction. To his great joy, George was asked by Miss Eather to look after the visiting priest. At times of relaxation, when both were off duty, they shared many thoughts and meaningful talks.

It was at this time that George felt the first faint hopes of one day becoming a priest. He recalls how the boys in the village were asked by their elders, 'Son! What do you want to do when you grow up? What are you going to be?' Proudly waiting his turn, George had said, 'I'm going to be a priest!'. His answer was said so seriously and earnestly that they all roared with laughter saying, 'You—a priest! You can't be a priest!' George ran away and wept bitterly. As Miss Eather recalled, 'At that time, it was the only longing in his heart'. When the time came for Fr Benson's return, Fr Brady left Gona to take up the leadership of St Aidan's Teacher Training College, at Dogura. All the people were glad to see Fr Benson back again. 'He was a father to us all,' wrote Miss Eather. 'The village people called him the smiling, loving *bada.*'

After his furlough, Fr Benson found that there was much work to be done to maintain and repair the existing buildings of the station. As a young man in Yorkshire he had trained as a painter, decorator and sign-writer, as well as a grainer of timber.[33] Through an apprenticeship, he had gained great practical knowledge. He set up a workshop at Gona where, according to Bishop George,

> he would take several boys for a couple of hours a week, to teach them how to use tools properly. In my case, the Church taught me how to build a house. The schoolchildren must learn how to saw the *sago* ribs...[34]

He recalled how he had learnt to use steel axes and knives in the school workshop; also, how he had saved the four pennies given monthly to every mission boy, to buy some tools. First he had bought an English Prayer Book, but after saving up again he bought a knife. Again, he 'saved and saved'. At last he was able to buy a steel axe which he lent to his father to replace the old stone axe. As Bishop George said, 'The steel axe was very sharp and wonderful'.

Both Fr Benson and Mavis Eather described how improvements and expansion of the station had been made at that time. 'Two new school houses were built,' wrote Miss Eather, 'and a very large cement tank to add to our comforts'. Henry Holland (an Australian missionary in charge of the inland station of Sangara and one of the Martyrs-to-be) came with a team of work boys to build a new church.

> ...a nice little church, and it is in the very best position, right on the edge of the station on the top of the hill as you approach the mission up the lane with the coffee bushes on the left hand.[35]

A Papuan builder, Stanley Tago, had also come to help Fr Benson with the building work. He stayed at the mission for some time and would tell stories of his life as a boarder at Duvira Mission Station at the mouth of the Mambare River. This was in the care of an English priest, Fr Romney Gill, in whose workshop Stanley had learnt carpentry and building. Miss Eather recalled how the mission boys would listen intently to Stanley's stories. George with his inquiring mind, always keen to listen and to learn, was one of those boys.[36]

The students were expected to help with the practical work on the station. Often they had to go far into the jungle to fetch timber for the new buildings. According to Stephen Tago, son of Stanley and later a friend of George, on these occasions the mission boys sometimes saw old people carrying home from the bush heavy loads of firewood or posts for their own huts. In Stephen's words,

> while the other boys would rather pass by, that male tower of strength, George, would stop and help the villagers. The other boys would leave him and arrive first back at the station, while George would carry the old people's loads as well as his own. He was always helpful.

Even as the Archbishop of Papua New Guinea, George was still the same —

full of compassion and sympathy for people. Maureen Ambo, his daughter-in-law, once told Stephen Tago that

> this old man can't change. We women expect him to sit down on the platform of the rest house, while we cook and prepare the food for him. But he can't. He can't stand men sitting down while the women are cooking over the fires at the back.

Many a time, Bishop George would climb down from the hut, assist the women with the cooking and order the other men in the rest house to go and do the same!

Maureen went on:

> So, for this man, now the Archbishop of our country, the humble service of others, all the small practical chores done in the background, are also of great importance. Even now, he can't stop himself helping those who serve.[37]

Bishop George has, right through his eventful life, remained a humble man, concerned to help equally with both the great and the humble tasks.

CHAPTER 5

Opening of Siai Mission

While James Benson was adding more buildings at Gona, in his heart he had a zeal for expanding the Mission into the vast inland areas untouched by Christianity.[38] Times were hard in the 1930s, however, and people in Australia had been hit by the economic depression. Support for the New Guinea Mission had dwindled, and in 1933 it had an overdraft of £8000. When local people asked the Bishop to send teachers or priests to their villages, he had to answer, 'No money and no men — maybe later on!'[39] Fr Benson's building plans for the station at Gona had to be curtailed in order to remain within the meagre budget allowed by the Bishop. Even so, his hope of placing evangelist-teachers in various isolated places persisted. As he wrote in 1938,

> I am thinking of putting Nathaniel [George's old teacher at Gona]
> up the river [Kumusi] until his retiring time arrives. It is his country
> by language, and he is far more useful as an evangelist and teacher
> of *Giu* [Religious Instruction] than he is at school work.[40]

On arduous journeys round the inland district, Benson would take George along as an interpreter. Together they visited the small Christian communities, widely scattered and isolated by thick jungle, rivers, swamps and long distances.

As a schoolboy at Gona, George was surrounded by a world into which the Christian Mission had hardly penetrated. Originally established in 1891 at Dogura, the Anglican Mission had expanded rapidly along the north coast of the Papuan peninsula, but spread slowly through the large inland areas of the northern part of the diocese. At the turn of the century, the Rev'd Copland King, one of the two founders of the mission at Dogura, had started an inland station at Ave near Ioma, on the upper Mambare River. That station was later closed.[41] In 1906, a second station was started by Copland King at Ambasi on the coast. From there, Henry Holland, an Australian lay missionary, ventured far inland to open a new station at Sangara on the slopes of Mt Lamington. He was given invaluable support by Andrew Uware, a local man from Ambasi, who became Henry Holland's lifelong friend. In 1928, together they started a new station at Isivita further inland. At that time, the Gona mission also was established with the building of a hospital and a school under the leadership of Fr Cecil Gill, an English priest and doctor. It was his brother, Fr Romney Gill, who established the mission at Duvira, near the mouth of the Mambare River. In that isolated place, about 350 km along the coast from Dogura, Fr Romney built a church, a boarding school and a large workshop, where his students could learn such practical skills as carpentry and building.[42] It was one of Fr Romney's keenest students, Stanley Tago, who later helped Fr Benson with the building work at Gona. Such was the slender extent of the northern mission in George's school years: only the widely scattered stations of Gona, Ambasi and Duvira on the coast, with Sangara and Isivita further inland.

In 1938, Fr Benson and George made a journey into the area behind Gona which yet had had almost no contact with Christianity. At Siai, a village half way up the Kumusi River, they unexpectedly found one Christian family: Isaac and Rebecca Tago and their three sons, Stanley, Randolph and Boniface. 'Five Christians,' wrote Fr Benson, 'with the nearest fellow Christians away on the Mamba River or at Isivita or at Gona, each about equidistant'. Stanley Tago

The Stanley Tago Family
Left to right: Philemon, Norah, Elizabeth, Evelyn (mother) with Cora, Stanley (father), David and Stephen (former Minister of Defence in the Papua New Guinea Government)
(Photo courtesy of Mr Stephen Tago)

29

had been appointed village constable of the Siai area by the Government Administration and was highly respected by all. Two white officials mentioned Stanley in their reports, having visited the area on separate patrols. One wrote, 'An excellent man in this sorcery-infested district,' and the other, 'The Rev'd Gill of the Mamba is of the opinion that Stanley Tago is fifty years ahead of the average Papuan in intelligence and reliability'.[43] Little did Fr Benson know that in four years' time, during the war, he would turn to Stanley and his people for help when he fled inland for his life. When the Japanese soldiers invaded Gona, the people at Siai were to provide a temporary hiding place in the jungle for the fleeing white missionaries.

During that first visit to Siai, however, all was peaceful. In the evening 276 people gathered to hear Fr Benson read passages from the Gospels. These were translated by George. While the people stood quietly around Stanley's prayer desk which he had placed in the centre of the village, they listened that night to the Biblical message. As Fr Benson wrote, '…the first time a white missionary had been in the district, and certainly the Mass next morning in the rest house was the first in Siai'. For Fr Benson and George, it had been a moving and unforgettable experience.

During the months following Fr Benson's visit, the people at Siai were, according to Miss Eather, 'crying out for a school and a church'.[44] Fr Benson promised that he would provide staff and equipment if they could undertake to put up the school, the church and the teachers' houses without financial assistance from the Mission. The station buildings at Siai were ready sooner than expected, mainly owing to the work and guidance of Stanley and his family.

In the school holidays of 1939, George Ambo's last year as a mission boy, a large party set off from Gona — 14 mission boys, George amongst them, 50 carriers and the three white missionaries, Fr Benson, Miss Eather and Sr Hayman. Mavis Eather described how they carried with them camping gear, school equipment and medical supplies for the new station.

> The procession set off in high spirits, but soon the rain came down
> in torrents. It rained the whole three days it took us to get there.

Miss Eather was often carried in a chair by the boys through patches of deep muddy water, lifted 'well above their heads'. At one place they came to a flooded river where the log bridge had been washed away. George and the boys cut down a tree, and they managed to get across: '…hand in hand, slowly side-stepping to keep the balance over the rushing water. One slip and we would have been gone,' she wrote. All the way to Siai, George Ambo carried Miss Eather's personal handbag and remained by her side, supporting and assisting her in every way.[44]

When finally they reached Siai, having travelled the last distance by canoe down the Kumusi River, the tired party received a warm welcome. Nathaniel Iaura, George's old teacher, had the villagers lined up on the bank in front of the rest house. As they saw the approaching canoes, their shouts of *Egualau* (welcome) rang through the air. As Miss Eather recalled, 'There was great excitement, for I believe we are the first white women to visit this inland village'. Stanley Tago and his family, the only Christians in that vast area, were first to greet the missionaries (see photograph on page 29). 'Stanley is an outstanding character and really has been the founder of this new mission station,' she wrote. In his home, where things were neatly arranged, Miss Eather saw holy pictures hanging on the walls in the bedroom and also the family prayer desk, which Stanley himself had made. 'Judging from the tone of the home, prayer was truly a part of their daily life.'[45]

On Sunday morning, Holy Communion was celebrated for the first time in the little bush chapel at Siai. Again in Miss Eather's words, 'It had been beautifully decorated with the altar, cross and candlesticks which Fr Benson had made himself and painted black and green'. Neighbouring villagers had arrived and after the service the new mission buildings were blessed by Fr James. Then, after the communal breakfast, the village people danced all day on what used to be the ancient fighting area. 'In the evening, the dancers presented their drums to the Gona people, inviting them to dance on the Siai grounds,' she wrote.

For George it was a happy and most meaningful experience. He reflected on the peace which had come to this land with the coming of the Christian missionaries. In the opening of this new Christian mission, a great achievement had been accomplished. Only a short time ago, these inland fighters had raided the coastal villages of his own people, killing or carrying away their victims to indulge in cannibalism. Now, they could dance on each others' ancient fighting grounds without any sense of fear.

At that time George was in Grade 5, which had only recently been introduced at All Souls' School. It was to be his last year. How lucky he was to have been educated at a mission school of such a high standard. In his 1939–40 report, the inspector wrote that there were 233 students, and that a 'remarkable quality of learning had been obtained'. It was also noted that the school was 'outstanding in the work achieved and in its outlook …' Although, in 1940, the staff consisted of only one trained teacher, Miss Eather, and seven untrained teachers, the standards were kept up with 'excellent results'.[46]

In terms of mission education, there being no other system available before the Second World War, the students at Gona were considered to be well-educated young men. Having completed Grade 5, the highest grade in the school, they were highly sought for outside employment at the end of their school days. European traders working at Sangara or Buna came to All Souls Station in search of reliable labour. The students were wanted for work at the plantations or for positions in government or any business run by white people, but George and his classmate, Alquin, were left behind, because they were smaller than the other boys chosen for employment.[47] The white mission staff now intended to send George and Alquin to St Paul's School, Dogura. Only there could they do Grade 6 and so finish their school education, but there were problems. As Bishop George explained,

> Oh, in those days the people believed in sorcery. Therefore, my family would not let me go down to St Paul's School. They believed the Dogura people would kill me with sorcery.

Fr Benson and Miss Eather tried again and again to convince George's family that, as he was a Christian, sorcery would have no power over him, but they had no success. George and Alquin were left at Gona with no plans for the future.

The belief in sorcery was always common amongst these coastal people. One dark, stormy evening, some of the mission boys at school with George gave Miss Eather an insight into their beliefs. She recalled that a cold breeze was blowing outside while the staff were having dinner together in the mission house. When the table boy came to remove the plates, he had whispered in fear to Miss Eather, 'Oh, Sister, the *binei* [evil spirit] is crying out! Listen, and you can hear it!' When the boys were doing the washing up, they explained that a *binei* was the 'spirit of sorcery'. Miss Eather wrote, 'It [the *binei*] was the evil spirit which did the work for the sorcerer'.[48]

According to the boys, when a young man died a natural death the people always believed his death had been caused by sorcery. His body was buried in the ground and, according to their belief, after three days they could communicate with his spirit. During the third night, as the men of the village chewed betel nut together, one of them would call out to the spirit of the dead person asking who had caused the death. Whoever received an answer from the spirit with the name of the guilty person had to take revenge. This he did by, in his turn, sending the *binei* to kill the sorcerer responsible for the young man's death.

The 'pay-back by sorcery' was an unending process, which the people believed could cause sickness, death or other troubles. Miss Eather wrote of one of these situations:

> We have a patient in hospital now who has a fearful abcess on the lower abdomen. Miss Hayman is having a dreadful time with him for he vows somebody has made sorcery on him and that he must die.

In cases of jealousy, the *binei* could also be sent to kill. George's family may have feared that should he, as a foreigner, go to study at St Paul's School and prove to be one of the most successful students, he might be the victim of such jealousy and sorcery. Little did George know that in future years, one of the most important tasks in his work as a bishop would be to fight his people's belief in sorcery.

Although George had been amongst the keenest and brightest students at All Souls' School, he now had a time of drifting about aimlessly, wondering what he really should do with his life. He was doubting the strength of his

Christian faith. Should he join the Mission as a medical boy? Miss Eather was keen for him to become a pupil-teacher, but he insisted on the idea of being a medical boy. 'My sister-in-charge, who was like a mother to me, insisted that I was born to be a teacher,' said Bishop George, 'but I didn't agree with her'.[49] His friend, Alquin, had become a medical boy, and George was impressed with the uniform and 'all the outward show' that went with that position. As there was a great shortage of teachers, however, eventually he gave in.

> Deep in my heart I knew that God really called me to be a teacher,
> so I joined the staff as a pupil-teacher.

At that time, George was still small for his age and the students he taught were far bigger than himself. He had to stand on an empty case while teaching the class. The big girls, especially, had been 'very naughty', because he was so small. So he was transferred to another class of smaller children where he enjoyed the teaching.

In August 1941, a plan emerged which would shape George's future life. The white staff at Gona were attending a special conference at Dogura. It was to celebrate the fiftieth anniversary of the arrival of the first Anglican missionaries in Papua New Guinea. For Mavis Eather it was a sad occasion, as she would not be returning to Gona. Time had come for her retirement and she was on her way home. Also attending the conference was a young teacher from Australia, Miss Mavis Parkinson (later to be a Martyr). She was to go back with Fr Benson to Gona to take up the position as the new Headmistress of All Souls' School. Before leaving for Australia, Miss Eather had urged Fr Benson and Mavis Parkinson to send George to St Aidan's College at Dogura for training as a teacher-evangelist. Even though fear of sorcery had stopped him from doing Grade 6 at St Paul's School, they thought it more important that he should now start his teacher-training course rather than worry about doing Grade 6. Having seen George's abilities as a pupil-teacher during the last year or so, Fr Benson did not think it mattered greatly that he had only reached Grade 5. In future years, this lack in George's formal school education would be a considerable source of sadness to him, at times causing a deep feeling of inferiority.

Sorcery was a ground swell in the culture both at Gona and Dogura. For fear of sorcery, George's father and brother had two years previously refused permission for him to go to Dogura. However, in view of the persuasion of the white staff and realising that George was now older and more mature, their opposition to his going away weakened. George himself had doubts about leaving Gona, however. Some new teachers on the staff who had recently trained at St Aidan's College warned that the district of Dogura was infested with women sorcerers. 'Much witchcraft was being practised by the women in that area,' they said. Two other pupil-teachers at Gona, Sylvanus Tumonde and Robinson Manudaba, had also been chosen to go to St Aidan's in 1942. Bishop George wrote,

Robinson was a very good person, known by all, but someone at Gona was jealous of him. Because of jealousy and gossip and fear of sorcery, he was prevented from going. He has since stayed in the village, living the life of a committed and devoted Christian.

So Robinson lost his chance for education.

Eventually, George agreed to go to St Aidan's on one condition — that Alban Jaipoba, his closest friend, would also be allowed to go to the college. Fr Benson, knowing they were like brothers, had often asked them both to accompany him on his journeys round the district. He knew Alban very well and had for a time employed him as a carpenter in his workshop. He agreed that Alban could go to Dogura with George. Alban's mother at first refused to give her permission. She had lost her husband and two daughters, and Alban and his younger sister, Marcella, at that time at school in Grade 3, were the only children left. Faced with the persistence of the white priest, however, she gave in.

During the five months while they were getting ready to leave, many people were discouraging about the wisdom of sending George away to study. Looking back, Bishop George recalled how his Christian faith at that stage was not strong enough to show him clearly the way to go. He was full of doubts about his future and apprehensive about leaving Gona.

> Our faith was weak but we offered it to God and God spoke to the
> three of us: Sylvanus Tumonde, Alban Jaipoba and George Ambo.

It seemed to George that he heard God's voice through some of his close family, through the white missionaries and through some of his schoolmates and pupil-teachers. In prayer and reflection it gradually became clear to him and to his two friends that going away to college was part of God's purpose for them all.

In September 1941, while George was still a pupil-teacher at All Souls' School, he wrote his first letter. It was to his old teacher, Miss Eather, who had by then settled in Sydney. This letter expresses much about the confidence he had in his friendship with a white person. In immaculate English, in a fine handwriting and with no spelling mistakes, George asked his old teacher to pray for him and his people in their 'sadness'. A sickness had spread in the area of Gona Bay but had not affected the mission station. As he wrote, 'eight Christian people and seven heathen people had died in Gona village'. Since his former headmistress was no longer present, he reminded her of the routine of life at the school. George mentioned at the end that he and Sylvanus would go to college in January (1942). 'Will you pray for us every day,' he wrote, 'and we will pray for you every day. God will bless you...Good Bye, I am your friend,' and he signed the letter 'George Koiawo' (his nickname).

George Ambo's experiences at the beautiful All Souls' Mission were to leave lasting marks in his soul. The following description of Gona by Bishop Philip Strong, the Bishop of New Guinea at the time, helps us to imagine the sort of imprint the place must have left in George's mind:

Gona was a lovely mission station...one of the brightest and most live spots in the whole of our work. I have never visited it without being thrilled by the reality of the atmosphere of devotion I found there, and by the enthusiasm and warmth of the large crowds of Papuan mission adherents for whom the mission station had become a centre of life.[50]

It was certainly the 'centre of life' for the young George, and the 'enthusiasm and warmth' were to be striking features of George's personality and work for the Church. The influence of the two white missionaries, Mavis Eather, his teacher, and James Benson, his priest, was to prepare the way for George's future churchmanship. Their genuine love and concern for people of the Gona District, would become the basis for his positive relationship with most white people. It was to be a relationship of mutual respect in which Bishop George never forgot Miss Eather's words: 'Never imitate white man, but learn from him. Always be yourself and be proud of being a Papuan'.

Bishop George later became a great friend and counsellor for many of the white people working in his country, but he always retained his own Papuan identity.

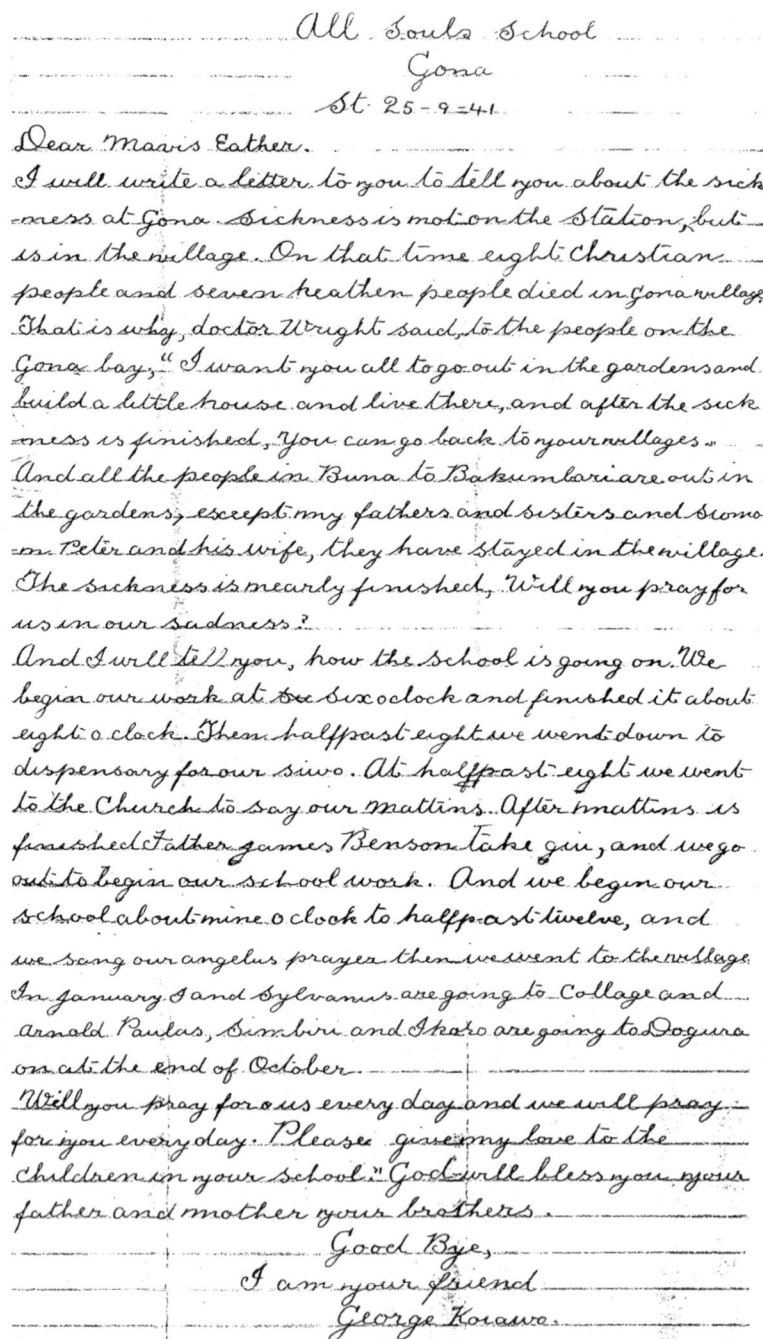

All Souls School
Gona
St. 25-9-41

Dear Mavis Eather.

I will write a letter to you to tell you about the sickness at Gona. Sickness is not on the Station, but is in the village. On that time eight christian people and seven heathen people died in Gona village. That is why, doctor Wright said, to the people on the Gona bay, " I want you all to go out in the gardens and build a little house and live there, and after the sickness is finished, You can go back to your villages " And all the people in Buna to Bakumbari are out in the gardens, except my fathers and sisters and Simon Peter and his wife, they have stayed in the village. The sickness is nearly finished, "Will you pray for us in our sadness?

And I will tell you, how the school is going on. We begin our work at six six oclock and finished it about eight oclock. Then halfpast eight we went down to dispensary for our sivo. At halfpast eight we went to the Church to say our mattins. After mattins is finished Father James Benson take giu, and we go out to begin our school work. And we begin our school about nine oclock to halfpast twelve, and we sang our angelus prayer then we went to the village. In January I and Sylvanus are going to Collage and Arnold Paulas, Simbiri and Ikaro are going to Dogura on at the end of October.

Will you pray for us every day and we will pray for you every day. Please give my love to the children in your school." God will bless you, your father and mother your brothers.

Good Bye,
I am your friend
George Koiawa.

Letter written in September 1941 by George Ambo
to Mavis Eather, then back in Sydney
(The letter can be seen in its original size in the Appendix)

CHAPTER 6

St Aidan's College — The Pacific War — The Martyrs

During the last two months before leaving Gona, the three pupil-teachers, George, Sylvanus and Alban, as well as all the people, had felt deeply anxious about rumours of war. For some time, Fr Benson had been giving them reports of disturbing events in Europe, where white people were fighting amongst themselves. Though sad, these reports had seemed rather remote. When early in December 1941 the Japanese attacked Pearl Harbor, the American naval Base at Hawaii, the threat of war became real. Chaos had been unleashed in the Pacific. A Japanese campaign of aggression aiming at conquering the whole of the region had begun.[51]

Only a couple of weeks before George was due to leave Gona war came to Papua New Guinea. On the 23rd January 1942, the Japanese invaded Rabaul in East New Britain. Although a government order had been issued for the evacuation of all white women in the country, the missionaries insisted on considering their position for themselves. Bishop Strong, the Bishop of New Guinea, soon made up his mind. On the last day of January he sent a radio message to his staff:

> I have from the first felt that we must endeavour to carry on our
> work in all circumstances, no matter what the cost may ultimately
> be to any of us individually...

Bishop Strong was deeply moved at the time by the letters and messages from many of his staff supporting his own conviction that they must stick to the work to which God had called them. Mavis Parkinson, the young headmistress at Gona, who was teaching there when George left, wrote to a friend:

> I was so sure the right thing to do was to stay, come what may...We,
> as missionaries, owe it to these people and the Church as a whole
> to stay and see this thing through. [52]

Little did she know at the time of writing, that in just over two months she and Sr May Hayman, the Gona nurse, would be murdered by Japanese soldiers.

These were anxious times for George, Sylvanus and Alban — their minds and hearts were overwhelmed with worry. Should they leave their people in such threatening circumstances? Bishop George recalled how, at different times as the war intensified, they saw Japanese planes or Allied bombers flying low over All Souls' Station. Rumours reached them of fighting in New Britain and in the area beyond the border between Papua and New Guinea, the Mandated

Territory of New Guinea, as it was then called. As Bishop George recalled the situation,

> There was always the fear of Japanese soldiers surviving a plane
> crash near Gona or of a small Japanese force landing to construct
> an airstrip in the area. Fr James Benson thoroughly explained and
> advised us of what to do if the Japanese landed on the Gona Beach.[53]

The calming influence of Fr Benson and the two Sisters, Mavis Parkinson and May Hayman, had a stabilising effect on George and his fellow pupil-teachers. Bishop George recalls how Fr James had kept urging them not to lose heart but have faith in God's plan for them. The knowledge that the three white missionaries would remain at their posts whatever happened gave the young men courage.

George knew and believed that God had sent the missionaries to Gona 'to teach and live the Bible'. Even in the hour of danger, they would be faithful to God's purpose and remain with their flock. Following the missionaries' example, George put his faith in God's plan for him, which he believed in his heart was to become a teacher-evangelist.

So, early in February 1942, with heavy heart and not knowing what dangers the future would bring, George left his family and friends at Gona. Together with Alban Jaipoba and Sylvanus Tumonde, he sailed away on the *Maclaren King*, the mission boat, down the coast in a south-easterly direction. St Aidan's College was situated on Bartle Bay, ten kilometres or so east of Dogura, in the Milne Bay District.

Bishop George recalls the sadness of that first parting with his home.

> The *Maclaren King* was anchored a little way off the shore of Gona.
> The beach was covered with children, single boys and girls and
> old and young men and women. Our relatives and families were
> crying and we also were crying. In that uttermost fear and sorrow
> we departed our beach.[54]

On its way down the coast, the *Maclaren King* called in at all the mission stations to pick up new mission boys for St Paul's School at Dogura, as well as new students for St Aidan's. At the first stop at Buna Government Station, they were joined by three new college students from the Northern District: Philip Tahima and Wilson Suja from Isivita Mission, and Maxwell Apota from Sangara Station. Philip and Wilson were accompanied by their wives, Marjorie and Dulcie; Maxwell was single. All three men would later contribute greatly to the development of their country, Philip as a teacher-evangelist, Wilson as a politician who later became a Member of the Papua New Guinea House of Assembly, and Maxwell as a teacher in the Northern District.[55]

Also on board was Bishop Philip Nigel Warrington Strong who, in 1937, had been enthroned as Bishop of New Guinea.[56] Anxious to visit his mission staff and people as often as possible in these uncertain times, he took every opportunity to go with the mission boat on its round trips from Dogura to all the coastal stations. Having just spent a couple of nights with Fr Romney Gill, the priest in charge at Duvira, the northernmost Anglican mission, he was now on the return trip. Little did George know that the bishop travelling on the boat with him was later to play a crucial part in shaping his future life.

At Menapi, the last port of call before Dogura, the boat picked up two more students for the college, Carson Osembo and Fabian Paisawa. Carson became a teacher-evangelist and later a village priest in the Mamba area. Fabian, also a teacher-evangelist, worked first at Menapi, later at Agaun Mission Station in the hills above Goodenough Bay, west of Dogura. He was the son of the Rev'd Amos Paisawa, an early Papuan priest, who had entered St Aidan's College in 1934. Fr Amos was regarded as 'one of the finest Christians on Cape Vogel'. Amongst other things, he had influenced Parata, a feared sorcerer of Cape Vogel, an area within sight of Dogura, to give up his evil practices and be baptised.[57]

At first the change to a strange environment had not been easy for the young George. Homesick and fearful of the unknown, he had to learn the ways of an area quite foreign to him. He clearly remembers their arrival at Wedau, the village at the foot of the hill of Dogura. A large crowd of people had come to the small jetty to see the mission boat arrive. These villagers spoke a language incomprehensible to the northern students. Their way of dressing in grass skirts was quite different from that of George's own people, who wore *tapa* cloth. Even the beach, covered with stones instead of sand, seemed strange as it stretched along the shore towards Cape Frere, the dark and mysterious mountain which formed the eastern border of Bartle Bay.

Bishop George recalled how the beauty of the landscape had impressed him and the other northern students—the blue bays surrounded by barren hills and mountains. It was all so unfamiliar after the flatness of Gona. High above them, perched on the plateau of Dogura, was the white Cathedral of St Peter and St Paul, bathed in the golden evening light. Its massive walls were set against the rugged hills, their razor-sharp ridges reaching down behind the belt of coconut palms which lined the beaches. The students had heard about the cathedral, completed only a couple of years before, and saw it from the sea as they were approaching the jetty. The sight of this proud building gave them hope for their future as workers for the Church.

After waiting some time by the jetty at Wedau, the new students were taken across Bartle Bay to St Aidan's College at Laronai, near Divari village. They had only a suitcase and a string bag with them as they transferred to the small boat owned by Reuben Mark, descendant of a South Sea Islands teacher who came to Dogura in 1893.[58] In Bishop George's words,

> Our heavy bags with food and other things would come later on the *Maclaren King*. We left Wedau jetty about 7pm and arrived at Laronai about 8.30pm. The former Principal, Fr AP Jennings, and Fr Oliver Brady, who had recently come to replace him, were together on the beach with the second- and third-year students to

greet us. They welcomed us by saying three times: *Eguclau, Egualau, Egualau* ('welcome', in the *Wedau* language), as we came in to shore.

Bishop George recalled his first sleepless night in the new place:

> My thoughts were not right and correct. I was afraid of and worried about sorcerers, magic and witchcraft for which the Dogura district was so well known. In the old days and even in my own generation the fear of sorcerers was very strong. They controlled whole communities. Our relations had taught and warned us to be careful if we met any of these types of people. Many young people died because they were afraid of the sorcerers. I was brought up in this situation and found it very hard to rid myself of such thoughts, beliefs and above all the feelings of fear in my heart. These false and evil beliefs were in me when I proceeded to college.

Another reason why George couldn't sleep was that the students had to lie on small pebbles, which the newcomers were not used to!

> We were tired and weary and had not eaten much. We had our wash in the sea and went to bed early but there were no real beds, only our own sleeping mats. We first had to carry the pebbles and put them on the ground to make it cleaner. Then we put down our mats which were very hard and not comfortable to sleep on.[59]

The rising bell rang at five in the morning, and after a wash the students went to the small bush chapel for Morning Prayer (Matins). Then followed the Holy Eucharist. Matins was in the *Wedau* language, and it was a bewildering experience for the northern students to follow Matins in a strange tongue. 'That was when I had to learn this foreign language,' wrote Bishop George, 'during the daily Services of Matins and Evensong'. The Eucharist was in English, which was also the language of St Aidan's College. After breakfast, the students were welcomed once more by the principal. 'Then, Mr Buckland, a white assistant teacher, presented our yearly programme.'[60]

The first month at college was so hard that George began to wonder whether he should remain at St Aidan's or go back home. Apart from having to learn a foreign language and sleeping on the pebbles, there were other difficult and unexpected aspects for the new students to cope with, such as 'getting used to eating vegetables which were not good, and the single boys' cooking which was not good'. Added to this, they spent the month of February mending old houses built of native materials and putting up new ones in the college grounds. Different ways of building had to be learnt by the young men from the north. They had to collect and carry back different types of bush building materials which were new to them, often from long distances. Bishop George writes further about the college:

> The college was situated on the plain near the beach and the ground was full of stones. There were ten houses on the station: four houses for married students, one dormitory for the single men, two staff

houses, one classroom, a chapel and a store-room for food and other things. They were all built of materials from the bush. Along the beach there were two villages on either side of the college with springs of fresh water, which we used to collect for cooking and drinking. The college whaleboat was lying on the beach in the shade of coconut palms and *mapa* nut trees. Nearby, a stony point jutted out in the sea. Rocky and barren mountain ranges rose behind the college. When the sea was calm and smooth, Bartle Bay was very pretty to look at. Several dozen goats kept by the principal would wander around the station, together with three horses which the students rode up to Dogura to fetch mail for the principal.

The following month was more encouraging. At the beginning of March the normal college programmes resumed. Bishop George recalled how impressed he had been with Fr Oliver Brady. 'My eyes were opened and my heart was opened too when Fr Oliver Brady gave his introduction lecture.' Then followed two days of tests given by Mr Buckland to find out the educational standards of the new students. The fine results which George obtained encouraged him to stay at the college. There were twelve new students that year and, including the second and third year students, the total was twenty-four. 'It was the biggest number of students the college had ever had,' wrote Bishop George.

He recalls how thankful he was for this new stage in his life — for this great experience which he felt had been given him by God.

> During the months from March to July, I was so happy in my studies and I put my whole heart to learn the Bible. Fr Brady's teaching was very clear to me and I thanked God that He guided, protected and encouraged me not to miss this golden and valuable opportunity.

Apart from studying the Bible, the students had to learn many other subjects, such as English, Reading, Writing and Arithmetic. However, the study of the Bible was for George his special and favourite subject.

During the months of March to June 1942, when George was settling in at St Aidan's, the war situation became more serious for Papua New Guinea. The civil administration had ceased. The old divisions of the German Mandated Territory of New Guinea and the Australian Papua no longer existed: they were now considered one area under the military control of ANGAU, the Australian New Guinea Administrative Unit, based in Port Moresby. According to Bishop George,

> both the Church and the new military government gave final warnings for all Europeans to leave the country. But Bishop Philip said, 'Those who want to go, they may go, but those who wish to stay they may stay'.[61]

In future years, it was to be a constant inspiration for George in his work for the Church that, faced with danger threatening their lives, the Anglican missionaries had remained at their posts.

Although worried about the war, the people at Gona did not feel in any immediate danger. A month or so after George had left, the Japanese invaded Lae and Salamaua, further up the north coast. As Mavis Parkinson wrote,

> The Americans are doing splendid work up at Lae and Salamaua. It really was marvellous that the advance was checked almost on our doorstep.

Ironically, some months after this letter was written, her youthful optimism would be shattered.[62]

On 22 July 1942, George Ambo and his fellow students at St Aidan's heard that Japanese forces had landed on the beaches at Gona, Buna and Sanananda near Killerton. The students were doing their night studies in the classroom when they heard the news on Fr Brady's radio. 'It was a great shock for us all,' recalled Bishop George, 'especially for the northern students'. But that was all they heard. For months after the Japanese invasion of Gona no news or letters reached the college. Bishop George wrote of the students' feelings:

> It was the saddest and most worrying time we had ever experienced. Our spirits were very low as we had no news of our families and especially of the white missionaries.[63]

It was as if a curtain had been drawn across the diocese, hiding the northern part of the mission. For months their mission sisters and brothers around Dogura were left in suspense, full of anguish and fear, not knowing for certain what had become of their fellow-Christians in the north. Bishop George said it all:

> But the faith of our bishop, our principal and other European missionaries was very strong and firm. Although they might be worried and frightened, they remained faithful to the work to which God had called them. Their faithfulness gave us courage.

Martyrs

The Japanese had invaded the Gona area on 21 July. The day had started in the usual way at the mission station: Fr Benson had celebrated the early Eucharist at the altar of the church, Mavis Parkinson had taught her classes in the school. At the hospital, May Hayman had cared for the sick. The work of the station was going on right up to the last moments. In the late afternoon, when Fr Benson was in his workshop, a mission boy shouted, 'Father! Father! Great ships are here!'[64] Mavis Parkinson later described the scene:

> There were four big ships not far out to sea, and another two on the skyline. Then the boats farther out opened fire on those nearer the beach; [there came] burst after burst of shellfire until the ground shook with the explosions. Soon an American Flying Fortress flew over and one of the transports opened up fire on her. Then followed a most thrilling sea-battle, the warships, both ours and the Japanese, seeming to move about like tiny boats, they were so quick. Then

the transports put out dinghies, and men got into them, so we decided we'd better move to a healthier spot.[65]

While enemy soldiers were coming ashore at Gona, the three white missionaries fled inland. After several days, having scrambled through swamps and dense jungle, they came to Siai Mission about forty miles inland from Gona. Having opened the station only a few years before, Fr Benson and the two white women were amongst friends. Again in Mavis Parkinson's words,

> As long as I live, I shall never forget the welcome they gave us. They hugged us and patted us for ages, and actually cried over us…they brought us food and hot water for a bath. May and I took off our filthy dresses and washed them, and while they dried, May wore a cassock of Fr John Yariri's and I wore an alb!

The white missionaries stayed for several weeks, hiding in a bush camp prepared for them by the Siai people. There they were safely cared for by the old pioneer teacher, Nathaniel Iaura, once George Ambo's teacher, and Fr John Livingstone Yariri, a Papuan priest, friend and assistant of Fr Benson.

The Japanese had landed on the north coast with orders to take Port Moresby by walking inland over the central mountains, along the Kokoda Track. As rumours came that they were approaching Siai, the missionaries decided to move on. With a group of other refugees, they made their way in a south-easterly direction. They were aiming for Port Moresby, hoping to cross the central Owen Stanley Ranges. After four days in the jungle, they were seen by an enemy patrol, and during the shooting the group scattered and were separated. For six days, Fr Benson wandered alone through the bush without food and water and having lost his glasses. Not knowing where he was, he at last gave himself up to a Japanese patrol.

The two Gona sisters had escaped the shooting but were soon caught by some villagers whose councillor bore a grudge against a white man. They were handed over to the Japanese authorities at Popondetta, at that time a small trade centre between Gona and Sangara serving the surrounding coffee plantations. They spent a night imprisoned in a coffee house. Early in the morning they were taken away to the nearby Ururu Plantation. There they were bayoneted by their Japanese guards and dropped into two freshly dug graves. Today, a simple stone altar by the roadside commemorates the place where they died.

A week or so after the invasion of Gona, the mission stations of Sangara and Isivita were also taken by the Japanese. For the last sixty years it has been generally believed that the version of the tragic events concerning the deaths of the missionaries is as follows.

Shortly before the enemy arrived, Fr Henry Holland, in charge of Isivita, fearing that his people might be punished by the Japanese for not handing over the white missionaries, decided that they must all leave the area. His plan was to walk over the Owen Stanley Ranges and so lead his party to the safety of Port Moresby. According to the account given in *The Road From Gona*, with him were Fr Vivian Redlich, Sr Marjorie Brenchley, nurse, Lilla Lashmar, teacher, John Duffill, missionary, as well as Lucian Tapiedi, teacher from Taupota Station near Dogura who acted as their guide. [66]

Having spent the first night in a village, as they were walking along the track towards the central mountains, they were joined by another group of fleeing expatriates. Persuaded by these people, Fr Holland made the fateful decision to change the direction of their flight. Instead of crossing the mountains, they all started walking together towards Oro Bay on the coast. After several days, they were joined by some hostile village men, who took charge of the party, secretly intending to hand them over to the Japanese. After crossing the Jewaia Creek near Embi Village, Lucian Tapiedi walked back to retrieve a box with mission records and money from Sangara, mistakenly left on the other side of the creek. He was stopped on the track by a group of villagers, one of whom killed him with an axe, and so he became one of the Anglican Martyrs. Shortly after passing through the villages of Embi and Dobuduru, the fugitives were handed over to the Japanese. According to *The Road from Gona*, some Japanese war diaries recorded that 'they were all beheaded on the beach near Buna by a Japanese soldier who volunteered for the terrifying job'.

Research done within the last couple of years into the fate of the Martyrs, however, shows that the above account is not correct in some important details. Until recently, it seems that the truth concerning the deaths of Fathers Henry Holland and Vivian Redlich has not been generally known. Bishop David Hand, in his book *Modawa* (page188), states that according to recent research, the two priests 'were not beheaded on Buna Beach but murdered by Orokaivans…'.[67]

According to confidential information given to the author in the 1980s by the local people, Fr Vivian Redlich escaped into the jungle and was never seen again. He did not join Fr Holland's party. Somewhere on the slopes of Mt Lamington, between the Banguho and Haijo Creeks, he was speared to death by some Orokaivans. Acting according to their belief that the Japanese soldiers were the spirits of their dead ancestors who had returned to their people and therefore must be obeyed, they had killed the white missionary. So what was earlier told the author supports Bp David Hand's contention in this matter, at least as it concerns the death of Fr Vivian Redlich. Elin Johnston was also informed by an Elder near Buna that Fr Holland was not beheaded by the Japanese, but the local people gave no further details.

There had been great need before the war to expand the work of the Church in this area and bring the Christian faith to more of its people. It is to be regretted that the money for this extension of the Church's work had not been forthcoming from overseas. Therefore, knowing some of the background of their heathen beliefs should help us the better to understand the actions of these Orokaivan people.

For George Ambo and the other northern students at St Aidan's the uncertainty as to the fate of their people and of their missionaries must have been deeply disturbing. Not until 1945, at a meeting of the General Synod in Sydney, did Bishop Philip Strong hear official reports that Fr Benson had survived captivity at the hands of the Japanese.[68] Already, towards the end of 1942, the Bishop had written to James Benson's father.

> You will by now have received the distressing and grievous news about your son...this is based upon native reports...the reports are...that he with Sr May Hayman and Miss Mavis Parkinson together with some Americans and Australians were annihilated on September 1st. Nothing further is known...[69]

(In fact, although harshly mistreated by the Japanese, Fr James Benson did survive the war; Chapter 8 gives an account of his subsequent activities.)

The bravery of the Anglican missionaries, their suffering and martyrdom, kindled in George's heart a fire which was to be a burning inspiration right through his life. It lit in his soul a zeal for his future work for the Church.

On 21 July 1942, the first of the invading Japanese forces landed here, on Gona Beach.
(Photograph courtesy of Bob Hay)

CHAPTER 7

George Ambo — Oliver Brady — Anglo-Catholic Church

The Principal of St Aidan's College, Oliver John Brady, was to influence George deeply — perhaps more deeply than any other of his white teachers. To understand some of the background for Bishop George's future churchmanship, one should look at aspects of Fr Brady's life and personality.

Intellectually, Oliver Brady was very capable. Born in Melbourne, Victoria, just before the turn of the century, he was educated at Melbourne Grammar School. Later he studied Theology at Trinity College as well as Arts at the University of Melbourne. In 1919, he graduated with a BA and became a Licentiate of Theology of the Australian College of Theology. The following year, he received a Master of Arts degree.[70]

Canon Oliver Brady
(Photograph courtesy of
Bishop Oliver Heyward)

Having worked for some years in a parish, Fr Brady initially visited Papua New Guinea in 1937. He was present when Bishop Strong held his first 'Native Anniversary Gathering' at Dogura. On that occasion, the course of Oliver Brady's life changed direction. As the bishop appealed to the national delegates not to look to Australia for all that they needed but to 'strive after self-support and the building up of an indigenous Church', Oliver Brady experienced a vision. He heard a call in his inner self to train and prepare Papuan men for Christian leadership. For the time being, he had to return to duties in Australia, but during the next three years the call persisted. His vision never dimmed.[71] He knew his life's work would be to help lay the foundations for a future Papuan Church. His training of George Ambo and other college students as teacher-evangelists would eventually bear fruit, bringing his vision to fulfilment.

As a graduate of Trinity College Theological School, naturally Oliver Brady had been influenced by its teaching. His nephew, Bishop Oliver Heyward, later declared:

> My uncle was a typical Melbourne Anglo-Catholic priest. The important features in his religious thinking were the sacraments…and orderly and decent worship with ceremonial and ritual framework — a great deal of pattern.

Already at college, meditation and prayer played a daily part in the young Oliver's life. Bishop Heyward continued:

> Every day he said Morning and Evening Prayer. They probably had Compline as well before going to bed. Oliver remained at heart a traditional Anglo-Catholic priest.

This religious school of thought, in which George was brought up at Gona and which he met at St Aidan's, was widespread in the Anglican Mission in Papua. The early bishops were all of the same tradition. Their common Anglo-Catholic thought could be traced back to England where, in the first half of the nineteenth century, a revival of certain Catholic doctrines, long forgotten in the Church of England, had occurred. During that period, a group of Oxford University Fellows produced writings called *The Tracts for the Times*. These led to the formation of a new direction within the Church of England called The Oxford Movement. The aim of 'the Tractarians', as they were called, was to shake the Church of England out of the indifferent and lukewarm state into which it had fallen. They emphasised the importance of prayer and the sacraments in religious worship as they sought to make the Christian life richer and more meaningful.

For Bishop George, one of the main tenets of the Tractarians was to form the very base for his ministry. Looking back to the ancient church as the source of their faith rather than to recent reformers such as Luther and Calvin, they claimed that Christ himself had instituted the Apostolic Succession. Christ himself, they preached, had authorised his Apostles and given them power to send others in His Name to carry on His work. Through the symbolic action of laying on of hands, a bishop at his consecration received this power and authority from Christ.[72] The belief that power was passed in unbroken succession from the first Apostles down to the present-day bishops gave authority to the leadership of the church in the New Guinea Anglican tradition. Right through his life as a bishop George Ambo was aware of God's power within himself, transferred to him at his consecration, which gave him the confidence and authority to carry out his ministry.

High-Church, Anglo-Catholic traditions have predominated in the Anglican Mission in Papua New Guinea. The first bishop, Bishop Montagu Stone-Wigg, who arrived at Dogura in 1898, tried to enrich the worship in the mission by introducing candles, crucifixes, silk vestments and incense. Furthermore, he stressed the importance of the bishop and his priests in providing pastoral care for their people. They must lead in worship based on the Gospels and the main sacraments such as Baptism and the Eucharist. Christians were encouraged to make Confession before a priest and to receive Absolution.[73] Such were the roots of the religious tradition planted in George Ambo by Fr Brady at St Aidan's College. These roots would later bear fruit in George's deep spirituality and compassionate care for his flock.

The course at the college was strenuous, demanding total commitment and obedience of the students. For four years, they had to learn academic subjects, educational principles and methods of teaching, as well as tenets of the Christian Faith. Thinking back on his college days, Bishop George recalled the hard training and the strict rules, such as not being allowed to leave the boundaries of the college without the principal's permission. But above all good spirit permeated the place. Former students wrote about the happy life, a kind of brotherhood life, devoid of negative feelings. One student wrote,

> You will never hear them [the students] bursting into a volley of abuse against their fellow brothers. They are always ready and willing to help each other in every bit of hard work.[74]

No doubt this atmosphere of commitment and brotherly love helped shape such features as the tolerance and self-discipline which are so prominent in George's personality.

Life for the students was highly regulated. The day began at 6am, with Matins followed by the service of Holy Communion. After an hour of physical exercise, such as the cutting of the grass in the college grounds with their bush knives, the students enjoyed a swim in the sea. Then classes were held in English till 2.30pm. The mission tradition was to teach in English: '...this opens to the native people a range of reading which is otherwise closed to them,' said Fr Brady.[75] In the afternoons, activities such as fetching firewood for cooking kept the young men busy. Only at night did the students have spare time for reading or meditation before the service of Compline and bed.

Owing to climate and difficulties with transport, one of the most serious problems at St Aidan's was the shortage of food. As Dogura is in the driest area of Papua, the ground is barren and hard during the long dry season. Although the students worked keenly in their food gardens, the plants frequently dried up. Added to which, the gardens were always being attacked by pigs. Bishop George remembered how once the food situation became so critical that Bishop Strong and Fr Brady decided to close the college.

> They made plans to move St Aidan's to All Souls' Station at Gona.
> During that very week, some northern students got dysentery and
> the plan was put off.

It was feared their move might have caused an epidemic amongst the people along the coast.[76]

Bishop George remembers how the situation had miraculously been saved. Fr John Bodger, the missionary priest in charge at Dogura Station, knew of a large supply of potatoes, planted by a goldminer who had since left the area. They were still growing in no-man's-land at a place called Kojgari, high up in the mountains behind Dogura. George, with most of the students, was sent up to collect the potatoes. It was a strenuous expedition. He still remembers crossing the Wamira River 35 times and spending the first night on the way in a mountain village. They stayed with Fr Japhet Koibua, the teacher-evangelist (later to be ordained priest), and his wife who welcomed them in 'the Christian spirit'. Bishop George describes it:

The freezing mountain cold was too bad. Some of us stayed awake all night, sitting around the fire to keep warm.

The whole of the next day, the students climbed higher up the mountains, walking up and down the steep ridges and reaching Kojgari in heavy rain.

We were hungry, cold and tired. So the prefect, Alan Bekau, gave orders that everyone must dig up his own potatoes and bake them on the fire for his dinner.

The next morning, he ordered that two students must carry back one sack of potatoes on a pole between them.

We had to dig potatoes and do our best to fill up our sacks. On the way down, there was torrential rain and the hills were very slippery and we found it very hard to carry those heavy bags.

The students arrived back at college the following day. 'We were all happy because, by the help of God, we managed to carry those heavy bags.' At Evensong, Fr Brady spoke to the students in the chapel, encouraging them by saying, 'God our Father in Heaven knows our troubles and problems. Let us all have our faith in Him and He will show us the future of this college'.[77]

In August 1942, the war came close to the college. Several thousand Japanese marines landed at Milne Bay, not far from Dogura but on the other side of the mountains. They were aiming at reaching Port Moresby along the south coast of Papua. First they had to gain control of the Milne Bay airfields. The fighting was fierce but short. Major-General Cyril Clowes, commander of the Australian forces in Milne Bay, issued his orders: 'No retreat or surrender, whatever the size of the attacking force!' His troops, inexperienced in jungle warfare, fought to defend the airfields. According to official accounts, for some time the battle 'hung in the balance'. In torrential rain, the Australian infantry held back the enemy in bitter hand-to-hand combat, forcing them back through swamp and sodden bush. Without sufficient support from ground troops, the battle was lost for the Japanese. Some nights later the last enemy forces were evacuated, but not all were able to get away. Troops remaining ashore were left to make their own way overland towards Buna and Gona. Most of them were tracked down and killed.[78]

News of the battle reached the students at St Aidan's. According to Bishop George, the fighting had been heavy and cruel. Many Japanese had been killed or wounded. Some of the wounded enemy soldiers walked away from the battlefields, hoping to cross the mountains and reach Gona, 350km or so from Dogura, to the north along the coast. Bishop George recalled that

the Australian soldiers at Dogura were ordered to hunt down the fugitives. Later, the students of the college heard that seven Australian soldiers had been killed during the hunt.

These were sad events interrupting the studies at St Aidan's during the last months of 1942. Once, reports reached Dogura that a group of 600 or so

Japanese were walking along the beach near Taupota Mission Station, further down the coast. 'Many of them were wounded and some died on the way,' wrote Bishop George. Some days later, spies reported that the Japanese had arrived at Lavora, a village on the other side of Cape Frere. Only the cape was separating the students and staff from the desperate fugitives. Bishop George described how the senior pupils were asked to give their service to the Australians.

> Six students offered to be spies for our soldiers. They had to find out how many Japanese were at Lavora. It was frightening to offer to help the Australian troops, but they did it by the Grace and Guidance of the Holy Spirit. On their return they informed the soldiers at Dogura. Then the Australians met the Japanese on the beach at Cape Frere. Six or seven Japanese were shot dead in the fight. The others escaped. One of our soldiers was shot in the arm. He was helped by the college students.

Bishop George recalls how, with some others, he took a few Australian soldiers to Cape Frere in the college whaleboat where they buried the dead Japanese.[79]

With wounded escapees roaming round the countryside, the situation at Dogura and St Aidan's was tense. Bishop George recalled one of the most frightening experiences of his life.

> A few days after the fight at Cape Frere, the Japanese tried to play a trick in order to get past the college on their way to Gona. They put on grass skirts and carried baskets on their backs. Our soldiers easily discovered them and the guards shot them. In the morning, we students found the dead Japanese and some wounded ones in the college grounds. They were in a very bad way, and I didn't like looking at them. I was sorry for the wounded ones. They were in a critical condition. The poor Japanese. They couldn't get away. They were shot dead as birds. We dug a hole on the beach and put them all in. That was our duty.

Compassion was ever present in everything George felt and did — even towards an enemy.

After the shooting in the college grounds, it was decided to move St Aidan's, first to Wamira village, but shortly after to Garogarona at the foot of the Dogura Hill by the main mission station. According to Bishop George, the students were not happy about moving the college, but felt they had to obey their church leaders, Fr Brady, Bishop Strong and Fr John Bodger, the priest in charge of Dogura. Slowly the students started to clear a new site. Then, one Sunday after Mass, when they went back to the old site at Laronai to collect belongings, they found some Japanese using the dormitories. Without being seen by the enemy, the students managed to run back to Garogarona. Bishop George told of this:

Soon after, those Japanese were killed by our soldiers. During the early months of 1943, the last enemy soldiers had either died or left Papua.

With the moving of the college and the uncertainty about desperate Japanese fugitives being in the area, he felt that '1943 was particularly unsettled and not good for studying'.

Throughout the period of war in Papua, St Aidan's College continued its daily work as best it could. Fr Brady carried on his teaching, preparing his students in academic as well as spiritual ways. Apart from learning such basic subjects as English, Arithmetic, Science and Geography, which in the future they themselves would be teaching, they also had to understand the meaning of Christian character. The Principal's main objective seemed to be the spiritual training of his students as future evangelists. Once, when asked what was his purpose in training the students, he replied, 'My real purpose is to plant Christ in the hearts of my men!' That was 'the essence of Oliver's vocation', wrote a missionary friend.[80]

Bishop George recalls how the influence of Oliver Brady deeply touched his students. He knew and loved each one of them, and shared with them their difficulties and any sorrows that might befall them or their families. His dedication to the task to which he felt called and his love of the people amongst whom he lived evoked in them a similar response. Bishop George described St Aidan's students' feelings about Oliver Brady:

> We honoured and respected and loved Fr Brady. He was a very patient man, spiritual and totally committed to Christ. He was kind and gentle. His sermons and his teaching, always in English, were very clear and simple. People could understand him. He was a saintly man. [81]

The friendship formed between Fr Brady and George lasted throughout Fr Brady's lifetime. Bishop George later named his first-born son Oliver Brady Ambo. Many opportunities occurred for the two to have talks together, either in the principal's house or in the classroom. During term, George would sometimes cook for Fr Brady. As a mission boy, he had been taught to cook by the European women at Gona. 'They wrote in my report, "he can cook" and they told Fr Brady about me,' said Bishop George. Dr Blanche Biggs, a missionary friend who sometimes had dinner with Fr Brady, recalled how George always cooked the meal and how he always did it with a smile on his face.[82]

On Saturdays, when the other students had gone away, George would often stay behind in the classroom to study. He recalled how sometimes Fr Brady came in with a cup of tea for him. 'In those days we didn't taste a cup of tea,' he said. 'That gave me a chance to ask a lot of questions.' They talked about serious matters of life, such as whether priests should marry, and about Fr Brady's belief that priests were more effective if they remained single. That was the belief at the time, and still is for a number of priests of a High-Church leaning. 'My son,' he told George, 'never give your body to young girls; keep it as a temple for the Holy Spirit'.

Bishop Ambo recalled how he 'thought and thought' about these words and wondered if he, as a teacher-evangelist or perhaps a future priest, should remain single. Although he had the greatest respect for his teacher, he always remained his own man, forming his own opinions. He did not slavishly follow others, but soon learnt to think out things for himself. For example, he decided to marry shortly after the completion of his course, in spite of Fr Brady's contrary view.[83]

At the end of 1945, Bishop Strong commissioned George Ambo and his fellow students to go to the various stations in the diocese. As licensed teacher-evangelists they were to teach in the mission schools and, as Bishop George said, 'above all preach the Gospel of Love to their people'.

George was sent to his home parish of Gona to help rebuild the station which had been destroyed by the Japanese. Before leaving St Aidan's, he briefly saw his old teacher, Mavis Eather, who had returned to Papua. She later wrote, 'I hardly knew him, he had grown so big, but still had that freshness and sheer joy for living'.[84] Joy of life has been a strong feature of George's personality right through his life. Whatever the circumstances, it would rebound with sparkling freshness.

Although his formal schooling had stopped at the end of Grade 5, through the example and teaching of Fr Brady George had been well prepared for his future ministry. The years at St Aidan's proved to be the most formative period in his development. He had stood out amongst the students. His keenness and joyful wholeheartedness had attracted the attention of Oliver Brady, who, in a vision, saw him as a future minister of the Church. Bishop George remembers this:

> He told me that one day I would become a priest. My vocation
> came clearly to me when I was in college.[85]

As a priest and later a bishop, he carried with him that indefinable stamp of St Aidan's, which, together with his natural charisma and spirituality, would make him a unique leader. One of Fr Brady's friends once said,

> Oliver's men set the quality of the native Papuan priesthood for
> the next generation. Out of these, his best and best-loved student
> was George Ambo.[86]

George Ambo and Fr Oliver Brady
at St Aidan's College
(Photograph from *Papuan Pastor*)

CHAPTER 8

So Gona's House Shall Rise...

So Gona's house shall rise, full fair again.
A living stone, for heavenly walls
     Of New Jerusalem.
Come comrades of all lands, be builders true
In love of God and fellow man
Make all things new.

James Benson
(Rabaul, January 1943)

Six months or so after George had left Gona to go to St Aidan's College, the Japanese had occupied the Gona area. Many of the local people had fled to Ambasi, a station 25 miles up the coast. On Sundays, Fr John Livingstone Yariri, the priest left in charge to do whatever he could during Fr Benson's absence, travelled the long distance to Ambasi by dinghy to take services for the local people as well as the Gona refugees. During 1942, nearly half of the Gona people at Ambasi were baptised.[87] Towards the end of the year, after the last fierce fighting on the beaches and annihilation of the Japanese by the Allied forces, the villagers returned to whatever was left of their old homes.

On their return to the devastated mission, the people were anxious to take up their former way of life and to revive the work of the Church. Led by Fr Livingstone and the teachers who had taught at All Souls' School before the invasion, they began the daunting task of building up the Church in the area. Leaving the old mission station by Kikiri Creek in ruins, they started two temporary stations at other places close by: one at Garara near Killerton, on the coast to the east of Gona; the other at Gomberu, a village by the sea, half a mile west of the old station. It was at Gomberu that George three years later would begin his work as teacher-evangelist, and at Gomberu he was to build his home.

For a time, the Christians met at these two separate stations of Garara and Gomberu. At Garara, Fr Livingstone and the teachers Godfrey Dabadaba and Horace Duega were in charge. At Gomberu, Simon Peter Awoda (George's brother), helped by the teachers Cecil Uiari (married to George's sister) and Michael Aguru (George's first teacher) led the work. Although divided in two groups, the Christian people were bound together by the tragic experience of losing their station and their missionaries. At that time there had been no news of Fr James Benson, who was thought to be dead. They worked together in a spirit of co-operation as if they all belonged to one station.

Soon after Easter 1943, Bishop Strong visited Gona. The sight of the station in ruins affected him deeply.[88] Pockmarked by bomb-craters on either side of Kikiri Creek, the mission had been devastated, with its buildings all wiped out. Only the hospital and Fr Benson's big white station cross, pierced by bullets, were still standing. As they walked along the beach, the Bishop and his fellow-travellers had seen the cross from 'a mile away...towering up over this fearful scene of death and desolation'. For the Christians at Gona, the white cross became a symbol of sacrifice of life, not only of the life of Jesus but also of the lives of the missionaries and the countless lives of soldiers who had died at Gona for their countries.

Near the station cross, and half hidden amongst undergrowth and orange hibiscus flowers, Bishop Strong found the concrete steps and platform on which the altar of the old church had once stood. There was also the wooden stump of the font.[89] 'At this old *bendoro* [a hardwood] baptism font my people were brought into the family of God,' wrote Warrington Manudaba, a teacher who later taught at Gona, 'and at these steps many received the Body and Blood of Our Lord'.[90] It was a moving occasion when, early the next morning after Bishop Strong's arrival, about 250 villagers knelt by these concrete steps to receive Communion from the hands of their bishop. When George Ambo returned from college early 1946, he was greatly encouraged to find that these foundations of the church — the cross, the altar steps and the font — still remained by Kikiri Creek. Bishop George recalled his feelings on his return to Gona:

> In my first week back in March 1946 I was thinking, planning and pondering how to start rebuilding the old station. I took a day off to see Fr Lester Raurela, the Papuan priest who had taken over from Fr Livingstone, to find out if he had any plans. I also wanted to hear if there was any news of Fr Benson.

While George was away at Dogura, doing his course at St Aidan's, all the students and staff believed that Fr Benson had been killed by the Japanese. Not until shortly before the students were commissioned at the end of 1945 had an official message reached the college, that he was still alive. 'When we heard the news, many people were crying — not for sadness, but for joy and happiness,' wrote Bishop George.[91]

Thinking back on his first position as teacher in charge of the school at Gomberu, Bishop George recalled how the whole of 1946 was a very hard and difficult year. He 'struggled along with the help of God'. Initially, George had arrived home full of enthusiasm for tackling his new job. He had experienced the joy of being guided into adult life by Fr Oliver Brady, the teacher he so greatly admired. The joy and blessing of that experience was always with him. He had a love for teaching. Gradually, however, he came to realise that life was not as easy as he had thought it would be.

After the talk with Fr Lester, George and his staff helped organise the clearing of the old mission grounds. They had to collect bush materials for the new buildings from the surrounding jungle. In Bishop George's words:

We were allowed to teach from Monday to Thursday in the classrooms. On Fridays, we had to help the village communities with the rebuilding of the station.

His only trained assistant teacher was Maxwell Apota. Having been at St Aidan's with George, Maxwell was now married and had a little girl. The rest of the staff were pupil-teachers whose educational standard was very low. On Thursdays, George ran teachers' classes 'to help the pupil-teachers to help me and Maxwell'. They had to make up their own teaching material, as there were no books or any kind of teaching equipment. In a telling note to the author, Fr John Wardman, who later succeeded Fr Benson at Gona, gives a brief glimpse of the difficult situation:

> Fr James told me how George and Simon Peter and others revived the school after the war before Fr James' return; with no equipment they used the sand of the beach, smoothed out as slates on which to practise writing.

In May, 1946, George sent a hastily written but illuminating letter about his work to his former teacher, Mavis Eather, who was then teaching at Wanigela, a mission station further down the coast.

> I wonder if you would like to know how my work is going. In my school there are 164 children. There are only two pupil-teachers together with three evangelists who are helping us. I'm trying to teach them [a] little bit on every Thursday afternoon. At present we are building [the] new station just near old mission station which was destroyed. While we are clearing the place we find many Japaneses [sic] bones and Australians lying in the grass. And I remembered Nehemiah in the moonlight with his young men went up the hill and found the pool.

It is evident from George's letter that Fr Benson was expected to return to Gona at this time. George continues:

> Russel [a local workman] is building Fr James Benson's house with work boys and some of the people are serving *kambira* [stalks and leaves of a plant like a *pandanus* palm for [the] roof with the help of the schoolchildren. At present the work is very hard but I'm feeling that God is helping me. Monday to Wednesday we are having school but Thursday and Friday we are helping in the building. Fr Dennis Taylor [the priest in charge of rebuilding Sangara and also responsible for the Gona area] told us to do this and help the building more quicker [sic]. In Holy Week I told the doctrine in Evensong and people came in their hundreds to hear me. Then on Good Friday the people came in their hundreds and I took three hours service. Then on Easter Day we have a happy time. I have very poor blackboard but I must be patient and God will give it to me in His own Good time. In Gona three people died, two were by sickness and one was by crocodile...[92]

Despite the difficulties, George was outstanding in his teaching and management of his school. This was noted at the time in a report on the school made by a visiting anthropologist and educationalist, Camilla Wedgwood, who was inspecting the mission schools for the government.[93]

In 1943, a Directorate of Research and Civil Affairs had been established in Port Moresby by General Thomas Blamey, Commander-in-Chief of the Australian Army. The purpose of the directorate was to gain information on which to base future policy. As General Blamey greatly valued the knowledge of such academics as Camilla Wedgwood, she was commissioned by the directorate to provide information on mission education in Papua. Between 1944 and 1947, she undertook four tours of inspection of schools. One of these took her to the Gona area. At Gomberu she was greatly impressed by George Ambo, both as a person and as a teacher.

Miss Wedgwood's report on George Ambo gives a clear picture of a conscientious teacher, born with a love of teaching and a natural ability for dealing with people. She also notes the enthusiasm which was always a hallmark of George's character:

> George is, I believe, exceptional both as regards personality and teaching skill...He is undoubtedly one of those people who have the gift of teaching. That became clear to me as I listened to him giving the school religious instruction. Although I could understand only a word here and there, the dramatic way in which he told the story of Joseph and his brothers made it possible for me to follow it, and the children, to whom the story was not new, listened with all their attention and eagerly answered in chorus the questions which George, with skill, threw out from time to time. In his English lessons, too, he assumed his dramatic and narrative gifts, with the result that his classes showed real interest, and jokes and laughter were enjoyed. Too often in native schools there is only boredom. Furthermore he was consistently quiet with the children and mistakes were corrected in a friendly manner. In this gentle courtesy he is very different to many of the native teachers in these and other mission districts. [94]

Camilla particularly noted that George taught his '162 pupils freely in the vernacular,' and that the children '...fully understood what they were doing in their English, Arithmetic and Geography...'. In a country with 850 or so different languages, the question of use of local languages in education as well as in church services was one of utmost importance. In areas where the Anglican Church operated, five major language groups dominated. At Dogura, before and during the war, teachers were trying to use English as well as the local *Wedau* language in the schools. Furthermore, an effort was made by the mission to spread these two languages, English and *Wedau*, right through the Anglican area for use in teaching, beginning with the youngest grades. It was hoped that *Wedau* could become a common language, a *lingua franca*, connecting the different language groups and districts of the diocese.

Not all teachers agreed with the view that *Wedau* should become a common language for the whole of the Anglican Diocese. Camilla Wedgwood firmly claimed that the youngest children should be taught in their own mother-tongue during their first years at school. She believed that language 'is an expression of a people's culture; of their physical, intellectual and spiritual life'. In her view, an ability to read and write their own language would be the means by which their traditional culture would be upheld and preserved for the future. She met in George Ambo a teacher with similar views.

Camilla had found at Dogura that English was not only the main language of teaching, but also of the services held in the Cathedral. All the hymns sung by the local people, as well as the liturgy, epistles, gospels and prayers were all in English.[95] She did not believe that the local congregation understood the English language, and wondered what was the value of a faith expressed in foreign words, mostly learnt by rote!

Such ideas on language would become very important issues for George in his future building of an independent Church. Deeply concerned to make the indigenous Church meaningful for his people, he, as a bishop, would later use his talents as a poet and linguist to write songs and hymns and translate biblical texts into his own language. Bishop George recalled, however, that

> as a young teacher at Gomberu, I was too keen on evangelism and teaching the children how to read and write to find time for composing any hymns. I did translate some hymns from English into the *Binandere* language (spoken in the Mamba area) and also into *Ewa-ge*, our own language (spoken by the 'sea-people' of the Gona area). The first one I translated was T*he King of Love my Shepherd is...* I also translated two songs in *Wedauan* into *Ewa-ge*, that was all.

From the start, George saw the futility of trying to impart knowledge to young children in a foreign language, and always taught them in their own mother-tongue.[96]

While George on his return had felt encouraged by the faithfulness of the Christians in his home area, he had also been distressed to find that evil beliefs and customs were still being practised by some.[97] He later wrote:

> I was a very young teacher and I tried to help my people give up their bad ways and keep only the good customs. I prayed that the Holy Spirit would guide me and give me Grace in my fight against such cases as sorcery, witchcraft and immorality. There was a famous sorcerer whose name was Jarugaba. His clan-name was Ijiba and he came from the Ope River area, which is in Ambasi Parish. I knew this sorcerer when I was a schoolboy. We children were warned by our parents not to go near him or to pass him when he was walking towards us. We were warned strongly to hide away in the bush and let him pass by. Everyone knew he was a great and dangerous sorcerer.

In 1946, when I came back from St Aidan's, Jarugaba still lived in the area and people still feared his evil power. During my pastoral care for them, I met this sorcerer. So I talked to him about the Christian Faith, but he treated me as a small boy and walked away, warning me to be careful with myself and in what I was trying to do. I met him a few times in the four years at Gomberu and Gona but he made up his mind not to see me. Even so, I kept on praying for him. Not until the year 1963, when as a Bishop I visited Gona and Ambasi Parishes, did I see him again. I made a special effort to visit him and warned that I would like to meet him in the near future. This time he was hoping to see me and talked with me about his evil practices. In the end he gave up sorcery. I thanked God for His guidance and because He gave me power over the sorcerer.

While George, as a young teacher, fought against his people's belief in witchcraft and sorcery, he valued many aspects of their culture. He loved traditional dancing.

If I thought it was a good custom, we would keep it, but if it was a bad custom, we would not keep it. In that way, I led my people. I said to them, 'You are dancing the good traditional stories, now I will teach you the old story from the Bible, written in the chapter of Exodus, of the Church going out in Moses' time'. It was the story of Mt Sinai that especially interested them.

In Papuan mythology, some mountains are sacred and spirits, moving in fog and mist over their pinnacles, must be obeyed. In a similar way, the voice of God came out of a cloud on Mt Sinai, proclaiming to Moses His Commandments. Expressed in dance, the images would come alive for the people. In George's words to the people,

You have been dancing our ancestors' story, practising it and imitating the ancestors, and this is good. Now we will try to practise dancing the stories of the Bible. That will teach you. Put yourselves into the story and you will see it.

Through traditional dancing, singing, drumming and miming, George took the first steps towards making the teachings of the Church clear and meaningful for his people. He did not know then that this idea would be one of his greatest contributions as a bishop to the indigenous Church. He said later,

I don't know how I got this idea. God put it in my head, but I started it. That was how it began in my early days.[98]

It was at this time that George was first aware of miracles occurring in his own life. His compassion for people who were suffering and his conviction that the healing power of God was stronger than that of sorcery led him into the sphere of spiritual healing. Bishop George still remembers how the first miracle occurred: 'One of our pupil teachers, Phanuel, had a little son. His son died — the first son'.

The death occurred on a Thursday while George was conducting his teachers' class:

> The mother was crying. We left the classroom and ran out to see what was happening. The baby, Nathan Siriga, had been ill with malaria. I had a strong feeling inside that I should take the child into the church. I grabbed the baby from the mother. All of us ran into the church where I led the prayers to God Almighty.
>
> The mother was crying—shouting outside the church building, 'Ai, George! Bring him out. He is dead!' She had lost her faith and was thinking in her heart that sorcery had caused the death of her child. Only witchcraft might bring him back to life. Inside myself I heard a voice saying, 'Go to the altar steps with the child and pray for him!' Phanuel Siriga and some of the teachers remained inside the church praying. Others left and went out. We prayed for over half an hour. Then I opened my eyes and saw the baby's condition was the same. I still had a feeling I could save it. I was praying like Elisha was praying for the Shunamite woman's son, using that story from the Bible in my prayers. This baby was their first one. I didn't know why he died. 'Why did you move me to come and do this?' I whispered in my heart to God. I shouldn't have taken the baby from its mother, but I had a feeling I could save it. When I took it, some of my pupil teachers put up opposition. They nearly refused to come into the church.
>
> The people's opposition to what I was doing was visible. 'You have a knife,' I had said to the mother. 'You can force me to give the baby back to you and you can take it to the witch doctor.' But inside I was crying for that child. He was very beautiful. Some of the teachers lost their faith and gave up praying, but two or three kept hoping that God in His Love would answer our prayers. In the end, the baby put his hand up and touched me on the cheek. I gave him back to his mother. Today he has a big position in the government. In the end God did answer our prayers and brought the baby back to life.
>
> That was the first miracle which happened during my ministry for His Kingdom. I became very well known in the whole district after that event. Some of the teachers believed in the miracle. They spread the news about it.

However, it seems that George's success was arousing jealousy in the community. While some of his staff and villagers acknowledged him as their leader and followed his teaching, others opposed him, resenting his growing influence. 'Many of my generation were against me, but I did not give up hope.' [99]

Bishop George continued:

> The second miracle happened later in the year, when I was walking with my school children to the bush. For some time there had been

rumours about a young village woman who behaved in a strange way. She was cutting her body with knives and bits of broken bottles. She had disfigured herself and lost her beauty. She was not a normal woman, but looked like an old lady. She had a sickness I couldn't understand.

One day, Fr Lester Raurela sent a message to Gomberu for George, his school children and staff to go to the bush to cut posts for putting up new houses on the station. George told what happened then:

> I was walking past her village with my children and teachers when I saw her with my own eyes. I felt very sorry for her. The young woman was sitting by herself on the sand. It was as if something had attacked her — an evil spirit? I don't know. Blood was pouring out from places on her body, on her head and on her face. She still has some scars on her skin. She began rolling on the sand in great pain. She was crying and rolling around as if she were crazy. Seeing the woman writhing on the ground, people were saying, 'Oh, what's going on? Where is this power coming from?' 'I'm not causing it,' I said. Then I snatched the knife away from her, and, kneeling down on the sand with my children and teachers around her, I began praying. We waited several minutes. It was not clear that this was a healing service. I only prayed.
>
> When I visited her again, she was no longer cutting her body. I assured her of our prayers for her to Jesus Christ and of His love for her. I told her that if she desired herself to get better she would. Here again, God in His love brought healing on her. She is now married to a good person and they have six or seven lovely children. These children are good Christians and she is still alive with her husband. She still remembers this happening and has always been very grateful to me. 'It was God who did it — not me!' I told her. I just prayed. That was the second miracle.

Bishop George recalled how the change from the serene world of St Aidan's to his life as a teacher-evangelist at Gomberu had not been easy. 'I had many enemies, especially amongst my former schoolmates and the young men,' he said. Two incidents, recalled by a former government minister, throw some light on the sort of conflicts which caused opposition to George and also to his brother, Simon Peter. Stephen Tago, former Minister for Defence in the National Government, was a young mission boarder at Gona when George was teaching there. Simon Peter had recently returned after completing the teacher-evangelist course at St Aidan's when the incidents occurred. Here is Stephen's account of them:

> I was a small boy, and these two names, George and Simon, were ringing in my head, getting bigger and bigger in my mind. In those days, they were the bright leaders and we had to listen to them. Both brothers were very, very strict. I remember, on one occasion,

they were walking along the beach. It was in the moonlight. The young people were dancing in a certain place by the sea called 'The Place of Entertainment'. It was like a club where young people met in social gatherings. They used to dance in the moonlight on the beach. This was more respectable than the disco-clubs today, but Bishop George and his brother stopped these social gatherings. They were very, very strict with the young people.

Another incident, which occurred shortly before George was posted to a new parish, left a deep imprint in Stephen Tago's mind.

We went to Matins in the church every morning, from prep classes up to the highest classes. We were all there and we all saw it. Fr Simon Peter caned his two sisters for having boyfriends. I still feel sorry about it today. In front of us all, he got up in church and belted his two pretty sisters, both assistant teachers, because their boyfriends had slept with them during Lent. They were their proper boyfriends whom they later married.

Although George had not been present in the church at that time, the two Ambo brothers supported each other closely, upholding strict ideals of Christian morality — too strict to be accepted by some of the Gona people.[100]

So his zeal for wiping out immorality created hostility towards George. He recalled it:

I tried my best to stop their bad and evil customs such as sleeping with the girls before they married. 'That is not the Christian way,' I said. They became very angry and hated me. Oh, they nearly killed me. They went mad shouting, 'Come on you George! Get out!' I had a pupil teacher staying with me. We used to walk around talking with them about the Christian marriage ideals. What I said, I tried to put into my own life. I tried to lead them but it was not easy. They nearly tore me to pieces. But my clan heard about it. 'If you tear me to pieces they will tear you to pieces,' I said, 'because they are a big clan, some at Kurou, some at Garara. They are all my Somboba Clan,' I said. As our clan was bigger than theirs, they dared not touch me or there would have been deadly fighting.

Although George was preaching and teaching about Christian marriage, most people, even some of the Christians, kept to their old ways. Mostly the girls were already pregnant when they sought the Church for their wedding. It was hard to stand by the Christian ideals, living as they did with their heathen parents.

There was the story of Ambrose Burogu, the pupil-teacher, and Mary Magdalene, one of the older school girls at Gona. They fell in love. It was against the mission rule for a teacher to have a close friendship with a student, and these two young people stood by their Christian Faith. They had to wait, of course, but Mary immediately saw the priest in charge. Following his wishes, she started preparing for the future when she would be a teacher's wife. After leaving school, she stayed on the station as a mission worker. Eventually, the wedding date was fixed. Then Mary disappeared. Her mother had taken her off to another district, hoping to give her away in exchange for a wife for her son! Mary had to obey. Such were some of the customs, the buying, selling and exchanging of brides, which George had to overcome.[101]

Bishop George considered that his first year—1946—was very difficult:

> Although God was helping me in my ministry, yet Satan, the cunning devil, was trying to interfere. Satan used some of the village communities and especially my own generation, married and unmarried, to go against my ministry. Their critical attitudes I offered to God my Heavenly Father, leaving it to Him to deal with them.

As Jesus saw Satan at work in people who were hostile to Him, so George saw Satan at work in many people who opposed him.

CHAPTER 9

Marriage to Marcella — The Return of Fr James Benson

During those first difficult months as a teacher at Gomberu, George Ambo strongly felt the need for a close companion with whom he could share the challenges, joys and disappointments of his everyday life. For some time he had been thinking about marriage. Remembering Fr Brady's words to him about keeping his body as a temple for the Holy Spirit, he had asked Bishop Strong for his view on this matter. Thinking that one day he might become a priest, he felt reassured when the Bishop had said, 'No, George, we do not allow you Papua New Guineans to become single priests. If you want to become a priest, you must get married'. George was thankful for his advice. After much pondering and soul searching, finally he made up his own mind. He later wrote,

> In the first part of 1946, I was praying to God to show me the right partner to help me in my future ministry. I prayed to God for guidance of the Holy Spirit — should I marry Miss Marcella Karau or another person?[102]

He had known Marcella for a long time. She was from Gona village (now Kausada), not far from his own place at Kurou. As it happened Marcella had already been thinking about George for several years. Her brother, Alban Jaipoba, was George's closest friend and fellow student at St Aidan's College. In 1943, she had written her first letter to George when he was away at St Aidan's. She had sent the letter to her brother Alban with a note asking his advice. It read, 'If you think your friend is the right person for my future, give this letter to him. If not, tear the letter and burn it'. Aware of the possibility that one day he might be ordained, George had not hurried into a close friendship with Marcella. In his reply to her he had indicated that no serious questions regarding a future partnership could be discussed at that stage. 'This is only correspondence; we will decide later!' he wrote. He recalled how he had told her that after his college years they would 'come together and talk in front of each other, because I thought then that one day I might become a priest'. They continued writing to each other during George's time at St Aidan's. 'She was the first girl to write to me,' he said.[103]

Marcella lived with her mother at Gona village. Her two sisters having died in childbirth, only she was left with her brother Alban. 'She was a fatherless child,' said Bishop George. 'Her mother was very strict.'[104] Wondering why two letters had started to arrive from St Aidan's College instead of only one from her son, Alban, the mother had guessed that the second letter to Marcella was from one of the other students. She then gave her daughter the following advice:

> Your body belongs to you. God has given the key to you, not to any other person. You must respect your body in the way God respects you. You must keep the key until you marry your husband. He will open your body and he will use it.

Urging Marcella to ask advice from her brother, the mother gave her daughter a final warning: 'Don't go after any young man who has a 'honey-tongue'!'

For George the decision to marry had not been easy. He had been praying intensely for guidance from the Holy Spirit during the first months at Gomberu.[105]

> Then one night God sent His angel to visit me in a vision. He said that my future partner would be Miss Marcella Karau. When I was saying Matins early the next morning, I asked God to reveal it a second time. Although I had two visions from God, yet I felt the need for a third vision. I used Gideon's prayer as an example, and God showed me again that I should marry Marcella Karau.

He continued:

> One Friday evening, Miss Marcella Karau came for Evensong. I met her after the Evening Prayer and let her know what was in my thoughts. Both of us agreed to let our relations and families know that we would get married.

A short time later, on a Sunday morning, when Fr Lester Raurela came to Gomberu for Mass, he interviewed the young couple and advised them to walk up to Sangara to see Fr Dennis Taylor, the priest in charge of the whole district. It was necessary to obtain his approval. 'This we did, and we were very happy and getting ready for our wedding,' wrote Bishop George.

However, before plans could progress in earnest, George's father also had to give permission for the marriage. He told George that he had to prove he was ready to marry; he had to make a canoe, and establish some gardens, so that his father could see that he was ready.

So George made a canoe in which to go fishing, proving that he was capable of providing food for a family. Bishop George described the process:

> I cut it out of a hollow tree trunk and made an outrigger. My father watched me and said that I had made a better canoe than he could have done. Because of that new way of going to school and learning how to use steel tools instead of stone tools, I had a good axe. I bought it as a mission boy and my father kept it while I was at college. It was still sharp and wonderful, so I made a beautiful canoe. It was on the beach, waiting for Fr Benson to come back and bless it. Then my father allowed me to marry.[106]

In May, 1946, George and Marcella both wrote letters to tell Mavis Eather at Wanigela about their plans. However, their views differed regarding the wedding date. Marcella wished to wait for Fr Benson's arrival at Gona so that he could take the wedding, whereas George was anxious to hasten the day. He needed Marcella to help him in his work yet seemed to feel guilty about wanting to speed up their plans. We sense his excitement in the letter he wrote to Mavis Eather.

> Now the other letter is written by Marcella who I'm going to marry her. She says when Fr Benson come home to Gona then we will marry, but I likes this year. What you think? The same girl I have told you all about. Please do not tell it to Father Andrew. Please, Please, Please…I'm your bad boy, George Ambo.

(Fr Hugh Andrew was priest in charge at Wanigela.)[107]

Marcella in her letter invited Mavis Eather to the wedding. She wrote in her mother tongue, *Ewa-ge*, as she had never learnt to write in English. Her time at village school had been interrupted by the war. She only had two years of education and although she could speak some English, she could not read or write it. Her letter follows:

> I am Miss Marcella Karau. I write to you to let you know that George Ambo is my true boyfriend…both of us love each other very much. We are hoping that when Fr James Benson will come out from prison then we shall get married. We would like you to attend our wedding service, but we know that you have plenty to do…When George told me during our conversation together that you are very kind and helpful to him, he said that he loves, respects and honours [you] as his mother. When I heard this I was very happy. I need a bag and *tapa* cloth very much. My love and best wishes, Your daughter, Miss Marcella Karau.[108]

'On the 21st July, 1946, the big and important day came,' wrote Bishop George. 'Fr Lester Raurela celebrated our wedding, and we became husband and wife.' In a second letter to Mavis Eather, written shortly after the great event, George gave some details of the wedding:

> Now Mother, I wonder if you would like to know about our marriage feast? We married on the twenty-first of July after Matins. I would have liked to wait one more year but my work is so big so I have married. After our marriage service we got the wedding dinner ready and sent messages around the villages. Some *ogabada* [headmen], some school children and some village people came to our wedding feast. It was a big feast and a good one because we got plenty of fish and plenty of shellfish too. So we had a good dinner on that day. I think she is a good girl and she will help me in my work.[109]

George and Marcella set up home at Gomberu Village, as he describes it.

Our first home was very, very simple. A little thatched hut, set up on posts, with two rooms in it. The posts were of *bendoro* wood, the walls were made of *sago* leaves, sewn together, we called them *kipa* walls, and the floor was split black palm trunks. I built it myself with the help of the village people and the school children.[110]

After the war, Gomberu Village was not in a good state. The houses were very tiny ones and there were no toilets. The people used the beach or the bush for going to the toilet. When I came, we built our toilet and we encouraged one or two to build theirs, but only a few did it. The huts were built around a central space with beaten earth, so that snakes wouldn't come in. But sometimes, snakes did come in the night. We also had problems with rats. They lived in the *kipa* walls of the huts or came in the nights from the bush where they sometimes had been eating the dead Japanese bodies. They spread that poison on the food dishes in the house, as we had nothing to cover our food with. Many people died of dysentery because of the rats.

Miss Eather had been pleased to hear of the wedding but had not been able to go to Gona. She had sent some useful gifts which included three Uiaku *tapa* cloths (made of bark and worn as skirts) and two Wanigela clay pots for cooking. Every day Marcella was cooking their evening meals in these clay pots, gifts from Miss Eather, over an open fire outside the hut.

Bishop George writes of those days:

Both of us were very happy and we were trying our best to minister to our people. Gradually and slowly our people were coming to our house for advice and help. It was at Gomberu that God in His love and mercy gave us our first baby son. He was born in the year 1947. Both of us were very happy. By that time, Fr James Benson had come back and he baptised our first son — Oliver Brady Ambo.[111]

It seems that his union with Marcella partly dissipated the hostile feelings towards George. Looking back on this period of his life, he later wrote,

Despite initial conflicts and hostility, my ministry amongst my own people was blessed. After one year I got married to a committed and devoted girl, the prettiest and most beautiful of her generation. Some people, even young men who had been against me, came to church and apologised. I was so happy at that moment and thanked God for His loving care and help in my ministry.[112]

Fr Benson returned to Gona at the end of August 1946 amidst overwhelming rejoicing. It had been his greatest wish that on release from the prison camp in Rabaul he should go back to his old place at Gona, once more to be with his Papuan people. His welcome had been tumultuous. Crowds covered the beach as he approached the shore that was so well known to him. Excited people thronged around him, affectionately stroking him and smelling him — signs of the traditional greeting of a close and special person.

Fr Benson was deeply touched by his welcome:

> As I looked at their happy faces and heard the warmth of their songs of welcome, I knew that all I had endured was so very much worth while. For I was home again at last.[113]

This had been the most joyful celebration in which George played a foremost part. This was when he danced the role of Gatara, the hero who overcame the evil forces of Kikiri, the wicked witch (see Chapter 1). At that moment, this ancient myth became symbolic, not only of Fr Benson triumphing over the forces of war but also of George fighting the dark forces of sorcery and immorality amongst his own people.

Though physically weaker, Fr Benson returned full of hope for the future. His determination to rebuild the mission station was strengthened when he found that the Christians had remained true to the faith he had taught them. He had suffered in prison and his weight had fallen through sickness and malnutrition to half his usual twelve stone. Yet he had gained in spiritual strength. Through daily prayers and communion with Jesus, he had sensed that Jesus was constantly with him in the prison cell, surrounding him with His love. This spiritual experience had given him hope for the future and deepened his understanding of the meaning of the Resurrection.[114] While he was still in prison, on scraps of paper given to him by Saguro, a Japanese interpreter, Fr Benson wrote a poem of hope for the resurrection not only of the church at Gona but of a wider spiritual Church — a 'New Jerusalem':

GONA

When bushmen ranged the coasts a thousand years,
Then fear and death and sorcery
Wrought only tears,
Till Christ the Lord did come, the Prince of Peace,
When love and life and liberty
Bid hatred cease.

So Love built up her house, not made with hands;
In Church and School and Hospital
Were Love's commands.
But war and hate burst forth across the main,
And aerial argosies of death
Brought tears again.

From the far north it came, at evening's time,
When blasting bomb and shattering shard
Wrecked Gona's shrine.
Life now gives place to death, and love to hate,
As trampling armies locked in strife
make desolate.

But the fair life of Love, God's Holy Son,
Lives still in many a humble heart,
Else hope were gone.
From jungle cot and river cave, Papuan men
Lift hearts amazed, but full of faith
And love to Him,
And God's own Sacrifice is pleaded still
In village church and forest shrine
From plain and hill.

So Gona's house shall rise, full fair again.
A living stone, for heavenly walls
Of New Jerusalem.
Come comrades of all lands, be builders true
In love of God and fellow man
Make all things new.

James Benson
(Written in prison in Rabaul, January 1943) [115]

The building work was now carried on in earnest under the capable leadership of Fr Benson. It was an immense task into which he threw himself. The new station was to be farther to the east and nearer the sea. The buildings were made of materials from the bush supplied by the local communities. The only exception was the roof of the church, which was of corrugated iron, rusty and old, obtained from disused army dumps. Working with his own hands, day after day alongside his workmen, Fr Benson used all his skills and practical abilities to the full. Approaching by boat, the visitor would see a new station cross around which the mortal remains of dead soldiers had been interred within an enclosure. The elongated church, the mission house and Fr Benson's house were all in a line behind an expanse of grass and a small bank of sand leading up from the beach (see photo, page 74).[116]

Fr James soon asked George and Marcella to leave Gomberu and move close to the main mission site so that they could be more easily involved with the building of the new station.[117] They now built a better and bigger house, also of bush materials. George and Marcella loved gardening around their home and on the station. Colourful hibiscus, frangipani and croton grew very well, but George's favourite flowers were roses and lilies. 'In those days, roses also grew very well,' he said. 'We encouraged our children and made them interested in gardening and in keeping the station beautiful.'

When the new station was dedicated at Gona on Sunday 12 October 1947, Fr James Benson was leading the procession and singing *Onward Christian Soldiers!* with his usual enthusiasm and zeal.[118] The procession had begun at the ruins of the old church and included in it were representatives of the Government, the Papuan Constabulary, visiting missionaries and local people. New staff houses, the dispensary, sportsgrounds and classrooms were blessed on the way to the new church. George, who was present at the great occasion, later wrote,

> The Station of All Souls was renamed Holy Cross after the old wooden cross, made by Fr Benson, which had kept standing as a witness to Jesus although bullets went through it during the bombing and firing of machine-guns.[119]

Bishop George recalled that

> at this time another white priest, the Rev'd Alfred W Clint, came to Gona. He was from Australia and came to help with the Co-operative Society in the Gona District. This was working well, and the people were very pleased and happy about it.

With the help of Alf Clint, Fr Benson pioneered and built up the co-operative movement in the villages of his district, which began at Gona after the war under his leadership. His teaching that all work should be consecrated to God and be for the benefit of others corresponded well with Papuan communal life. In the not-so-distant past, the tribal spirit of working together for the common good was all important for survival when tribal fighting or famine had frequently to be faced.[120]

In the period between the end of the war and the devastating eruption of Mt Lamington in 1951, there were over 30 co-operatives working in the Gona district. which covered some 60 miles of coastline and stretched over 30 miles inland. From here the idea had spread to other Anglican Mission areas.[121]

George Ambo was a great supporter of the co-operative movement. He saw in it a reflection of early apostolic times, when Christians shared with each other and had all things in common. He was sorry and disappointed when after a period of time it became clear that the co-operative movement was not working. 'The Anglican Church was the first to see the picture of people's need, but through jealousy and selfishness the leaders used their power wrongly,' wrote Bishop George. He did not know that one of the main causes for the failure of the co-operative system in Papua was, according to James Benson, that certain Church groups in Australia suspected it was linked with communism and therefore would not support it.[122]

While George was at Gomberu, rumours about this energetic and compassionate young teacher-evangelist spread through the Northern District. 'Most of all,' wrote Fr Benson later, 'he was noted for his charming and utterly unself-conscious goodness, as well as for his lovely smile'.[123] It had even become a common expression in the community, when somebody had acted in a particularly kind and virtuous way, to say, 'Yes, it is just like George, isn't it!' After George and Marcella had moved from Gomberu to the main mission site, George, assisted by Godfrey Dabadaba, became the teacher in charge of the main mission school. 'I was really in charge of all the education,' said Bishop George. 'Godfrey did the administration. I ran the teaching part until Sr Marjorie Govers, a European teacher, arrived.'[124] It was a measure of George's success as a teacher that some of his students were accepted at the Martyrs' School at Sangara. They were the first from Gona to attend the Anglican Secondary High School, opened in February 1948. George was proud of their achievements:

> Out of the first young men I sent to Martyrs', five became priests in the Church of God, and the rest gained important positions in the police force and with the government.

One day, a white manager of a plantation in the Northern District needed a reliable storekeeper. Having heard about the young teacher, he went to see George about the possibility of employing him. Intending to lure him away from the mission by tempting him with money, the trader first asked about his salary. Amazed to learn that a teacher's pay was five shillings a month, he offered five pounds a month. George's reply was, 'Thank you, *Taubada* (Master), but I am God's man, and I must do God's work!' Trying once more to persuade George, the trader said his company could pay ten pounds a month to an honest man with brains like him. 'Thank you again, *Taubada*,' replied George, 'but it would be just the same if you were to offer me one hundred pounds a month; for I am sent here by God to do His Will and nothing will move me from that'.

Amazed at George's commitment and sense of duty to God, the trader went to see James Benson. Admitting that he had tried to steal his teacher, he exclaimed, 'That lad's religion is real, he really believes it. I'd no idea your mission work could get so deep!'

During one of his visits to Gona in 1947, Bishop Strong asked George if, at some time in the future, he would consider training for ordination to the priesthood. With his usual humility — always so typical of George — he answered the bishop:

> I would like to test my vocation to the ministry, but there are some teachers who are more committed and devoted than myself. Also, I am a very young teacher, so I will pray about it.[125]

It would be two years or so before another step was taken by George towards his future destiny. This was when he was asked to leave Holy Cross to take charge of an isolated out-station, inland towards the mountains. At that time, two white missionaries arrived to help Fr Benson: Elsie Manley, a teacher, and Nancy Elliot, a nurse. During the year, Fr Alfred Clint and Marjorie Govers, a teacher, had also joined the staff. Fr Benson was eventually succeeded by Fr John Wardman, who was married to Mary, Fr Benson's niece. So it was that Gona Station entered a new era. The prophecy of James Benson, 'Gona's house shall rise, full fair again', had been fulfilled.

George Ambo (at that time teacher-evangelist at Gona), Albert Maclaren Ririka
and Simon Peter Awoda (George's brother). In the background is
Fr Benson's new Church of Holy Cross, dedicated 12th October 1947.
(Photograph courtesy of David Wetherell)

Beating a thin piece of bark to make *tapa* cloth at Gona Village (now Kausada).
This was Marcella's village.

Painting the *tapa* cloth with charcoal and traditional colour.
(Photographs courtesy of Bob Hay)

The rebuilt Gona Mission Station. Note the rusty iron roof of Fr Benson's Holy Cross Church, and the new mission cross close to the beach. The *St George*, Bishop Strong's mission boat, is in the foreground. (Photograph courtesy of Bob Hay)

The Annunciation painted on *tapa* cloth by Fr James Benson for the Lady Chapel of Holy Cross Church. (Photograph courtesy of John Wardman)

CHAPTER 10

Eiwo and the Eruption of Mt Lamington

After four years in his home parish of Gona, George Ambo was transferred to Eiwo, an inland mission station beyond the Kumusi River. Eiwo was in the Isivita District which stretched towards the mountains as far as Kokoda. Fr Dennis Taylor, an English priest, who came to rebuild the ruined stations at Sangara and Isivita after the war, had opened several new out-stations in the area. Amongst these were Waseta on the main Kokoda Road, Sasembata further around the side of Mount Lamington from Isivita, and Eiwo across the Kumusi River (see map, page xiii).

After the expulsion of the Japanese, there had been a sudden wish for the establishment of Christian missions. Hundreds of Papuans with no knowledge of the Christian faith had come forward, asking the Church for teachers and evangelists for their areas. Some were successful in their requests, and as they received instruction in the Bible and the Christian doctrines, they first became 'hearers', then catechumens. As catechumens, they were allowed to start building their first church. In these post-war years, many new churches and mission stations were established in the Northern District.[126]

In March 1949, a year or so before George took up his new position at Eiwo, Bishop Philip visited the Northern District. He was to dedicate several of the new churches in the Sangara and Isivita areas. Amongst these was the first church at Eiwo. With the wave of people asking for Christian missions, Bishop Strong was anxious to prepare Papuans for leadership in the church. During his visit he asked Albert Maclaren Ririka, head teacher at Sangara, and Ambrose Burogu, teacher-in-charge at Sasembata, if they would consider at some time in the future doing further studies for ordination to the priesthood. Both men had assisted Miss Eather as pupil-teachers at Gona when George was there as a mission boarder and both agreed with the Bishop's plans for their future.

A letter written in 1949 by Nancy White, an Australian teacher at Sangara, reveals that Bishop Strong had even greater ambitions for George Ambo:

> The Bishop will send George to take charge of a rather difficult out-station with another language. He is so good, intelligent, keen, and an excellent teacher, but has so far been teaching in his own district, with his own language. The Bishop wants him to be tested pretty hard. I believe various people have their eye on him as first native Bishop.[127]

This would have been one of the earliest hints of George Ambo's future consecration. During the intervening time, he was to be tested indeed.

During a second visit to the Northern District later in the same year, Bishop Strong asked George if he would go to Eiwo. Bishop George later wrote,

> I didn't have a clue where Eiwo was but Fr James Benson explained it to me. I was not happy to go up to Kokoda area. My father and my wife's mother were not happy either. They didn't want us to go, as they took it for granted that people up there were still savages and cannibals.[128]

By the end of the year, George and Marcella, after much consideration and with concern for their families' feelings, agreed to transfer. 'The Holy Spirit worked through Fr James and Fr Alfred Clint, an Australian priest helping Fr Benson, and we accepted our posting.'[129]

Bishop George describes the journey to Eiwo:

> It was not an easy way to travel. In those days we had to carry our bags etc. ourselves and walk. My wife packed. We went up to Popondetta. On the way to Sangara, the Ambogo River was flooding at Double Crossing. We had a baby son, Alban, two weeks old, and we were worrying about our son. Fr Dennis Taylor had picked us up on the way. His truck stuck in the river, where we sat for two hours. Then we managed to push it through and we arrived in the night at Sangara.[130]

They spent the weekend there with Marcella's brother, Alban Jaipoba, who was then teaching at Sangara, and his wife Anita Joyce, George's sister. It was a happy family gathering, a brother and sister having married a brother and sister. It was one of the last occasions for George to be with his closest friend: dark clouds were brooding on the horizon.

The journey from Sangara to Eiwo was also slow and difficult. Fr Sydney Smith, an Australian priest at Isivita, drove them part of the way in the old army truck. After some miles down a rough track to the Kokoda Road they reached Agenehambo Village. Then, after some further distance, they passed Waseta Station, and another eight miles or so of rough and stony track through five rivers took them to Wairope by the Kumusi River. 'The truck was left this side of the Kumusi,' said Bishop George, 'and we walked across the cane bridge to the opposite bank'. It could not have been easy to move along the narrow cane walkway of the suspension bridge, slung between great posts on either side of the rushing river, carrying the baby and all their bags. After a short distance, a jungle track off the main road led them for four miles or so along the bank of the Eiwo River to the station.[131]

Bishop George recalled how the people were happy to receive their new teacher and his family.[132]

> They were waiting for us and expecting us to arrive. They were very kind. Very generous. They respected and honoured us, but they didn't know the meaning of truth. They didn't know what was true. They believed in the power of sorcery.

When they arrived, George and Marcella found the station was run down and in urgent need of attention, with the houses all deteriorated, in bad condition. Many people suffered from sickness and infections such as conjunctivitis, sores and ulcers with pus running down their legs.[133] It was evident that medical help was needed.

The head teacher and evangelist was called Alexander Rekiembo. He was himself sick and due to retire shortly after George's arrival. There had been considerable trouble between Alexander and the Assistant District Officer at Kokoda, Mr Yeoman.

Bishop George told of the tensions:

> He was anti-Anglican Church. He was himself a Roman Catholic. He came down to Eiwo regularly and rebuked Alexander, the village schoolteacher. He rebuked him very severely with nasty words. One day he spat on him.[134]

Cane bridge over the Kumusi River at Wairope. The photograph was taken on 6 October 1951; the bridge was washed away the following day! (Photo: the late Nancy White)

Alexander had complained to Bishop Strong about it and George believed that this sad situation was behind his posting to Eiwo.

George described the steps he and his wife took to bring about an improvement:

> Slowly we trained the people in my new area. Gradually my wife taught them how to cook properly. She showed them how much salt they could put in when cooking the vegetables, how to squeeze coconut milk into the food, and how to make soup and so on. She was teaching the wives while I was working in the school. It was a very low standard. They didn't know the letters of the alphabet because the first teacher in charge, Alexander, a local man, had very limited education. He did his best and was a wonderful man, committed to his work, but I had to try and lift up the standard of education.[135]

While George was at Eiwo an event happened which to him was another miracle:

> One day a hostile sorcerer came to me. He threatened to kill me. I said, 'Sorry, I came here as a Christian teacher because God sent me to teach people to live better lives, to teach the Christian way and to

uplift the standard of education. I will not interfere with you. You can do your business, I will do mine, so you leave me alone!' He went back to his village.

That particular night he got very sick. How it happened that he became ill I didn't know. He called for me to come. I went there in the night to his home and taught him about the Bible. After that, he called for me many times. I gave him instruction. I'm glad to say that Fr Brady taught me very well about the Bible. All the Bible passages are still in my head. So I went to the sorcerer and talked to him, coached him and gave him examples. He wanted me to come again and again. In the end he converted and became a Christian. That sorcerer would have killed people, but on that particular day, when he came to threaten me, I went to him in the night. [136]

Girls and Boys of Martyrs' School, Sangara — Speech Day 1948
Left front: George Nixon Simbiri (later ordained priest) Fr John Rautamara* (son of Fr Peter Rautamara, first priest in Papua), Albert Maclaren Ririka (head teacher at Sangara and later ordained priest with George Ambo), Sr Nancy Elliott with two Taylor children, Ross* and Russell*.
Left back: Fr Sydney Smith (priest at Isivita), Margaret de Bibra* (headmistress of Martyrs' School, Fr Dennis Taylor* (priest-in-charge of Sangara), Nancy White (teacher at Martyrs') * denotes killed in the eruption of Mt Lamington
(Photograph courtesy of the late Nancy White)

George believed that it was God who had given him the courage to go into the bush at night to face this dangerous sorcerer. He was convinced that he was God's chosen instrument, through which He worked his divine purpose. That conviction never failed. It gave him courage throughout his life to face even threats of death.

At this stage, the Ambos had a holiday:

> We served at Eiwo during 1950.[137] Towards the end of the year, we walked down to Gona for a month's holiday. In the middle of January we walked up again, not back to Eiwo but first to Sangara Mission Station for a refresher course for teachers. It was to last a week

The first Anglican Secondary High School had opened at Sangara in February 1948. It had been established as a memorial to the Anglican Martyrs who had lost their lives in the war, and was given the name of Martyrs' School. Its first Principal was Margaret de Bibra, a teacher from Victoria in Australia. She had organised the refresher course for the teachers from Martyrs', from the Sangara Preparatory School and from the out-stations of the district.

In front of St James' Preparatory School, Sangara, 1950
Left to right: (village man), Alban Jaipoba (brother-in-law of George Ambo, later killed in the eruption), Jerome, Didymus, George Nixon Simbiri, Arnold, Ambrose Burogu (teacher-evangelist, who taught for Mavis Eather at Gona before the Japanese invasion and who was later killed in the eruption), Philip Tahima, Augustus Wasita (Photograph courtesy of the late Nancy White)

Little did the Sangara people know that after a week, on Sunday 21 January 1951, a terrible disaster would strike, claiming most of their lives.

Bishop George wrote,

> It was that very week we saw the trees and bush around Mount Lamington go brown. There were 19 teachers altogether, and although we were attending the course at the same time we were anxiously watching the mountain. Then on Wednesday that week, the trees were falling down towards the valley. Also rocks and stones were rolling down to the valley. On Thursday the stones were still rolling down and we began to get worried. Some people from the villages at the foot of the mountain fled to the Mission Station for protection.

> It was on Friday that smoke started to come out together with an earthquake. The earthquake and smoke were getting worse and worse. The smell of sulphur fumes was terrible. We did not sleep well as we had never before experienced anything like this in all our lives. On Saturday the smell and the smoke covered all the villages around the Sangara Mission Station. Some of the teachers were getting worried and frightened, especially the married ones. Some of us teachers had very young children with us. My wife and I had two little sons, Oliver of two and Alban of one. We too were worrying and concerned about our children.

Later in his life, when Bishop George looked back on these devastating events, it seemed to him that he and his family had been snatched from death by God's Divine Hand. In the afternoon of Saturday 20 January, Fr Robert Porter, the priest in charge of Isivita Station, had sent a message to Fr Dennis Taylor at Sangara. Fr Porter asked for the two teachers, George and Albert Maclaren, to come to him at Isivita to help him as interpreters for the refugees. As Bishop George recalled,

> A lot of people were fleeing from the mountain side and coming down to Isivita Station for protection. So Fr Dennis called Albert and myself to see him. He said to us, 'Your priest needs you at Isivita as the Station is full of refugees'. Then he warned me not to take my wife and sons with me, because the distance from the top of Mt Lamington to Isivita is only 6 miles, whereas Sangara is 16 miles away and therefore, they thought, Sangara was a safer place.

But George answered Fr Taylor with determination, 'I will take my family with me and wait and see what this mountain will do in the future'. Then they all had a meal together. Bishop George described it.

> We left Sangara about 4.00pm, and arrived at Isivita after Evensong. That night we did not sleep. We stayed awake all through the night, because the earthquake made the house shake.

The temptation to flee the area would have induced many of the people to leave, but they were encouraged by mission and government staff to stay.

The Papuan teachers and their families all remained on their posts. Bishop George later wrote,

> We were taught at St Aidan's College that if we were truly called by God to serve our Lord and Saviour, Jesus Christ, we must bear our troubles and sorrows with Jesus. Our St Aidan's cross on our chests reminded us of this. *'MA VIPATUTU'* or 'BE FAITHFUL' is written on the cross. So we all stayed together on the mountain with our brothers and sisters until the end.

As the earth-tremors, smoke, flashes of fire and bursts of steam had gradually built up, there was no panic amongst the Papuans although many were frightened. After the early service on the Sunday morning of 21 January, Peggy (Margaret) de Bibra was writing a letter:

> We are carrying on our work as usual, though we run outside from time to time to watch it... At the moment it is scientifically interesting, and when we can see it, very beautiful. Since it broke out quietly and gradually we don't anticipate it becoming dangerous...

She continued to describe how one church councillor had said,

> The mountain people do not understand. They are afraid...Our fathers did not know of it. The trembling of the earth — yes, but not the fire. At night it is like a torch, and we do not understand the sign.

Towards the end of the letter she expresses her worries for the future:

> What of our work here — the Martyrs' School, which has seventy boys from distant places? Will they be afraid to return after the holidays? Will we be able to feed them?... I think...we have a troubled year ahead. Will you think of the people here... Pray for them and for us that out of this, good may come, and as the dead mount came to...

At this point the explosion occurred. The letter ended abruptly.

It was not only at Sangara that people had believed there was no immediate danger. Also at Isivita there was considerable confidence that no catastrophe was about to happen. As Bishop George recalled,

> It was Sunday morning, the 21st January 1951. We had our Holy Eucharist and straight after the Service, Fr Porter announced the district commissioner's message concerning the volcano: 'Do not be afraid. It will be all right. If you would like to go back to your homes, you may do so'. But the priest, Fr Porter, gave his opinion. His advice was to wait for a few days on the station and then go back. Those who believed the words of their government left the station and started walking towards their villages. Those who believed their priest stayed back.
>
> About one hour later, Lamington blew up. Of those Isivita people who were walking on the mountain 87 were killed. This happened

before they reached their homes. The eruption was terrible, nasty, dirty, filthy. We all got a shock and were very frightened. Many people did not care about their old fathers and mothers. They fled for protection and safety.

It was an unexpected and unusual type of eruption. Instead of erupting upward, one whole face of the mountain had exploded sideways.[138] A cloud of incandescent dust had devastated an area of 68 square miles surrounding the crater. People died from burns and suffocation, not being able to breathe in the atmosphere of superheated dust and ash. Forests and gardens were flattened by glowing rocks and lava. At Sangara Mission and at the nearby Higaturu Government Station nobody survived. In Bishop George's words,

> Seventeen teacher-evangelists were killed. Two priests and their families died and I would say about 4000 people.

Soon after the explosion, George and Marcella had news of the deaths of their friends and families at Sangara, which George wrote about later.

> Our brothers and sisters and all those who were working there had passed into Paradise. Fr Dennis Taylor with his wife and children and Fr John Rautamara, son of Fr Peter Rautamara, who was the first Papuan priest to be ordained, were all killed. My dear wife lost her mother and her only brother Alban with his wife Anita Joy (George's little sister) and their two young children. Her sister's daughter, Priscilla, who was staying with Alban, also died. They all died together.[139]

Many a time afterwards, George and Albert Maclaren, together with their people, would sing the haunting *Lament of Lamington*, which Albert Maclaren composed in the *Ewa-ge* language shortly after the disaster:

> The Song of our God and the Mountain, and of our Friends
> Who found Him there:
>
> *Nango einda Sangara da a —*
> *Dada ewora e*
> *Naso nanonamendi de e*
> *Usari nati e*
>
> Chorus:
> *Nango jo e*
> *Nango jo e*
> *Nango jo e*
> *Bada iso o ingodare.*
>
> (Here at Sangara, the place where we gathered
> with our brothers and our sisters —
> It has become our community —
> The community where we have been gathering to live together
> and work for God

Chorus:
Have Mercy on us—
Have Mercy on us—
Have Mercy on us—
Father, we are in your Hands –
So we are at your Mercy.)

Iso itari dirida a
Matu nango ga e
Bada iteso bugira a
Nango dududu e

(The handmaid of your creation of the mountain
Of long ago, we never knew—
You have brought us to realisation
We were shocked.
Have Mercy on us—
Have Mercy on us—
Have Mercy on us—
Father, we are in your Hands
So we are at your Mercy.)

Diri wasiri etira
Ungoi petetera
Ungoi petetera
Ungo da kinapeinade e
Inono torera.

(The mountain shook and exploded
They stood their ground
They stood their ground
They with their wives and children
Walked together through the Gate) [140]

Bishop George tells of what happened after the explosion:

After the explosion the priest gave permission for the staff to take their children to a safer place. I heard Fr Porter's message that we must take our families down to the main road. I took my family, my wife and two little sons, and left Isivita Station. But we did not take the path that leads to the main road. Instead we went along the Sasembata Track—we were looking for Albert Maclaren and thought that he might have tried to reach Sasembata Station. He had left his pregnant wife and youngest children at home at old Gona Village after the Christmas holidays, and had taken with him only two older children when he left to attend the teacher training course at Sangara.

As we made our way towards Sasembata, my wife carrying one child and I the other, we were stopped by a village policeman. He was from the Managalas area, right round the mountain on the southern side. He ordered us not to go to Sasembata but to walk down to the main road. 'You'll walk down to Agenehambo,' he said. That's where all the people are going. Albert Maclaren is there. We'll go there together.' When we were walking, he disappeared. We heard later that people had been killed on the Sasembata Track.[141]

We walked for about 15 minutes towards Agenehambo. Then thick darkness covered the area. The volcano had thrown up mud which blocked the light from the sun. The darkness was awful. It was very frightening. The mud was falling down on our bodies and our heads. We were covered in ash and mud. I was scraping it off my wife and myself and our little boys. The trees had fallen down and were blocking the path. We couldn't find our way through. So we joined a group of people and sat down under a garden shelter. During that thick darkness, people were praying for forgiveness and protection. Others were crying for fear. We believed that any minute we would be dead.

Local people had always feared the mountain. They believed the eruption had been caused by the anger of the spirits inside the volcano. They called it Mount Sumbiripa. It was the home of the departed spirits of all the hill peoples. In their ancient legend, Sumbiripa was a man who misbehaved while hunting. In punishment, the mountain grew up around him, trapping him inside. The mountain people, even the Christians amongst them, believed that Sumbiripa became Lord of the Dead. To offend him and the spirits would result in punishment. They believed the explosion was the punishment for their own wrongdoings.

Much later, during Bishop George's years as Bishop of Popondota Diocese, he would come up against this belief amongst the people of the mountain. As a Christian village elder some three decades after the disaster was heard to say: 'In the eruption, Sumbiripa and the other angry spirits killed many people in villages nearby'.[142]

Bishop George recalled how after two to three hours the darkness passed.

Although anxious about my wife and sons, I decided not to continue down to the main road but to walk back to Isivita Station to see Fr Porter and the two lady missionaries, Sr Pat Durdin and Mrs Lane. Just as we reached the little spring of water which was at the edge of the station, we heard people say that Fr Porter had sent out a message of warning, that everyone should hurry down to Agenehambo Village for protection. There would be a second blow-up. It was feared the second one would be worse than the first.

So we turned round again and this time I took my family down to Agenehambo where we found Albert Maclaren and his two children. At last we met again and we were wondering and worrying about the Sangara staff, both national and white missionaries. While we were there at Agenehambo, Rod Hart, an Australian mission engineer, arrived from Popondetta in his old wartime jeep. He asked Albert Maclaren and myself to take a letter up to Fr Porter at Isivita. Leaving our family behind, we started to walk up with the letter. While we were walking in the night, a second explosion occurred. So we hurried back to Agenehambo. Later, we tried a second time and managed to get through to Isivita with Rod Hart's letter.

Having received the letter, Fr Porter immediately asked us help load his jeep and trailer with badly burnt and wounded people. Luckily the jeep started and he set off down the mountain for the main road. It was sad that Fr Porter had to leave many injured villagers behind. The track had been blocked by fallen trees and bushes, so Fr Porter asked me and Albert to clear the path and cut a way through, so that he could get down the mountain. So we were clearing the track. Some of the trees were very big. We chopped with our knives for some time, until Fr Porter told us to go back to the station to fetch the mission axe.

As we were making our way back, suddenly the Managalas policeman stood in front of us on the path. He was the same policeman who had stopped me and Marcella before when we walked on the track to Sasembata. Albert and I were surprised. We were not in the Managalas area, but here was a Managalas policeman, carrying a brand new axe![143] He said, 'George and Albert! Where are you going?' When we told him, he said, 'This is a new axe. You take it and cut the way through'. We believed he was an angel.

All the people had fled from the whole district. No one was there. Only that policeman with a Managalas face and uniform. We saw it clearly. God had sent an angel in the form of a Managalas policeman. We took the axe and cut the way through for the jeep. The injured people were taken down to the main road. Sad, downhearted and frightened, we felt that God was with us. He had given us a sign and His Holy Spirit was calling us all to Waseta Station for immediate shelter.

Shortly after the eruption, Bishop David Hand was asked by Bishop Strong to take charge of all the rebuilding work in the devastated mission areas. Bishop David had been consecrated the previous year, 1950. Having served for some time in the Sangara district, he had learnt the language of the local Orokaiva people, which helped him in his work with the hundreds of shocked refugees.[144] Soon the Government established a large camp for the homeless people at Wairope by the Kumusi River Crossing. After a short time, the camp had to be moved due to flooding of the river. It was set up on the other side at Ilimo, further up the road towards Kokoda.[145] Little did George know that Bishop

Mt Lamington after the eruption, January 1951. In the middle foreground are two uprooted trees by the Martyrs' School playing field. The school and Sangara Station were destroyed; only the mission house is still standing.

Martyrs' School, Sangara (foreground), totally destroyed in the eruption.
The new mission house is still standing. 22 January 1951.
(Photographs on pages and the one opposite courtesy of the late Nancy White)

David in future years would play an important and guiding role in his life.

George continues the story:

> It did not take long for the first government officials to arrive from Port Moresby and for the first loads of blankets, water, food and other things necessary for the refugees to be airlifted across the mountains.[146] After two days, Dr Gunther, the Director of the Papua New Guinea Health Department, came to Waseta. He ordered the coastal teachers, medicals and other mission workers to go back to their homes by the sea. Many of the best coastal teachers had been lost, so he wanted us to go back and be safe.

> We spent two days at our homes. Then Bishop Philip arrived at Killerton. He knew already that Albert and I were there. When he came, we walked over to meet him.[147] This is what he said, 'George, you ran away!' I was being criticised. He thought I had deserted. I felt strongly about that. 'Father, you said I ran away! Who told you about that? Well Father, I'm going back to my village...!' Someone gave the wrong message that Albert and I ran away. 'Albert, I'm going,' I said. 'If you want to, you can stay and talk with him.' I just went. I walked to my uncle's home at Garara Village. Who had given the wrong message, I wondered?

> A short time afterwards, the Bishop sent his Papuan helper, Lawrence Modudula, to tell me that he was sorry. The message was: 'George, I'm sorry! Someone gave me the wrong information'. I sent the message back: 'Bishop, you'll find from Fr Porter what really happened. You'll know then what we did during the eruption'. So the Bishop went up to Fr Porter who told him the whole story. Later on, Bishop Philip apologised to me. He should have interviewed me before making a judgement. 'So are you ready to go?' he asked me. 'I'm ready to go,' I said, 'as long as you trust me'. 'George! I trust you,' he said.

The following day, George and Albert were flown from Popondetta to Kokoda, for George had been asked to go back to Eiwo, his own station. This was a turbulent time for George. Having left his wife and family at Gona, he experienced his first flight. 'I left my wife and my two sons behind in the care of my old father and my brother Simon Peter, who was teaching at Holy Cross, Gona,' he wrote. Albert Maclaren was posted temporarily to the refugee camp at Ilimo as teacher in charge of 600 or 700 school children. Ilimo was the headquarters for the government team of officials, medical staff, nurses, pupil teachers and other helpers. Temporary buildings had been put up with a hospital and a school. Fr Porter and Fr Hugh Andrew, a priest from Australia, were there with Sr Pat Durdin, Albert Maclaren and Ambrose Isoroembo to assist thousands of refugees.[148]

The wonderful work of rescue and healing, shared by the missionaries, government officers and Papuans, had begun. Unfailingly, they played their part during that first week of devastation and danger. According to Fr James

Benson's account of the distressing events, Sr Nancy Elliott, the nurse at Gona, had walked during the night after the explosion the twenty miles from Killerton to Popondetta, hoping to reach Fr Dennis Taylor who was known to be badly wounded. Only Simon Peter, George's brother, had the courage to accompany her. He carried boxes of medicines for the suffering victims. On arrival in Popondetta, they found Fr Dennis dead. 'They were joined next morning by Sr Jean Henderson, and a jeep load of medical orderlies from the Mission hospital at Eroro,' wrote Fr Benson, 'all ready to help the wounded'. Rodd and Maddy Hart (Australian missionaries) and the three other Europeans at Popondetta '...had been working through the day and through the night, in the fogs and the dust of the sulphurous smoke, driving trucks and jeeps, like so many figures in the inferno'.[149]

About July, the crowds began to disperse, as Bishop George recalled.

> The volcano was cooling down.[150] It was still not safe for the villagers to return to the mountain, but they built their homes and gardens along the main road. Slowly the floodwaters of the Kumusi River were going down and the people could swim or walk across. At that time, I walked to Gona to bring back my family. George Jambara, who stayed with me at Eiwo, was my companion. My dear old father did not agree to allow my wife and two children to go back with me. After four days, however, my brother Simon Peter made him see reason. We walked up to Popondetta where we stayed the night. It was not a quiet night because many soldiers and police had arrived in town. Some of the Orokaivan people refused to go past Mt Lamington because of their fears of the mountain and its spirits. Gradually, the Church and the Government persuaded them to go up to Ilimo to be with their brothers and sisters in Christ. The next morning we left for Agenehambo.
>
> It was not an easy journey back to Eiwo. My wife was loaded with her string bag, cooked food for the journey and sleeping mats. I was carrying a pack on my back, my elder son Oliver Brady on my shoulder, and a bush knife in my hand. Our second son, Alban, one year old, was carried by George Jambara. Very slowly we arrived at Agenehambo, where we stayed the night. At dawn, we left for Eiwo, very, very early. Our people cried for joy because they saw that by the Grace of God we had reached Eiwo safely.

In spite of the terrible upheavals and problems of communication and transportation of supplies due to the flooded river, George built up the station with his usual energy and strength. Shortly after Marcella's return, Sr Pat Durdin, the nurse at Wasita, visited Eiwo, and wrote,

> The station is in perfect order. A wide stretch of neatly-cut grass, with coconut palms in two rows along one side; tidily swept paths, with gay shrubs on either side, mostly crotons and hibiscus of all colours; the school buildings at the far end of the station; the well-

kept teachers' houses, and the beautiful church...The licensed teacher in charge is George Ambo, one of our outstanding Papuan teachers...[151]

Marcella was again at her husband's side providing support and hospitality, as she did through their working life. She and the station women took Sr Durdin to the rest house where, as she wrote, she found

> delicious things like pineapples, papaw, a huge bunch of bananas, tomatoes, corn, a water melon, as well as the essentials such as *taro* and sweet potatoes. Marcella provided eggs from her little poultry run ... The station was a place of peace and beauty.

From Sr Durdin's account, it is clear that George's days were filled with hard work. He did not spare himself. Apart from running the school, he had supervised the building of a small dispensary. Every morning for an hour or so before teaching, although he had no medical training he treated the children and village people for sores and injuries, trying to prevent bad ulcers breaking out. First of all, however, he was an evangelist, spreading the knowledge and belief in Christ in the largely heathen area. On the Sunday at Matins, Sr Durdin had seen 'a very big congregation of catechumens and hearers from all the villages in the district...'

A brief glimpse of George's work in the school is gained from another report, written a few months later by an Australian teacher, Nancy White.

> It was always a joy to get to Eiwo. George had three pupil-teachers to help him with the 257 children I saw and tested...I was glad at the end to be able to watch for a little while, George taking his class for PT. That was a joy, splendidly done, finishing with leapfrog games, and making pyramids, all happy, energetic and enthusiastic.[152]

The new Church of St David, Eiwo, started by George Ambo (Photograph courtesy of the late Nancy White)

Joy, strength, energy, enthusiasm — those were the features which the white missionaries found in the young teacher. Today, these qualities still radiate from Bishop George's personality.

Before leaving Eiwo, George had begun the building of a bigger church. He had made a new altar and started work on the candlesticks though they had not been finished. The following year, when he was no longer at his station, he wrote to Nancy White:

> Will you also let me know about the Eiwo people and their new church for God's work which they are building. Have they finished it?…When you visit them will you deliver my love and greetings to them and to the teachers and their wives too. I always remember them in my daily prayer.[153]

Towards the end of 1951, George received a letter from Bishop Philip Strong written to Fr Porter: 'Send George next year to be trained as Deacon!' Next year, in 1952, George would be called to go to Newton Theological College, which was being established at Dogura and where Fr Eric Cassidy, a priest from Australia, would be in charge. Albert Maclaren Ririka and Simon Peter, George's brother, were also asked to go. When this call finally came, George had become unhappy at the thought of going so far away from his own area. He felt anxious about his old father, whose body was weak and incapacitated by elephantiasis in his legs. If he and his brother Simon both left, he thought, the father would have no sons nearby to help him. So George wrote his refusal to Bishop Philip:

> I'm not coming. If this is a failure, forget about me. I put my father first. Of two brothers, one must stay back and look after him. I am the youngest. I am staying back to let my older brother go and finish his training, or it will be too late for him.[154]

Pressure was put on George to accept the Bishop's offer of training for the priesthood, however. As George later put it,

> Fr Benson, Fr Oliver Brady and Fr John Wardman, who had arrived from Australia to take charge of Gona, they all wanted me to go. They wanted us both to be trained together. I was very unhappy about it. I wrote to my father from Eiwo, 'I'm not going away. Don't worry. I'll be with you until Simon Peter is ordained'.

George decided to give up his work for the Church and go back to stay in the village, and he described the plans for his departure.

> That very night, at Eiwo, when I had written to my father that I was coming home, we were going to have a farewell dinner with the Church Councillors. My wife had prepared food and put out all the dishes in a line on mats on the floor.

George had hung up the hurricane lamp above his head and lit it. As he was waiting to say Grace, a snake appeared.

We didn't notice it at first. The snake was creeping over the food. Then we saw it. As I jumped up, I hit the light and it went out. In the moonlight we could see the snake gliding over the dishes of food. Everyone rushed out. I lit a light from the fire outside and looked for the snake. It had gone. We threw all the food in the rubbish hole. Instead we had two big, ripe pineapples.

George did not tell anybody about the incident with the snake, but he kept wondering what it meant. Why did the snake come to spoil the farewell meal? 'It was an unusual thing to happen,' he said. 'I could hardly believe it. Was it a sign that I was not meant to say farewell to my calling?' Shortly after this, George heard that their younger sister had arrived to look after their father. He wanted both his sons to go away to train for ordination and assured them that he could manage. 'So we both went, but I was not happy,' said George. 'Deep in my heart I was not a happy man.'

George Ambo with Alban, Oliver Brady and Marcella,
Eiwo 1951
(Photograph courtesy of the late Nancy White)

CHAPTER 11

Newton College and Ordination

Early in 1952, some months before George started his theological course, Bishop Strong had succeeded in setting up the first Anglican Theological College. This had been established at Ganuganuana, a site at the foot of the Dogura Hill, close to St Aidan's College. It was a great advance for the Church. Before then, students had lived up on the station at Dogura as best they could. During the later years they had been prepared for ordination as occasion offered and they had always been without the support of college life. Bishop Strong gave to this new establishment the name of Newton College, because, as he said, no-one had been more deeply concerned than Bishop Henry Newton with the foundation and growth of a Papuan ministry.[155]

Henry Newton's span at Dogura had stretched over a long time. As Vicar-General, he initially assisted Bishop Montagu Stone-Wigg, first Bishop of New Guinea from 1898 to 1908, in whose episcopate the vision of an indigenous Church led by Papuans was first expressed. Bishop Stone-Wigg wished to prepare the local people for holding authority within their own Church.[156] Thus, from the earliest days of the Anglican Mission in New Guinea, the aim had been to train Papuans for the ministry.[157] Both Henry Newton and Montagu Stone-Wigg believed that the creation and survival of an indigenous Church largely depended on Papuan priests, who were best suited to make the Church meaningful for their people.

As early as 1903, Henry Newton, had been teaching Papuan students to prepare them for the ministry. His first three Papuan students were told by Newton that 'foreigners could not properly enter the lives of New Guinea people, and therefore Papuan clergy must shoulder the responsibility'. Later, as a bishop himself, Henry Newton continued training Papuan men for ordination. Even when he lived in retirement at Dogura, during the first part of the episcopate of Bishop Philip Strong (bishop from 1936 to 1963), Henry Newton continued his theological teaching, almost until his death in 1947.[158]

Over the years, Papuan men had come forward for training for the priesthood. In 1914, the first two Papuans were ordained deacons: Edwin Nuagoro and Peter Rautamara. Some years later, they were the first to be ordained to the Anglican priesthood. By 1928, there were ten Papuan priests. All were from the south-eastern part of the diocese.[159]

However, two great disasters, the Pacific War and the eruption of Mt Lamington, interrupted the move to ordain indigenous people. Although as an old man Bishop Henry Newton carried on his clergy training right through the war years, few ordinations took place then.[160] Furthermore, the deaths in the eruption of some of the most promising Papuan candidates for priestly training, such as Ambrose Burogu and Alban Jaipoba, both from Gona, were great setbacks to the development of an indigenous Church. Added to this, there was the tragic loss of Fr John Rautamara, the Papuan priest who was also killed at Sangara; he had been regarded as one of the most important leaders for the future.

Despite the tragedies, it seemed that out of suffering and disaster came new growth in the Anglican Mission. New people, such as George Ambo, came forward for theological training. In some ways, he and Marcella had been sad to leave Eiwo. 'We loved the people and they loved us,' wrote Bishop George. The two weeks when George and Marcella were preparing to leave had been a time of mixed emotions for their people — a time of great sadness at the departure of their teacher, but also of pride. They were proud that God had chosen their teacher-evangelist to be amongst the first men ever from the Northern District to undertake priestly training.[161] George Ambo, his brother Simon Peter Awoda and his friend Albert Maclaren Ririka, all from Gona, were the first from the large northern part of the diocese to undertake theological studies at Newton College.

At Gona, they had an unforgettable send-off organised by Fr John Wardman, an Australian priest who had taken over from Fr Benson. While the mission boat lay at anchor off the coast, crowds of people came to the beach to farewell the three teachers and their families. Cheering and waving, the people expressed their mixed emotions of affection and sorrow as the canoes took the northern men away to the waiting boat. It was the second time George Ambo had left his homeland to train near Dogura. Ten years previously, he had been a single student of twenty; now he was a mature man with family responsibilities. He had proved himself a leader of his people. Now, much was expected of him.[162]

During the journey down the coast, George was plagued by feelings of doubt and guilt. Was it right that he should desert his father?

> Although the God of love and mercy had called me to do this important work, I was worrying about deserting my old father, leaving him by himself at home. In my heart, I was thinking, pondering and praying that God would guide me to make the right decision according to God's good will.

Having called at every mission station on the north coast to pick up passengers and mail, the *Maclaren King* at last arrived at Wedau jetty. Bishop George recalls the occasion:

> The mission's old truck came down from the Dogura Hill and took us to Ganuganuana. Our houses were not ready; for example there was no gravel on the floors and the grass was not cut. We put down our things and slept on our mats on the bare ground for the first night.

There were no festive shouts of *Egualau* (welcome), like the welcome that ten years ago had greeted the northern men on arrival at St Aidan's College. These three teachers from Gona were the only students to start the course. 'The Principal, Fr Eric Cassidy (a former vice-principal of St Francis' Theological College, Brisbane) allowed us the first day off to settle in,' wrote Bishop George.[163]

At first the modest settlement of Newton Theological College comprised three traditional bush houses for the northern students and their families, as well as an unfinished chapel and the Principal's cottage. Fr Cassidy's notes in the college logbook, beginning with February 1952, give some insight into the difficulties encountered with the supply of food and materials, and the harsh conditions under which the three students had to cope with their theological studies (see Appendix 3).

The small settlement, beautifully situated just above the shingles of the beach, was sheltered from the sun by coconut palms and mango trees. Casuarinas and *mapa* nut trees lined the coast. The air was filled with the scent of pink, white and yellow frangipani flowers and the gentle sound of waves lapping the coral sand. The place was glorious, but the northern students would have little leisure time during the next three years to enjoy its beauty.

Under Fr Cassidy's leadership the college gradually developed, and new buildings of a more permanent type were constructed. The chapel was enlarged, a dormitory was built for the single students and a kitchen where they did their own cooking. The married men lived in four small, one-bedroom houses. A library was built for study and two classrooms were erected on the beach. There was also the principal's house. The buildings were lightly constructed of wooden frames, covered only on the outside by cement sheeting. The galvanised-iron roofs were visible above the polished cement floors—there were no ceilings, nor any glass in the windows. Push-out shutters let in light and air, although little air circulated in the hot interior.[164]

Fr Cassidy must have had high expectations of George Ambo's practical and intellectual abilities. Apart from coping with a theological course, he was called upon to do time-consuming duties for the principal. Bishop George described these responsibilities:

> When we arrived at the college, the principal made a roster for the three of us. Two of my brothers were to look after outside jobs and I was to sweep Fr Cassidy's house and to cook his meals. It was not an easy life because of such jobs as collecting firewood, enough for the three of us with our families and for the principal. Besides all this, grass in the college area had to be cut by hand and chickens fed so that eggs could be sold to help the college buy books, etc.[165]

Thinking back to his college days, Bishop George recalled how he had found some duties very hard:

> Some of the jobs I had to do were terrible indeed. I had to collect the chickens' dung and put it in a drum with water. It was left

there for some time. We would then get it out with a twig and put it on the vegetables. The smell was awful! Although the earth was dry and dusty, we tried hard to make the vegetables grow.

George's ability to cope with studies and innumerable other duties as well as cooking for Fr Cassidy was remarkable. As he later said,

I was at the college for three years and was also the cookie-boy. I was living with my own family, but I used to go to Fr Cassidy's house in the morning to cook his breakfast, attend my lectures, cook and serve his lunch and dinner. Previously, at St Aidan's, I had cooked for Fr Brady, but I shared the cooking with someone else. I didn't cook all the time, and only in term-time. But for Fr Cassidy, I cooked for three years. Father used to say, 'Scrambled eggs, please George! And pudding — this kind of pudding please'. Fr Cassidy was lucky because I knew something about cooking for Europeans.

The following letter which George wrote from Newton College at the beginning of 1953 to Nancy White, then teaching at Sasembata, reveals some other pressures with which he had to cope:

My Dear Sister,

Thank you very much for your lovely letter to me. I received it after Christmas and I'm so pleased and thankful about the very helpful book which you gave to me. It will help me very much in my study...

Just at present we are having little tests on Human Behaviour (or Conduct) and after that, tests on Christian Doctrine and Old Testament. It is very hard work for us because we are studying in a foreign language so we need your prayers very much. Father Cassidy is doing his best to teach us in this hard work.

We start our work with Matins first and straight after that Mass begins. After the Mass, I cook Father's breakfast and Albert Maclaren and Simon Peter do garden work. It is a very dry place for growing something but we are trying hard. After breakfast we wash up the dirty things, inspect signs of white ants, and then we have half an hour for meditating and then our lecture begins.

Then we have half an hour break and during that period we dig or cut grass. Then the bell rings and we write notes and have a lecture again until 12 noon. Then about half-past one to 3 o'clock on Monday and Thursday afternoons, we go out to find firewood for Father. At four o'clock we read the notes through which we have written until five o'clock. During that same period I try to cook Father's dinner and at five o'clock we have Evensong. After Evensong while I'm seeing to Father's dinner, Simon Peter and Albert Maclaren do a little bit of garden work again until 6 o'clock.

At half-past seven to half-past eight we have a lecture again, and we finish with Compline. So you see, there are only three of us and the work is very big indeed and we need your prayers to help us do this work for God. The rules say I must put the light out and say my prayer and go to bed. May God bless you always in your work for Him. With best wishes and greetings from the family to you...

Good bye, I'm your sincere brother in Christ,
George Ambo Somboba

Bishop George continues to describe the problems:

It was hard for Marcella. I did not have much time to spend with her and our two children, Alban and Oliver. In 1954 when our new baby boy, John Laban, was born, things were even more difficult. But Marcella is very sensible, she never grumbled. She was always with me, right through Newton College and right through my time as a priest and a bishop. She has always been supporting me, right through till this day. I am thankful I married a good woman.[166]

In another letter, this time to his old teacher, Mavis Eather, written at Newton College in April 1954, George also refers to his third son, John Laban. He writes,

I and my wife have 3 children and all of them are boys. The first-born is Oliver Brady, he goes to school at Dogura and he is 6 years old. The second is Alban and he is 4 years old...The third is John Laban and he is 10 months old and he is growing fat like other babies do, and also he is walking about.[167]

There are no other references to John Laban, however. Neither in his personal writings nor in his interviews does Bishop George mention him. According to Oliver Ambo and Helen Ambo, George's son and daughter, John Laban as a little boy of two was given away to George's brother and sister-in-law, Simon Peter and Jennifer. Oliver recalled that his uncle and aunt were asked by George to a small dinner at their home at Newton College.

Dad always had a hard brother. He loved his brother, but uncle sometimes didn't agree with what my father was saying. He would get angry but Dad always had time and love for his brother. Because he and Jennifer didn't have any children, George gave them this little son, John Laban. Dad wanted to show that he loved his brother.[168]

Helen Ambo also gives her view of this event.

It's really a question of love, of how much you love your brother. It is very hard to give a child away. Auntie couldn't give birth to any child, so the other uncles and aunts decided to give one of their children each to live with them. So Dad didn't ask Mum for her permission or views. Auntie and Uncle were having dinner with us that night and Dad said, 'That's your son!' He was between 2 and 3. My mother keeps her sorrow inside. She was pregnant with the one who died at the time of Dad's ordination.[169]

Perhaps it is as well to bear in mind that giving away children for adoption to childless members of the family is a common practice in Papua New Guinea and is in most cases an expression of love.

Missionaries who knew Fr Cassidy during his time at Newton College describe him as tall, thin and austere. To some, he was even frightening.[170] He was also very abstemious. Having been a member of the Community of the Glorious Ascension at Goulburn, New South Wales, before he departed for New Guinea, he still bore the stamp of the monastic life. 'He never really left that behind,' according to Fr Charles Helms, the mission priest who succeeded Fr Cassidy. 'He was so abstemious that he didn't allow himself to enjoy life.' Although Fr Cassidy was invited to social functions at Dogura Station from time to time, he rarely accepted such invitations. 'I think it was probably a one-way traffic,' said Fr Helms. 'It was part of his self-image, that he was monastic and penniless, and so he couldn't reciprocate. It wouldn't have been proper for him to have done so.'

Fr Cassidy was most conscientious in his teaching and had a strict sense of duty regarding the academic development of his students, but his serious manner was reflected in the atmosphere of the college. Bishop George, looking back to his time at St Aidan's when he was doing the teacher-evangelist course, made some comparisons:

> At St Aidan's College we had a hard training, but the spirit was good and we honoured, respected and loved Fr Brady. In Newton College, there was also a man who knew his job well, but there was very strict discipline. In the beginning we didn't like Fr Cassidy. Gradually, we began to see what he was trying to do. We came to respect him as our father and love him — in some ways.[171]

Being of High Anglo-Catholic churchmanship, Fr Cassidy believed in the importance of personal confession. He had placed a confessional in the small bush chapel. Sr Jean Henderson, an Australian nurse visiting the college, later recalled how amazed she was to find a small enclosure with a grill inside the chapel. This would have been quite usual in a Roman Catholic church, but not in the Anglican Church. The principal would sit behind the grill to hear the confessions of his students. 'It seemed as if we were back in the Middle Ages,' said Jean Henderson. 'I had never seen this before in the Anglican Mission. Fr Cassidy was a true conservative.' [172]

At times George reflected on the difference in attitude to study between his former and present principals. At St Aidan's College, Fr Oliver Brady's main purpose had been 'to plant Christ' in the heart of his men and develop their pastoral abilities. He had been less concerned about academic training. In contrast, Fr Cassidy, when training the future priests at Newton College, was primarily concerned to raise the academic level of the course.[173] He hoped eventually to present a course of such high standard that his students could obtain a ThA (Associate of Theology) diploma or even a ThL (Licentiate of Theology). These aspirations could not be fulfilled till later years, however, when candidates came to the college after receiving a higher standard of education. Some time would go by before a group of students would pass a ThA at Newton College. So it was that George Ambo never gained the ThA diploma or any other officially recognised theological qualification.[174]

He found it very difficult to cope with the course. Although he had trained at St Aidan's College as a teacher-evangelist and had experience of teaching at mission schools, his knowledge of the English language was still basic. Right through his life, he felt limited in his knowledge of English and therefore inferior to more highly educated people. George later wrote,

The Ambo Family at Newton Theological College, 1954 — Marcella with John Laban, George, Oliver and Alban
(Photo courtesy of the late Nancy White)

We didn't like Fr Cassidy because we couldn't understand him. He was teaching the theologians and it was beyond our grasp. Besides, he didn't have a clear voice.[175]

Fr Cassidy's limitations in teaching methods were obvious to some expatriates. Dr Blanche Biggs, a mission doctor, wrote, 'He would talk exactly the same way whether he was talking to the Queen of England or to a Papuan boy'.[176] Fr Helms recalled that the material which Fr Cassidy delivered to his students in class was often over their heads. 'It lacked colour,' he said, 'and was very theoretical, very cerebral and not tied into life'.[177]

Fr Helms continued with his description of Fr Cassidy's teaching methods:

The difficulty might also have been the time of day that he taught, because he taught subjects like Christian Ethics and Morality in the afternoon, when the heat is on. Even just getting the breeze from the sea wasn't enough to keep people awake. They all used to go to sleep over the benches in his class room, but Fr Cassidy never faltered or halted.

Only through great determination and strength of mind did the three northern students complete their course. In Bishop George's words,

> We gradually and patiently used our minds to think wisely about our work and the life of the college. I thanked God for sending Fr Eric Cassidy to be my principal for the future of my ministry. He was a man of prayers and he was a very highly educated and learned person in the Church's doctrines.[178]

This ability to be positive in difficult circumstances has helped George Ambo to accept people as they are and face the hardships of life. Such wisdom is an important part of his personality.

After two years in Newton College, George, Marcella and their sons went back to Gona for a holiday. George found his old father very worried, especially about the poor state of his home. The white patrol officer had recently ordered him to rebuild his house within two months. 'I thanked God,' wrote Bishop George, 'for making the time available for me to build a new house for my father'. During the month at home, George realised that his father needed one of his sons to stay at home with him.

It was with heavy heart that George and his family returned to college for his final year. As he wrote,

> I was worrying about my dear old father. I was praying to God to show me if it was His Will for me to leave the College. One day, I told Fr Brady, still at St Aidan's College nearby, about my worries. He advised me not to give up my studies but to trust in God and leave my father in God's Loving Hand. Then one night, I was lying on my bed and I heard a voice saying, 'If you love your father and mother more than me, you are not worthy of me'.

Shortly afterwards, George's prayers were answered.

> God knew my father was an obstacle to my work for the Church and took my father away from this world to set me free. Two weeks before I was made a deacon, my father passed away into His Kingdom.

George was not able to attend the burial. He later remarked to Dr Biggs that at every important advancement in his life in the Church, he had suffered the loss of one of his family.[179]

Two weeks later, he was made a deacon at Dogura Cathedral together with Simon Peter and Albert Maclaren. As he wrote, 'We were the first men from the northern part of the diocese to be ordained deacons in the Church of God'. Many people came to Dogura from the parishes in the Northern District. Bishop Strong arranged for the two mission boats, the *Maclaren King 2* and the

St Laurence, to pick up 120 people from Gona for the ordination. 'The great Cathedral of St Peter and St Paul was packed,' wrote George Ambo. 'It was a big and important event in my life. I was filled with God's Holy Spirit to do my best to help my people and nation.'[180]

Shortly before his ordination as deacon in 1955, George had a deep disappointment which would have a serious, restricting and dampening effect on his inner being, curbing to some degree the artistic and expressive side of his personality. Eric Cassidy forbade George to dance the traditional dances. Still with sadness in his voice, Bishop George recalled the words of his principal:

> 'As a deacon, you will not dance! As a priest, you will not dance! You will give that up!' So I gave it up ever since. I gave it up for ever. To this day I never danced, because the priest who taught me told me not to do it. In some ways I doubted the fairness of his words. Why did he tell me not to do it?
>
> My father was *Ya Bajari,* Master of the Dance. My grandfathers and great grandfathers were all Masters of the Dance. I had been dancing from my youth. It was in my blood. But I gave it up. I was very sad but I showed complete obedience. I have in me obedience from my youth, my school age, my dancing age. I try to keep law and order. I never danced again.[181]

Bishop George, as an older man, thinking back on the occasion of his ordination as deacon, recalled that only nine years before this event he and his group of dancers had danced the ancient story of Kikiri and Gatara (see Chapter 1). That was in honour of Fr James Benson, to welcome him back to his people at Gona. Fr Benson had praised George as the hero Gatara who overcame Kikiri, the evil witch, exclaiming he was the finest dancer of that role he had ever seen. He had hoped that George, if he became a priest, would continue to perform the ancient dance. The words of Fr Cassidy at George's ordination prevented this hope from being fulfilled. Though George himself did not dance during his ministry, it is perhaps ironical that one of his greatest contributions to the future indigenous Church would be the introduction of traditional dancing into the Anglican services. He himself taught the dancers to perform during the worship to make it more meaningful for the people. In this way, as a teacher of dancing, he partly continued the tradition of his ancestors.

After the ordination, the three new deacons, Simon Peter, Albert Maclaren and George, returned with the visitors to Gona. Their first task was to assist at the Holy Communion service in their own parish church. At this memorable service, Fr Wardman celebrated, Albert Maclaren read the Epistle, Simon Peter read the Gospel and George preached. 'And then,' as Fr Wardman recalled, 'for the first time, the three deacons administered the chalice to 563 of their own people in a very reverent and moving manner'. Later in the day, there were cricket and football matches finishing with traditional dancing and a great feast. The following day, Albert left to take up his duties with Fr Robert Porter (later Bishop of The Murray) at Agenehambo Station, opened in 1952 to replace Isivita. Simon Peter stayed at Gona to assist Fr Wardman, who later wrote, 'He [Simon Peter] has wonderful gifts as an evangelist and is one of those rare persons who has honour in his own country'.[182] Only George sailed back to Dogura to take up his new duties as a deacon.

This year, 1955, when George Ambo was made a deacon, Fr James Benson died in London. He had stayed on at Gona for a time after handing over to Fr Wardman. With the help of local people, Fr Benson completed the translation and printing of the prayer book into the *Ewa-ge* language. His final and mammoth task was to beautify the cathedral at Dogura by painting the murals in the east end above the sanctuary. Then he returned to England, the land of his birth. His last appointment in life was as temporary rector at St Paul's, Knightsbridge. It was there, shortly before his death in October 1955, that he had the joy of knowing that the first three of his spiritual sons from Gona had been made deacons.[183]

James Benson had been one of the three main formative influences in George Ambo's life. Thinking back on his boyhood, Bishop George reflected on his first vague feelings that one day he might become a priest. He wrote:

> My vocation first came to me when I saw Fr James Benson in his daily devotions and in his commitment to his call. When he took my friend, Alban Jaipoba and myself visiting the out-stations, his pastoral care for the people opened my eyes. In the same way, the committed life and Christian example of my first teacher, Miss Mavis Eather, affected my thoughts and feelings. But they were not clear to me then, because I was just a schoolboy. I was pondering on the vocation to the priesthood, but at the same time I felt I was just a boy, a grandson of a cannibal. In those early days, I didn't see a clear picture of myself. Later Fr Oliver Brady's life and preaching helped me to see my goal clearly.

It seems George's formative years had been influenced more by his experiences at Gona and St Aidan's College than by those at Newton Theological College. Under the warmth and caring guidance of his first three white teachers, George's spirituality and great pastoral sense were developed along with his outstanding teaching abilities. James Benson, Mavis Eather and Oliver Brady were the inspirational lights of his life.

George was commissioned to work under Fr John Chisholm, Sub-Dean of the Cathedral at Dogura. It was the practice of the mission that deacons should for a time train and gain experience under a priest-supervisor before some of them might proceed to priesthood.[184]

Fr Chisholm had been made a deacon in Australia. He had then gone to London, where he had been priested, then served in a parish for four and a half years. When leaving England to go to Papua, he had been highly praised, and he was greatly missed by his vicar and people for his many contributions to parish life.[185] He was a man of musical and artistic talents, with a sense of humour and great warmth who made a considerable impression on George.

A few months after his arrival in 1952, Fr Chisholm was left in charge of Dogura.[186] According to Bishop Strong, 'He quite won the hearts of the native people in that area and had a wonderful influence on them in that short time'. It was especially Fr Chisholm's concern for people which made a great impact on George. He later wrote, 'I thanked God for posting me to work with Fr Chisholm, because he helped and taught me to become a true pastor'.[187]

An important part of the priestly training was the development of a keen pastoral sense. As there was a great shortage of staff for the many new mission stations recently opened in isolated areas, it was of utmost importance to develop an efficient patrol ministry. Clergy and mission workers were required to make frequent pastoral visits, often at monthly intervals, to these new Christian communities. George Ambo walked on several patrols in the isolated mountain areas behind Dogura. He recalled how he had been visiting some out-stations with Fr Peter Robin, an English priest who had come in the early 1950s to the Mission. Fr Robin, still remembering doing this patrol with George, wrote,

> George most certainly initiated me into patrolling, accompanying me into the mountains, staying in two or three villages and meeting the people, taking Communions, teaching and preaching and so on. It was a wonderful initiation for me, being with such a charming and sensitive Papua New Guinean man under training himself as a priest. I made a fair collection of errors but never felt judged. He got sick near the end of the patrol and needed help to get home. It was tough travelling, and malaria was around.[188]

Bishop George also recalled how he had come home with sickness and had found himself in hospital:

> I was so sick I nearly died but there was a good and committed Christian nurse in St Barnabas' Hospital, Sister Pat Rawlings. She looked after me very well and I got better and started the more academic part of my training for the priesthood.[189]

Having gained experience in patrolling the out-stations, George now had to remain at Dogura to study the prescribed subjects. As Bishop George puts it,

> Deacon Albert and Deacon Simon Peter arrived from the northern part of the diocese, and together we began attending our lectures. We were taught by Bishop Philip himself and Fr Edward Dams [an English priest who was with the Diocese of New Guinea from 1956]. The course of study which the three deacons had to follow fell in four parts: (a) Bible Studies (b) Doctrine (c) Pastoralia (d) Spiritual Life. Again, I thanked God for the lectures which I received from them. Their words gave me a great deal of help in future times of my ministry.

The subject of Pastoralia included 'The working out of instructions for hearers, catechumens, confirmees. The guided preparation of a sermon each month. The keeping of a diary each day, listing pastoral visits, etc...'. It was especially his pastoral abilities and understanding of people which already had distinguished George Ambo and which would form an important part of his future work.

The ordination occurred at an important time in the life of the Anglican Church in Papua. It happened on 25 January 1958, which was St Paul's Day, the patronal festival of the Cathedral. On that date it was also the diamond jubilee of the diocese, because it was sixty years since the first Bishop of New Guinea, Montagu John Stone-Wigg, had been consecrated in Sydney. Large crowds from all the mission districts gathered together at Dogura for the anniversary celebrations, for the ordination and also to attend the diocesan conference, held every second year. Over one hundred white missionaries, and twenty or so Papuan clergy as well as other church workers arrived for the festivities.[190]

The conference started with a two-day retreat conducted by Bishop Strong. Then, after twenty-four hours of continuous intercession in the cathedral, the ordination took place. Four deacons were to be ordained: the three Papuan men from Gona — George Ambo, Simon Peter Awoda and Albert Maclaren Ririka — as well as Douglas Jones, an Australian missionary who had trained at St Francis' College, Brisbane. It was the first time a mixed ordination had taken place in the diocese.

Fr Jones recalls how the large church was packed, even the gallery being filled with people. The four deacons assembled outside, while Bishop Strong vested in his episcopal robes. The service started with the great procession through the nave towards the sanctuary. Fr Jones described the occasion.

> It was very moving. I know I was nervous, I felt the occasion. The bishop was an old-fashioned Anglo-Catholic. We had the full traditional solemnity. During the length of the litany, we lay, face down, on mats on the floor before the sanctuary [see photograph opposite]. After the prayers of thanksgiving, as we were kneeling in turn in front of the bishop, he and twenty priests, white and brown, placed their hands on our heads. At that great moment of ordination, when the bishop said, 'Receive the Holy Ghost...', you felt you could almost see the Holy Ghost pressing on you.

It was a moving experience for the newly-ordained priests when they concelebrated with the bishop at the Eucharist which followed. Great was the joy when, at last, boiling in the heat, the four priests came out of the cathedral to join the people at a communal breakfast. Then they watched the dancing and drumming all through the day, finishing with a great feast. Fr Jones recalls, 'It was a wonderful and memorable day'.

After his ordination, George Ambo was commissioned by Bishop Strong to serve as assistant priest under Fr Norman Cruttwell, a priest from England, in charge of Menapi Parish. Menapi District covered a large area on the southern coast of Cape Vogel, the peninsula stretching far out into the sea and forming

The four ordinands lying prostrate at their ordination at Dogura
    Cathedral, 25 January 1958
Front, from left: Simon Peter Awoda, George Ambo, Douglas Jones,
    Albert Maclaren Ririka
Kneeling at step: Canon John Chisholm, Bishop Philip Strong
At right: Canon Oliver Brady, Archdeacon Byam Roberts
Far right: Fr Peter Rautamara (first Papuan priest)
            (Photograph courtesy of Bob Hay)

The Cathedral of St Peter and St Paul, Dogura
(Photograph courtesy of Martin Chittleborough)

Bishop Philip Strong with the four newly-ordained priests
From left: Simon Peter Awoda, George Ambo, Douglas Jones,
Albert Maclaren Ririka
(Photograph courtesy of John Wardman)

the north-western side of Goodenough Bay (see map, page xii). Before he could start his first posting, however, a tragedy struck which nearly made George Ambo give up his work as a priest.

In 1954, after the birth of their third son, John Laban, who was given away to Simon Peter, he and Marcella longed to have a daughter. Two years later, their wish was granted. A baby girl was born to Marcella on 30 January, 1956. She was baptised Mary Gloria Embota Ambo.[191] 'She was very pretty,' wrote Bishop George, 'a beautiful girl. Her skin was light and she had beautiful long hair like my mother. We loved her dearly'.[192]

Their happiness was short lived. As George and Marcella were getting ready to move from Dogura across the bay to Menapi, their little girl suddenly became ill. Bishop George wrote of the sadness suffered by him and Marcella.

> My first dearest daughter was attacked by malaria. She got sick on Tuesday in Holy Week and died on Wednesday in Holy Week. I lost my beautiful daughter. We were very, very sad. All of a sudden she died, only two and a half years old. I was very angry with God. I nearly gave up serving as a priest. My faith and trust in God became vague. It seemed to me very unfair. God gave me the first daughter in my family. Why did he take her away?

He continued,

> A lot of people came to support us. My wife was nearly dying from sorrow. I remember Fr Oliver Brady, standing behind me, saying, 'Son! It's your Cross. Carry it through. Carry it with the help of Jesus'. Wherever I went, people were crying, but I wiped my tears. I wept in my heart.
>
> Then Bishop Philip Strong came to bury my daughter, Mary Gloria. He conducted the Burial Service and said the following words which have stuck in my mind and heart till this day: 'My dear Father George and Marcella. God in His wisdom chose you and Marcella to bring this child into the world. But Mary Gloria was not your daughter. She belongs to God. He has a purpose for her future. It was part of God's plan to take her back to Heaven. You have many friends and relations who pray for you in Paradise. You also have many who pray for you on earth, but here their prayers are not perfect. God took your daughter away from you so that one of your close family can offer perfect prayer for you in Heaven to help you and your future Ministry'.
>
> That was the way he put it, but I didn't believe his words.

The burial of Mary Gloria Embota was one of the rare occasions, perhaps the only one, when George Ambo could not control his emotions. His eldest son, Oliver, at the time a student at Dogura Primary School, recalls how the only time he had ever seen his father break down was at the sudden death and burial of his little daughter. A grave had been dug near the cathedral. Oliver remembers seeing his father sitting there, his eyes bloodshot and red, with his dead daughter in his arms. When she was to be buried, he refused to let them take her out of his arms and put her in the grave. He kept refusing to let her go. Eventually, Bishop Philip succeeded in calming him down. He took the child and buried her.[193] As Bishop George himself later admitted, 'Only at the death of Mary Gloria did I show a lot of emotion. I tried to control myself, but tears were just falling'.[194]

After the burial, George Ambo grappled with the problem of suffering. Why had God made himself and Marcella suffer in this way? 'My heart failed,' he wrote, 'and I was pondering and thinking very critically about my future ministry'.[195] Many of his fellow-workers at Dogura suggested to Bishop Strong that George and Marcella should not go to Menapi, but stay at Dogura. However, the Bishop's answer was, 'We shall leave the decision completely to Father George himself!' George Ambo recalled how the white missionaries had offered their support, visiting every evening and trying to help him and Marcella carry their cross.

> This we did, offering our sorrow to God and asking Him to help us make the right and fair decision regarding my ministry, according to His Will.

Then, as Bishop George recalls it,

> ….one day, I was meditating after the Holy Eucharist and three thoughts came to me: God speaks to His people 1. through Bible reading, 2. through sermons, 3. through Sorrow. I was pondering these thoughts with my wife, and I heard a voice: 'Fr George! If you really love me carry your Cross and follow me'.

Shortly after this, George Ambo told Bishop Strong that he and Marcella would go to Menapi. 'Very well done,' answered the Bishop, 'by the Grace of God you and Marcella overcame your temptation'. Then he took George and his family across to Menapi in his own boat.

George's life as a parish priest would soon come to an end, however.

CHAPTER 12

Parish Work and Interruptions:
Menapi, St Aidan's, Boianai

As assistant priest with Fr Norman Cruttwell at Menapi, George Ambo was well on the way towards the fulfilment of his destiny. The distance to the top of the Church hierarchy would prove to be short, yet hardships loomed ahead.

The main concern of Fr Norman Cruttwell was to establish contact with the vast areas in his district which had not been reached by the Christian Mission. He opened several new stations in the mountains behind Menapi, some of which were in the isolated Daga country. With great perseverance Fr Cruttwell made strenuous journeys, often of three or four days, into the remote areas to start preparing the people for the Christian teaching. He was assisted in this pioneering work by Mrs Christian Cruttwell, his mother, who was living with him. She also undertook rough journeys either on foot or by boat, and was indefatigable in her efforts to help the women gain support and strength from each other through coming together for Christian fellowship. In this way, she developed the Mothers' Union in the Diocese.[196]

Although George did not complain about conditions at Menapi, life was hard for him and Marcella. George's pay of £4 a month was not enough to cover their basic needs. In that dry, barren country one of their main concerns was the shortage of food. George recalled how, sometimes, committed Christians brought vegetables for them, while at other times they had nothing to eat for several nights. Once, they had gone to bed without dinner and he was lying awake, pondering what he could do for Marcella and the children. He was thinking of sending them back to Gona for six months until their new food-garden was ready.

> That particular night God sent a stranger with cooked food and vegetables for us. When I asked him where he came from, his answer was 'from Banapa Village,' [a village in the parish]. This happened on Friday night. On Sunday morning at Church, when I thanked the Banapa people for sending food by their church councillor, they answered that they had sent nothing.[197]

For George this incident was a miracle, a sign from God which gave him courage to carry on and complete his posting to Menapi. As he wrote,

> I thanked God that by His Grace we had not given up or lost our faith or been angry with the priest in charge. My wife and I shared our problems and troubles and again we carried our Cross with

Jesus. We did not know then, that in the future we should receive rich blessings.

The following event which happened in George's first and only year at Menapi, indicates how support for the Church was growing in that district. In the months following the 60th Anniversary celebrations at Dogura in January 1958, Bishop David Hand was visiting every district in the Anglican Mission. He told the widely scattered communities about the significance of the consecration in 1898 of the first Bishop of New Guinea, Bishop Montagu Stone-Wigg, and the birth of the Diocese. Before leaving every parish, Bishop David received the thanksgiving offerings given by the local Christians in support of the Church.[198]

When, in August, Bishop David arrived at Menapi, a crowd had gathered on the wharf to greet him. Many of these people had come down from the mountains, especially from the large Daga country. As Bishop George recalled,

> When the Bishop came on shore and gave the Blessing to us all, he...shook hands with every person who had come down from the Daga country. As there were more than 300 communicants and about 600 people wishing to worship, the altar had to be moved out of the church and the service was held outside. Afterwards, Bishop David sat on a chair in front of the altar. The people came in their lines in twos and knelt down in front of the Bishop, and as he blessed them they gave their jubilee thanksgiving offering. Menapi Christians gave £224 and our brothers and sisters from the mountains gave £57.[199]

This was a defining moment in George's life for he saw the future possibility of an independent, self-supporting Church in Papua. He noted that such large sums of thanksgiving offerings showed that his fellow Christians could give enough money to support the Church in their own country. 'We must encourage people to give what they can to help Christ's work,' he wrote. 'We must try to stand on our own feet.'

A few years later, however, after his consecration as bishop, he was less hopeful about a Papuan Church being self-supporting. Seeing things in a more realistic light, he stated that support from Australia was urgently needed. Without it, he could not do his work for the Church. All his life George was to be caught in this conflict—on the one hand was the need for his Church to be self-supporting, on the other was the realisation that this would be impossible for a very long time, and that outside assistance would be needed far into the future. This was a worry to George, as outside help inevitably would weaken self-reliance and initiative. Still today, the tension exists between the idealistic concept of Papuans being responsible for their own Church and the economic necessity for foreign help.

After almost a year at Menapi, circumstances changed George's life. He was asked by Bishop Philip Strong to go back to St Aidan's Teacher Training

College at Dogura to upgrade his standard as a teacher. And so he found himself in a rather humbling and surprising situation. A new education ordinance had been introduced which required that all teachers, trained by the mission, would have to pass a government examination in order to qualify for government registration.[200]

The Education Ordinance of 1952 came into effect in 1955. In it, the government claimed the ultimate authority over all education in the Territory, including that of the mission schools. The ordinance, amongst other things,

> provided for the setting up of schools...by the Administration. It provided for the compulsory registration...of all schools conducted by educational agencies other than the Administration; and it provided for grants to be made by the Administration to missions or other educational agencies.

According to Dr David Wetherell, until 1956 financial assistance was provided in the form of a grants-in-aid scheme by which the assistance granted depended on the subjects taught by a master and the standard of his training, also on the number of pupils in the school. By December 1956, the terms for the giving of these grants were changed. From then, money would only be available on the basis of the number of government-registered teachers at the mission schools. So, staff teaching at mission schools had to qualify for the grant. As priests frequently had to take the responsibility for education in the mission areas due to shortage of teachers, this new situation affected George.

To understand the need for him to go back to being a student, one must look at the changes which began to occur after the war. Through the 1950s, a general growth was happening in social and economic conditions. With an increase in European enterprises, new opportunities for employment opened for the Papuans within such areas as agriculture, mining and general business. For these they needed higher educational training. The process of taking up land by foreigners had been made simpler than before the war. Therefore, many Europeans availed themselves of the opportunities for establishing plantations and engaging in various forms of agriculture. An example of this development was a soldier-settlement scheme by which Australian ex-servicemen could easily and cheaply obtain blocks of land for cultivation of cash-crops such as cocoa. The resources of the country were also being developed and mining operations expanded. As progress was made in the provision of housing, health and education services for the growing European population, so, to a certain degree, this progress demanded improved standards in health and education for many indigenous people.[201]

As part of this forward move, the education ordinance had been introduced by the government in the 1950s to raise the standard of education. At first, the new policy caused concern in mission circles: whereas in the past mission schools had received some government grants based on the number of children in the school, that assistance would now cease. In 1956, Bishop David Hand wrote, 'Until 1956, we used to receive a lot of money in that way. Now it is different. The government has started "Registration" of all teachers, and the grant is now only given for the number of registered teachers we have'.[202] Not only the teachers had to be registered, but the mission schools also had to qualify for government registration or they would miss out on any financial help with materials or equipment. If the mission schools failed to meet government standards, they would be regarded as non-existent!

Missionaries feared the new education policies and strongly opposed the government's intention to secularise education. 'If standards are too low, maybe the government will close our schools,' wrote Bishop David. 'Then if we lose our church schools, how will our country grow to be a strong Christian country?' Although priests and Christian teachers were allowed to give some religious instruction in the government schools, it was only for one hour a week. Fr Cruttwell at Menapi was most concerned with this restriction in teaching of religion:

> How could that...wean a primitive people from their belief in
> sorcery, and build in them a faith strong enough to save their souls,
> in the incredibly difficult period of transition through which they
> are passing today?[203]

For the time being, the government had decided that St Aidan's Teacher Training College should continue to train Anglican teachers, provided they passed the exams for government registration. Changes in Fr Oliver Brady's teacher-evangelist course inevitably occurred, which he and his students found difficult to accept. In 1956, he wrote to Dr Blanche Biggs:

> The government business about registration of teachers, the upset
> of courses etc. has rocked the men greatly. I feel that if I walk out
> on furlough now, they will feel that all solid ground is swept from
> under their feet...I feel that I have to stand by my men...I know
> that I can hold the men and keep them...on an even keel.[204]

So it was that, at the end of 1958, some teachers and priests—George Ambo amongst them—were asked to go back to college the following year to prepare for government examinations and registration. It was difficult and somewhat demeaning for George and Marcella to have to adjust to college discipline and student life. Together with two deacons from Gona, Deacon Nicodemus Umbusuba and Deacon Ronald Kaiae, George started studying again. Without complaining, he simply wrote, 'We three were older men and we were now training with Martyrs' School boys who had recently completed Grade 9'.

Stephen Tago, later a Minister for Defence in the Papua New Guinea Government, was amongst those young students from Martyrs' School who had just started their first-year studies at St Aidan's. He recalled how he observed Fr George at college, and his account paints a clear picture of the older man:

> He was a very humble person, a good listener, honest, open and a hard worker and I mean a really hard worker. No matter how busy he was, he always showed respect for all, young and old, and he and Marcella had open home. They were loving and caring for the students. They were really father and mother to all.[205]

Stephen continued,

> George Ambo praised and spoke highly of other people, but he was never afraid to speak the truth. Sometimes after Evensong, we would come out and sit on the grass, and all the young students would listen to Fr George…'You young people of the Northern District,' he said on one occasion, 'you will all have equal opportunity for a good education, but as far as leadership is concerned, you Orokaivans will be dragging behind. The future leaders will come from the Binandere people, the coastal people, the Tufi and Musa people. You Orokaivans will be the last to produce leaders'.

As Stephen Tago reflected,

> In speaking his mind, George did not fear jealousy or hostility from others. He would talk truthfully about complex and sensitive matters such as the differences, as he saw them, between white and black. He didn't hide anything but was open. What he said was correct. It always happened. He was a man of truth.

Characteristically, George took the government's new regulations as a challenge and as part of God's plan for him. Some mission teachers were drawn away into government institutions and employment, where they could get higher pay and better conditions for personal advancement. But George remained faithful to the Mission. He was not one to switch his loyalties from Church to government. Faced with change and difficulties, he forced himself to adapt to the new situation. With his usual positive attitude and courage he went back to school, applying himself wholeheartedly to his studies.

A new principal, David Durie, had arrived with his wife from Australia in September 1957, to take charge of teacher-training at St Aidan's.[206] Bishop George wrote, 'We were lucky to be trained by David Durie in the Teachers' Registration Course. It was not an easy course, but I had full confidence in God for my training'.[207]

Athough George appreciated the teaching of David Durie, at the same time he felt sad he was no longer taught by Oliver Brady, who had retired a few months before George came back to St Aidan's. The official reason given for the retirement was ill health.[208] The real cause, however, for leaving his beloved college after seventeen years as principal may have been unwilling-ness to adopt the new government policies in teacher-training. Whereas his foremost aim had been, and always would be, 'to plant Christ' in the heart of his students, the purpose of the new course was to produce highly-trained teachers rather than devoted evangelists.

In March 1959, Oliver Brady wrote from Hobart:

> The parting was harder and more painful than ever I could have imagined...I can still see that disconsolate little group standing on the Wedau jetty crying out 'Father, Father!'...I am tempted to wish that I didn't love them so, for love always brings pain with it...My heart will always be in Papua and my soul, half Papuan.[209]

The new principal, though educated with a Bachelor of Divinity degree, was not ordained. He was planning to go back to Australia the following year to train for the priesthood.[210] As he would be away in 1960, there would be no teacher-training course that year. Therefore, the pressure was on in 1959 to get as many men as possible through the government examinations.

It was a particularly strenuous year for George and his fellow students at St Aidan's, with almost everybody taking either the Registration 'A' or the Registration 'B' Course. Towards the end of the year, the students were getting ready for examinations. They were under great pressure to pass so that they, as well as the mission schools where they would be teaching, could qualify for government subsidies.

As Bishop George wrote,

> The examiner came from Samarai and he stayed for four days at the college. Our first test was oral questions and on the second day we had written exams. The last day we did our practical teaching in St Paul's School, Dogura. Then the announcement was made throughout the country of the results of the 1959 teachers' exams. I thanked God that I passed my course through His Grace.

With typical modesty, he added the following words in brackets: '(In 'A' Course I came top in the whole country)'.[211]

His name appeared in several places in the end-of-year issue of *Komboro*, the St Aidan's College Magazine: 'SPECIAL CONGRATULATIONS to Rev. George Ambo, who received the highest marks of all the 'A' candidates in the Territory...'. George also won praise for his personal example to the younger students. This was expressed in a farewell message written by Stephen Tago who, by then, had finished his first year at St Aidan's. Stephen said,

> We thank you, Rev. George Ambo, our loving Father in God, for your very good example to us every day; an example not only from you but also from Mother Marcella and the children, to our whole college. No doubt your actions have been speaking louder than your words to us through this year...The sort of life the ministers live and that WE ought to live, you have shown us. Your light has shone before us all...[212]

In his life as a bishop, George Ambo often emphasised his belief that one must teach by personal example and not by words alone. 'Do as you preach,' he would say, and then he would add, 'I try to live what I have preached'.

So it was that George, having gained government registration as a teacher towards the end of 1959, returned to parish work. However, he did not go back to Menapi but was asked by Bishop Strong to re-open the Boianai Mission, which had been closed for some years. The station lies approximately 26 km west of Dogura by Goodenough Bay, on the north coast of Papua.

Since the early days, Anglican missionaries had lived at Boianai. When Romney Gill, an English priest, arrived in 1911, there were just under 300 Christians.[213] When Fr AP Jennings came to take over from Fr Gill eleven years later, he found the station running smoothly with a thriving school and frequent celebrations of the Eucharist. Romney Gill had built up an effective system of running the church and the station, in which the people themselves played an important and responsible part.

Between 1925 and 1929, the first cement church in the Anglican mission was built there by the Boianai people. Collecting coral in the sea, they made lime for the concrete, and by their good workmanship produced a building which is still standing near the beach today.[214]

In spite of these sound foundations, giving every optimism for the future, the situation at the station declined during the following decades. George had heard rumours about the Boianai people's bad ways from his friends and fellow workers. As he recalled,

> I was not happy to go because the station had been closed for four years for evil practices and they were still practising their evil habits.[215] However, when Marcella and I had prayed about it, we both felt strongly that it was God's Call that we should go and try our best by God's Grace to help the people convert.

Bishop George recalled in detail what was wrong:

> One of the evil practices at Boianai was called *eriama*. It means 'the exchanging of wives'. Husbands would exchange their wives for the sake of committing adultery.

George asked Bishop Strong to pray for him and Marcella, warning the bishop that he was only young, and still inexperienced to fill such a difficult and important position.

George Ambo had been commissioned as the priest in charge and head-master of All Saints' School, Boianai. He recalled the feeling of despondency which overcame them on arrival:

> It was a very poor show, and both of us looked at each other and bore it patiently. Only two people came to help us carry our things to the mission house. The grass around the house was not cut and the floor inside had not been swept. That evening, a man called Samuel and his wife, Chrisander, came to see how we were settling in. We thanked God for these two committed Christians.

So you can imagine that the condition of the Mission House was pretty bad and it was not fit for us or any family to live in. For five years it had not been looked after. White ants went through the building and rats and snakes used it as their home. Our first night was troubled and disturbed. Dozens of rats running to and fro made us stay awake until the morning. During that first night we killed three snakes.

Therefore we used downstairs for our lodgings, and by God's guidance I was able to make plans to repair the house. Although we were both depressed and downhearted during our first week, I felt that God had trusted me with this parish and left it to me to re-open it for His Kingdom. But it was very hard. The snakes chasing after rats in the mission house made us stay wide awake for the sake of the children. I kept a bush-knife beside my bed and I killed many of the snakes. Soon the village cat found the rats and caught many of them, so, after some time, they left the house. The village cat helped us and we were very thankful to God for sending the cat.

After a week, I called the first church councillors' meeting. It was in the mission house on Sunday after the Holy Eucharist. Some of them did turn up, but others refused. We opened the meeting with prayer and then proceeded. It was a short meeting because some came with an un-Christian spirit. The chairman asked me some questions: 1. Which is your home parish? 2. What is your name? 3. How long were you ordained?

Bishop George continued,

I was smiling when I answered his questions. Then he warned me, saying, 'I am very sorry, Father. You are a very young priest. I am afraid you will not last long. Our pretty young girls and women will tempt you and you will not last long in this parish'. Some church councillors were not happy with him. Anyway, I took it with a smiling face and we ended the meeting with prayer and thanksgiving.

Although the surroundings of Boianai were beautiful with palms lining the grey, sandy beaches and views of soaring mountains, it was not an easy parish in which to pay pastoral visits. As he wrote,

It is a mountainous district, but I made my plans to visit every chapel. Sometimes I would arrive as planned, but when it was the rainy season I found it hard. There are three big rivers in the district. During the heavy rains, when they all flooded, I found it very hard to reach the villages or to go home. Three times, I had to spend the nights in a cave with my carriers.

Through patience and prayer, George gradually built up a relationship of trust with many of his parishioners. The chairman of the church councillors visited him and apologised for what he had said. Bishop George tells of the meeting:

> He brought some vegetables and some cooked food for us. We had a happy dinner with him and his wife and I took them home. That night, Marcella and I knelt on our knees and thanked God.

> At the end of the year, a good number came and made their confessions. Slowly people began coming to church. There was an encouraging spirit in the place and I thanked God for His Divine Grace.

In early December 1959, things were getting easier for George. He wrote a letter from Boianai to his old teacher, Mavis Eather. This shows that he had some help in the school and also with pastoral work:

> ...It is very big work for a young priest like me, but I'll try to do my best and let God do His part. I know most people are praying for me and I know you will too...There are 2 male teachers, Stephen and Ananaias, and 4 female teachers, Ilma Violet, Dulcie Freda, Ida Mary and Lionella. The Rev. Edward Dams is spending his holiday at Boianai...he is visiting Boianai out-stations and helping them in their needs. He is doing very good work for Boianai and its district...[216]

In the same letter George also refers to three of their children:

> I left Oliver Brady and Alban at St Paul's School, Dogura, because there are no Standard 4 and 5 at Boinai. My little daughter, Gloria, is walking about now. She is a year and three weeks old...

He makes no mention of his third son, John Laban, who had been given away to his brother and sister-in-law, Simon Peter and Jennifer, while George was still at Newton College training for ordination.

According to a second letter to Mavis Eather, written on 25th February 1960, the situation at Boianai had greatly improved through Fr George's hard work as headmaster and parish priest. There were 179 children in the school and four registered teachers. Four pupil-teachers were assisting both in the classrooms and in the church.

> The pupil-teachers are all girls and they are doing very good work for their people...We are all doing well and I'm teaching Standard 4 at 8.30am–3.00pm including doing my priest's work as well. I have got all the books I need except a nature study book...

At home things were also going well, and George and Marcella felt pleased with their two sons. As George continued,

> My little Oliver has passed the Martyrs' entrance exams and has gone to Martyrs' School in Agenehambo in the Orokaiva District. I'm very pleased about that. The younger one, Alban, has passed Standard 4 exams and he is in boarding school at Dogura.[217]

With their sons away, George and Marcella felt blessed to have a new little daughter with them at home. She was a little over one year old and had been baptised 'Gloria', as distinct from Mary Gloria whom they had lost at the time of George's ordination to the priesthood.[218]

Boianai Station and parish life had, by the great efforts of George and Marcella, been built up and strengthened. Christmas 1959 had been a very happy time when the church was packed with people. 'We had *amgogona* on the grass,' recalled Bishop George. *'Amgogona'* means 'eating together on the grass for Christmas dinner'.

But there were still many problems for George which were hard to deal with. For some time, he had been troubled by the superstitious beliefs and false teaching among the people in the mountains behind Boianai. In his words,

> In these particular areas, the cargo cults, witchcraft and sorcery were very bad. These beliefs were so evil and immoral. Many men and women were adulterers, especially the leaders of cargo cults. It was nearly like the ancient times of Israel when the people worshipped Baal and other false Gods.

Cargo cults were a fairly recent phenomenon. They were nourished by confusion in some people's minds, caused by the blending of the new Christian teaching, Western materialism and traditional beliefs, also by memories of experiences in the war, when ships and planes had brought great loads of goods. It was thought that Christ (or in some cases ancestral spirits) would bring 'cargo', that is, gifts of food and material things to the members of the cult, providing for all their needs. Symptoms of this delusion could be seen in the destruction of food-gardens, pigs and other property, as the people believed they would no longer have to worry about necessities for their daily lives.

Bishop George recalled that

> It was at Udubi Village I dealt with my first cargo cult case. A married woman, very thin and middle-aged, was saying that she was going to give birth to baby Jesus. The people in the area believed her and worshipped and praised her as she visited their homes and villages. They believed that when the Christ-child had been born, a great flood would bring about the end of the world. On top of a hill, they had built what they called an 'ark'. It was a traditional house, in which they would be 'saved,' when the flood came. They had killed their pigs and destroyed the food-gardens, as soon they would no longer have any needs as they would be in the care of the Christ-child.
>
> As Udubi Village was on a very steep mountain, I sent a message asking the 'pregnant' woman to walk half-way down to meet me. Her followers walked with her shouting *Kaiva, Kaiva* (Welcome, Welcome). They were shouting and singing, holding flowers,

brightly coloured croton leaves and branches of trees. As she came to Ikara Village where I was staying for the night, I went out to meet her. Some of the people of that village did not believe her but quite a good number did. I did not interrupt her welcome but I warned the local church councillors to watch her carefully until after Evensong.

Then after Evening Prayer I interviewed her carefully, and her answer was that she was going to deliver the baby Jesus at 12 o'clock midnight. So I warned very strongly the church councillors to keep watching her during the night. I and my group stayed wide awake until midnight. When I went and saw her and asked if she had given birth to Jesus, she said that it would happen at 6am in the morning. Here again, there was no baby and her husband was a very worried and troubled man.

Fr George had been telling them about the teaching of the Bible, that before Christ would come again, the Gospel must be preached in all the world. Even then, no man would know when He would come. Despite the teaching of their priest, they had persisted in their false beliefs.

But George was not deterred by their blind persistence. Although he was a man from a different place, whom the mountain people would instinctively distrust, he overcame cultural barriers. Somewhat incredibly, he managed to persuade the 'pregnant' woman and her husband to give up their fears and go with him to Dogura. To them this was a foreign place and traditional enemy land.

On a Sunday in May, 1960, they arrived at Dogura. Fr George saw Bishop Strong about the case. Then he took the woman to be inspected by the mission doctor, Dr Ken Houston, who had come from Ireland to take charge of the hospital. Bishop George recalled the result:

After he had examined her, he pronounced that 'no egg had formed in her womb' and she was not pregnant! Her husband was very ashamed because of his wife's gossip and lies.

Then Bishop Strong wrote a letter for Fr George to read to the mountain people:

...I am greatly troubled by the false teaching that you have been believing...Christ is God's only son...He was born as a little child. That happened once only. The Christ will indeed come again at the end of the world...in all His great glory as God...no man will know when He will come...I desire that you will obey Fr George's word and the word of me, your Bishop, and that you should at once give up this false teaching and never follow it again.[219]

After a week, Fr George set out again to visit the mountain districts carrying the letter with him.

I visited all the villages which were involved with cargo cults and false prophets and tried by God's Grace to explain in the *Wedauan* langage the Bishop's letter to them.

This cargo cult case had been a test for George, who had acted as a highly competent and responsible parish priest. Bishop Strong had seen for himself one example of the effectiveness of George's ministry in a strange and difficult situation.

Back at Boianai, George had to plan his programme for All Saints' School. As the headmaster it was his duty to have meetings with the teachers to discuss the school year. As he wrote,

> It was not easy for me to teach children in the classroom as well as looking after the church and do my pastoral work for those whom God had entrusted to my care.

Gradually, George was building up the station by his determined efforts and obtaining positive results. Before long, Bishop Strong called at Boianai to see his young priest, who recalled the visit.[220]

> The visitation of the bishop was unexpected. We were doing our daily duties as usual. I was teaching in the classroom, when we heard the engine of the *St George*, the bishop's boat. My wife walked up to the school to let me know that the bishop was on board the *St George*. She did not go into the classroom but stood outside and made a sign. Then she walked down to the beach and welcomed the bishop. He went up to the mission house, then he walked up to the church and round the station before going back to the mission house. The teachers and I met him there. He spent about one hour with us and then he returned to Dogura.

It seemed that Bishop Strong had gone to Boianai on the spur of the moment. Could it be that he wanted to see for himself the depth of George's faith and his ability to cope with the difficult situation at Boianai? Knowing from the past George's unique qualities of leadership, could it be that in the corners of his mind were taking form the faint glimmerings of a picture of a future Papuan leader of an Indigenous Church?

As the work of the Mission had increased in recent years, Bishop Strong had for some time felt that the task of governing and administering the Church in his Diocese, together with the weight of pastoral work, had grown too big for him.[221] No longer could he afford the time to visit all the Christian missions, recently opened in the mountains and inland areas of Papua. No longer could he fulfil such responsibilities as blessing and dedicating new churches, or the confirmation of old people unable to travel to the head stations.

Although Bishop David Hand had been consecrated at Dogura in June 1950 to assist Bishop Strong, he had been unable to offer much help. Almost immediately after his consecration he was involved in the restoration work in the northern district following the disaster of the eruption of Mt Lamington.

Then he was in charge of the work of the Church in New Britain and the highlands of northern New Guinea. Having opened many new out-stations and established the mission in remote, heathen highland areas, Bishop David was needed to build up and care for the work that had been started. Because of this, he could not assist Bishop Strong in Papua.

Overburdened by the huge task before him, Bishop Strong felt the need for a second assistant bishop. The more he prayed about it, the more firmly he believed that God eventually would provide the answer. As he wrote to his staff:

> I have felt that in God's good time He would show me whom He would have for that sacred office and work, and whom I should choose and appoint, for I have always felt that I must not choose myself. I must wait for God to show me...[222]

Bishop Strong had never thought that the time was ripe for the appointment of a Papuan bishop. He had felt that it must wait till the standard of education in Papua had been raised and an educated elite had emerged with matriculation and degrees, from among whose ranks a suitable bishop could be found. In the same letter, he told his staff how he had always felt that, while they could hope for more and more Papuan deacons and priests, 'it would be many years yet, perhaps two or three generations, before a Papuan could be called to the episcopate'.

Boianai was not far by boat from Dogura, the seat of the Diocese, and Fr George would go there for special occasions such as church festivals and diocesan conferences. Little did George know, as he set off for the annual conference from the beach at Boianai one day in late June 1960, that it was at Dogura that the seed would be sown for the most profound change in his life.

CHAPTER 13

Consecration of the First Papua New Guinean Bishop

It happened on St Peter's Day 29 June 1960, in the Cathedral of St Peter and St Paul at Dogura, that Bishop Strong had a vision which would deeply affect the Church in Papua New Guinea. The mission staff had come from all the widely scattered stations to meet for the annual conference. Dr Blanche Biggs, one of those attending, wrote,

> Our Conference ended up with a wonderful Thanksgiving Evensong. We sang and we sang...At the end we had a procession and a long, long hymn and the Bishop just sat in his throne and watched it. All the time he was puzzling over this need for an assistant bishop and he didn't have anyone suitable.[223]

As the Bishop's eyes followed the people processing through the vast cathedral, he suddenly heard a voice. In his own words he described this deep experience:

> On St Peter's Day in the Procession at Solemn Evensong something seemed to say to me, 'You have not got to wait till then. You have your man NOW'. I looked down the Cathedral and my eye fell upon Father George Ambo, and God seemed, I thought, to say, 'He has the qualities. It is not education or a graduate's degree that make a Bishop. There is something indefinable, and it is in him'.[224]

Through this spiritual experience in the Cathedral and through reflection and prayer, Bishop Strong understood that God had reversed his previous judgement.

> I have come to see that...God, in His inscrutable wisdom , and for reasons known only to Him, had raised up among the Papuan clergy one man, and ONE ONLY, long before the time when we might normally look for such, to whom He had given the qualities and spiritual capacity for the high office and calling in the Church...I feel that God has given us just this one, and that if anything was to happen to prevent it, there is no other in the present or foreseeable future.

Although Fr George had no secondary or university training, he was now recognised by Bishop Strong as the only Papuan of his time suited to hold the office of a bishop.

> He is the most knowledgeable of all our Papuan priests, and has the best knowledge of the Faith and Theology and he is always keen and eager to learn more. BUT ABOVE ALL ELSE he has within

him what I call THE INDEFINABLE QUALITY and with it too the essentials of deep humility and wonderful dedication with complete loyalty, balance and level-headedness.

These remarkable qualities have remained with Bishop George through-out his life. No number of academic degrees could alone have created the wisdom, spirituality and that 'indefinable quality' needed to be a bishop, which have been marvelled at by all who know him. Several Papuan Bishops, much more highly educated, were to follow. They came after the independence of their country and their Church. George Ambo preceded them by many years — he was truly a man before his time.

It was four weeks or so before George, back at Boianai and unaware that he was close to the climax of his destiny, received a letter from Bishop Strong. He was asked to go to Dogura. Bishop George tells what was involved.

It took me about half a day's walk. The beach from Boianai to Dogura is twenty miles long and it is a stony beach. I arrived before Evening Prayer and the Bishop met me after Evensong. He told me to go up to his house after dinner. He was very happy to see me.[225]

Before talking to me, both of us knelt down in his small, private chapel and spent 15 minutes in prayer. After that, he revealed his vision to me. I got a shock. I did not answer him. I waited for 10 or 15 minutes and then I said, 'Father Bishop, I knew that one day I would be a priest in the Church of Christ. But to become a Bishop is not my hope and belief. It is your vision from the Holy Spirit. Being a Bishop is a very holy and high position. A Bishop must be a university graduate. I am only a very simple bush priest. I am an ignorant man. My education is not high enough and I am not worthy to accept this high position.

The Bishop firmly believed that God, through the Holy Spirit, had revealed to him in a vision the future of my ministry. Humbly, I took in everything he said to me that night, after the prayers. Then he blessed me and I walked back to my uncle Roland Somboba's home. He was a teacher at St Paul's School, Dogura.

Oliver Ambo, Bishop George's son, remembered his mother's reaction when, back at Boianai, George told her about the Bishop's vision.

She broke down. She broke down because she was wondering how she could take all that responsibility upon herself. She was very frightened and cried. It would have been frightening for her. The Bishops were all white people, and she would have to go to white man's place and eat at white man's table. That was frightening and different to the Papuan custom where women eat after the men. The thought of having to go overseas to white man's country was too much for her at that time. Now, she is used to it. She can now sit back and watch the other bishops' wives performing and she tries to help.[226]

George spent the following days praying and meditating on the Call. He wrote,

> Then, one night, God the Holy Spirit spoke to me in a dream. He encouraged me to accept my Call. I heard a voice saying, 'I have called you to be the first Native Bishop in the Anglican Church of Papua New Guinea. If I have called you to be a Bishop, then I will give you knowledge, wisdom and power to help you in your Ministry'.

George reflected that the Disciples were ignorant men without much schooling. God had helped them, so He would also help him.

> Then after a day, I took off to Dogura to reveal my dream to the Bishop. On August 10th, at Evensong in the Cathedral, Bishop Strong announced his vision and my acceptance of the Call. The local people from Wedau and Wamira came up to the station for the service. The students from St Aidan's and Newton College came as well as the girls from Holy Name School.[227] Those serving as priests, deacons, nurses, teachers, lay workers and St Paul's School children all attended the service. The Bishop preached a very inspiring and moving sermon which touched many of us.

Bishop Strong himself wrote an account of his sermon in a letter to his staff. He began with the words, 'This is the Lord's doing, and it is marvellous in our eyes (Ps118, v23)'. Then, starting with the landing of the first missionaries of the Anglican Church, Fathers Albert Maclaren and Copland King, 69 years previously, he went through the history of the Anglican Mission, building up to the moment when God spoke to him in the Cathedral. He then spoke of Fr George's humble acceptance of the Call. He concluded:

> And so I give you the MOMENTOUS NEWS that soon there will be a third Bishop in this Diocese and that he will be a PAPUAN BISHOP, and will be the first native Bishop in the South Pacific, for as yet there is not a native Bishop in either of the Dioceses of Melanesia or Polynesia.

After Evensong, George experienced the mixed reactions which he would face frequently in the coming year. As he wrote,

> Many Christians came and greeted me but the local people of Wedau and Wamira walked away in bad spirits. They criticised me for lack of education and wondered how I would cope in the future. Their jealous and evil attitudes spread quickly to nearly all the parishes in the Dogura area. I thanked God for His Grace which He gave to me at that time, which enabled me to carry my Cross. Although they were very jealous and took my name in vain, I tried to understand them and did not blame them. The Gospel of our Lord, Jesus Christ, was first planted by the Anglican missionaries in the Dogura area. The local people were right in thinking that the first Bishop of brown colour should be one of their own. But God sees not only the outward appearances of human beings, but

considers firstly the inward parts. I rewarded their ill feelings with love, prayers, patience and forgiveness.

Despite some ill-feeling, the announcement was big news. Stephen Tago, who had studied with Fr George the previous year and was still at St Aidan's, recalled the great excitement most people felt at the announcement.

> This excitement went on for a long time; it was there after his Consecration in Australia and when he came back. We didn't think about an independent Church at that time, but a Papuan Bishop had been appointed and that was something good. I still remember the text used by Bishop Strong. It was in the paper and I felt it was indeed true: 'This is the Lord's doing and it is marvellous in our sight'.[228]

Bishop Strong, realising the loneliness and isolation which George's high position might bring, urged his staff to give him all possible support. As he wrote,

> ...it will be a greater spiritual and physical loneliness than would fall to the lot of a European similarly called, for there will be few of his own people in whom he can fully confide and who will be able to have a deep and full understanding of all that is involved for him. We must therefore...surround him with prayer...

Soon after the announcement of the coming consecration of Fr George, preparations began for the journey to Australia. Despite his close contact with some white missionaries, George Ambo now had to learn many new customs which were part of life in Western society. For example, he had to adjust to wearing European dress. As he recalled,

> They had to show me how to wear shoes. I had never worn shoes in my life. Bishop Philip said to me, 'George, try and walk properly so that I can take you to Australia'. It was very, very awkward for me but I practised wearing shoes and gradually learnt to walk properly.[229]

Then, one morning, Bishop Philip and George left Dogura and sailed in the mission boat to Samarai. George describes the trip:

> [Samarai was] a small, pretty island surrounded by dozens of other islands scattered in the blue sea ...The little town of Samarai was well established in Milne Bay Province. It was my first trip to see a town in Papua New Guinea. Oh, what wonderful houses and well-planned streets. I was amazed and marvelled at it all. Would I have a home like those houses one day I wondered? Staying at the Rectory, we were looked after by Bishop Henry and Mrs Ray Kendall. They were very kind to me. They taught me how to behave in the European homes.[230]
>
> From Samarai we flew by seaplane to Port Moresby. The trip was very frightening. A strong south-easterly was blowing, but the pilot

managed to take off and Bishop Philip and I arrived safely. It was the first time I saw a big city like Port Moresby. I was staggered. In comparison, Samarai seemed like 'something nothing'. I watched the traffic and couldn't go to sleep because of the noise of cars going to and fro. I had never seen anything like this in my life.

During the next few days, Fr Kenneth Lashford, an Australian priest in Port Moresby, and his wife, Sandra, looked after George. They helped him get his passport and see government officials. Despite their kindness, it was a time of anxiety and doubt.

Although I was getting ready for Australia, I was pondering and wondering if I would fit in or be able to cope with the European way of life. I opened my eyes and ears and I was able to learn many things from Fr Lashford, his wife and the Franciscan Friars. I learnt from them how to behave at meals, how to handle knives and forks. 'When you are sitting at the table,' they said, 'and the food is served, you do not start to eat straight away but you wait until the head-woman in the family says "do start". Then eat as they eat, but don't eat quickly'.[231]

Then the day came to board the plane for Australia. It was an old type of plane that sometimes broke down but we took off safely. The sunset was glorious as we arrived over Australian soil. I was sitting by the window, Bishop Philip beside me. 'George, look down,' he said. As we looked to our right and left, I opened my eyes wide. Being a newcomer to this civilised nation, I felt I needed four eyes to see the beautiful Australia. It was about 7.00pm when we landed on Brisbane airstrip. When I saw millions and millions of lights in different colours in Brisbane city, I couldn't believe it. I couldn't talk. I thought I was entering Paradise.

After a week, we flew to Sydney. Again it was towards evening. The sunset gave glorious views of the city with millions of sparkling lights. I looked through the windows and thought the sky was upside down. Again, the glittering lights gave me the impression that I was entering a heavenly world.

The first night at the ABM (Australian Board of Missions) head-quarters in Stanmore was a very cold night. I couldn't sleep. The next day we caught a train to go to the heart of the city. I had never seen a train before. I kept wondering and thinking inside myself: 'Is Sydney a real city of this world or am I dreaming?' When I saw people walking fast, all in a hurry, traffic lights with different colours and thousands of cars and trucks going to and fro, I found myself walking fast too.

We then arrived in Melbourne to see various people. Amongst them was a lady, Gladys Hammond, who was going to make my cope, mitre and bishop's garment for the Consecration.[232] I was amazed at the size of Melbourne. I knew it was the second biggest city in Australia but I hadn't a clue how big and wide an area it covered compared with Sydney. I managed to survive for two weeks. We stayed with the Sisters of the Holy Name. I enjoyed staying with the Religious Orders because their devotion, prayer life and meditation helped me a lot. But I found it very, very cold, especially at night. I stayed wide awake all through the first night. Three blankets and a hot water bag were not sufficient. 'How did you sleep?' they asked me in the morning. 'Oh, Sister, not well,' I answered. 'The cold was too much for me. Could I have six blankets for tonight, please, and an extra hot water bag?' The blankets were heavy but I didn't care. They looked after us very well.

Bishop George still remembers some aspects of life which he noticed especially while staying in homes connected with the Australian Board of Missions. The polite manners, respect and love, which the family members showed each other, impressed him. Also the way people's lives were so well organised seemed remarkable to him. His hosts and their families were always clean, tidy and well dressed, the meals regular and well cooked. Above all, he noticed that they didn't waste time. He wrote what he observed:

They try to be on time for work and important engagements. They try especially to be on time for Church. European societies have learnt very well that time is God's good gift to them, so they must use it well.

George Ambo never forgot what he learnt in Australia. As a bishop in Papua New Guinea, he was, for example, always most particular about time. He could be very critical of other bishops or priests if they were late for work, for church or for meetings. 'Why is that bishop lazy?' he would say. 'Why did he not get up in time? In his concept of time as a God-given gift not to be wasted, he was different from many of his fellow-countrymen. As a bishop he would not tolerate unpunctuality amongst the workers of the Church. Expecting much of himself, he expected much of others.[233]

In October, Bishop Philip and Fr George at last flew back to Brisbane. He recalled,

It was a little warmer there, and I was feeling much better. I stayed with the Rev'd Eric Hawkey, the Secretary for ABM.[234] He and his good wife helped me with the preparations. He put all his careful thoughts and prayers into the planning of my Consecration Service. He asked me which hymns I would like. I suggested these four: 1. *Love Divine, all loves excelling* 2. *Come down, O Love divine* 3. *Thee we adore, O hidden Saviour Thee* 4. *The Church's one foundation*. I will never forget what he did.

After a week, I flew to Cairns to meet Fr Oliver Brady. I was going to stay with him for my retreat before the Consecration. He was then the Chaplain at Yarrabah, a Government Settlement for

Aboriginal people near Cairns. I had especially asked him to conduct my 'Quiet Days'.

George Ambo felt very much at home staying with his old teacher and friend at Yarrabah. With its heat, colourful tropical vegetation and views of the sea, it reminded George of Menapi.[235] A letter from Fr Brady to Dr Blanche Biggs gives glimpses of George's visit in the beautiful surroundings. It also shows his innate understanding of human nature and his wisdom in dealing with people. Fr Brady wrote,

> My Rectory garden is a riot of hibiscus, crotons, poincianas etc.etc., and you look out to sea from the wide verandah through a fringe of coconut palms. George loved it. I had laid in a stock of rice, sweet potatoes, paw-paws etc. to be used in conjunction with our own kind of food. Again, George loved it. I had plenty of eggs and the Aboriginals brought lovely fresh fish (salmon and barramundi) almost daily. How wise George is; so restrained and so apt with the right thing to say and do. I had feared the aboriginals might be jealous. They could have been but George soon remedied that.

Fr George was always grateful for the advice and teaching of Oliver Brady at that important time.

> He helped me understand how I could become a true Spiritual Father to my people.[236] I thanked and praised God for giving me the right Spiritual Guide to get me ready for my future Ministry. His Retreat was very encouraging, his addresses really inspired by The Holy Spirit.

At first, Fr Brady went through the Consecration Service with George. Daily, they discussed its significance and the meaning of the old-fashioned words. Between the hours of instruction, the daily Services of Mass and Offices, George would walk along the shore or in the bush. Fr Brady wrote,

> He was fascinated by the lovely Australian bush. Then came the three days Retreat. It was a closed Retreat with complete silence...There were four talks by me per day and conducted Meditations. It ended late on Saturday and on Sunday George preached at a crowded Sung Eucharist for Aboriginals and white staff.

On Monday morning they both left for Brisbane for the consecration.

It was a moment of great joy and excitement when, at Brisbane Airport, George was at last united with his close family. As he wrote, 'My dear wife, Marcella, with my elder son, Oliver Brady Ambo, and my elder brother, Fr Simon Peter and his wife, Jennifer, were all there to greet me'. They all stayed together with the rest of the consecration party at the Canberra Hotel. Mrs Ray Kendall had been asked to assist Marcella and her sister-in-law, who had journeyed the long distance both in time and experience. Coming straight from their thatched bush-huts, they had only a few days to adjust to the modern amenities of the nine-storeyed hotel. Overnight they had to learn to cope with wearing western clothes and shoes and many other aspects of a new way of life.

The last few days before the Consecration were filled with fear and feelings of inferiority. Bishop George recalled,

> I was thinking and pondering it over very deeply that I was not good and worthy enough to be a Bishop in the Church of God. When I saw the cities of Brisbane, Sydney and Melbourne and I experienced the European way of living, I felt unworthy. My lack of education also worried me. I wished I had gained high academic results and knowledge. Above all, I felt I did not deserve the respect and honour shown to me by the white people.
>
> In my prayers I asked God for His help. Through Bishop Philip Strong and Bishop David Hand, God in His Love and Mercy answered my troubled mind. It became clear to me that they were sent to our country by God to be our true Spiritual Fathers. I owed very much to both of them for their guidance, love and respect for me. They were born to be leaders in the Church. They proved this by the way they served my people.
>
> Two days before my Consecration we had the main rehearsal. This practice was very important to me personally, because I was lost. The big cities, the high standards of living, of education and knowledge were too high for me to understand. Deep in my heart I felt I should not have accepted the Call. With tears in my eyes, I offered my humble prayers to God. The night before my Consecration the answer came to me: 'I have chosen you. You did not choose yourself'. That night I took courage and humbly offered myself to God's loving and holy Hands.

The Consecration occurred on the 28th October, 1960, the Day of St Simon and St Jude, in St John's Cathedral. In simple words George described what must have been the most elaborate and glittering occasion — perhaps the highlight of his life.

> The Big Cathedral Bell was ringing. The Christian friends were flooding into the Cathedral. Soon all the seats were filled. The Governor of Queensland, Sir Henry Abel Smith, and his wife were there. So were my dear wife, Mrs Marcella Ambo, my brother, Fr Simon Peter and his wife, Jennifer, all sitting in front of the Cathedral seats. They were crying of joy. Mrs Ray Kendall was sitting with them and other missionaries were near them to give spiritual support. The large Cathedral was packed. Many had to stay outside.[237]

The Lady Chapel had been given over to George for his use before and during the Service. The Chapel of Reservation was given to the Bishop-elect of Carpentaria, the Rev'd John Matthews, also to be consecrated on that occasion. Two hours before the start of the great ceremony, George had been in the Lady Chapel, meditating and praying. Fr Oliver Brady was with him. In his role as George's chaplain, it was his duty to see that the episcopal regalia were all arranged on the Lady Chapel altar, ready for the great moment. Bishop George wrote,

> I thanked God that Fr Brady was chosen to be my Chaplain. The Service was almost beyond my understanding. It was Fr Oliver who stood near me, advised and guided me all the way through the Consecration.
>
> What was happening was wonderful. The Cathedral Choir had already taken their place. St Francis College students also joined in the singing. The great Procession of Bishops with copes and mitres was moving towards their seats in the Sanctuary. At the end of the line came the Primate of the Australian Church, the Most Reverend HR Gough, his train carried by Oliver Ambo, my son, and Tony Matthews, son of the other Bishop-elect. The singing was wonderful — very inspiring and moving. It lifted and encouraged me to go forward for my Consecration.
>
> After the reading of the Collect, Epistle and Gospel, the Primate of Australia preached the sermon on the text: 'God dwelleth in us so we can do all things...' I was inspired and moved by his words.
>
> While Archbishop Halse of Brisbane took his place by the Chancel steps, the Bishops-elect were led back to the Chapels and clothed in the purple cassocks, rochets (white garment worn over the cassock) and pectoral crosses. My presenting Bishops were the Right Reverend Philip Strong and the Right Reverend David Hand. They led me to the Chancel steps and presented me to the Archbishop (see photograph, page 132). When I saw over five thousand Anglican Christians praying for me I took courage.

Following the form of Consecration in the Book of Common Prayer, the Bishops-elect took the oaths of obedience. This was followed by the Litany and Examination by the Archbishop. Having again been led back to the Chapels, the Bishops-elect reappeared wearing their copes. Kneeling before the assembled Bishops, they heard the singing of the *Veni Creator Spiritus* (Come, Holy Spirit). The most moving and holy moment of the Service had come.

'At this moment I was ready in Spirit for my Consecration', wrote Bishop George. Feeling the light pressure of the Bishops' hands on his head, he heard the Archbishop's words:

> Receive the Holy Ghost, for the office and work of a Bishop in the Church of God, now committed unto thee by the imposition of our hands...And remember that thou stir up the grace of God which is given thee...for God hath not given us the spirit of fear, but of power, and love, and soberness.

From that moment, and through his life in the Church, George drew strength from the spirit of power and love imparted to him by the laying on of hands. Awareness of its presence in him brought forth his innate confidence and dispelled his fears. 'When God calls a man to high office like this,' he said, 'I believe He gives him the strength to do it'.

Oliver Brady described the end of this important occasion for the Papuan Church:

> The Procession out was very fine. The Archbishop leading George and Carpentaria by each hand. The 10 Bishops followed…After the Governor had congratulated George, he (George) went back in cope, mitre, ring, cross etc (me carrying his staff) and blessed about 3 or 4 hundred people who came up.
>
> An outstanding feature of the whole thing was George's dignity and self-forgetfulness. In his face was a complete awareness of God and an utter un-awareness of the people, Bishops etc. He walked with God.

Fr Brady continued:

> Another feature was the complete success of Marcella and Jennifer and Simon Peter. The women were wonderful and a great honour to Papua and the Mission. So was Simon Peter.[238]

Marcella had been deeply moved, watching the laying on of hands and seeing for the first time her husband wearing a cope and mitre. Was she fearful for the future? Did she realise then that as a bishop's wife, she would have to share her husband with many other Christian souls for whom he was to be responsible? It seemed, from that moment, she determined to give him all the support a wife could muster through their life together.

131

Fr George Ambo being led to his Consecration by
Bishops Philip Strong and David Hand
(Photograph courtesy of Blanche Biggs)

Bishop George greeting his son, Oliver, after the Consecration at
St John's Cathedral, Brisbane
(Photograph from *Papuan Pastor)*

CHAPTER 14

First Years as Bishop

The first official engagements for Bishop George began on the day he was consecrated. He appeared to face them with the same dignity and assurance that would be the hallmarks of his public performances throughout his life. Yet underneath, there must have been times when he felt overwhelmed and bewildered, especially when away from his own land.[239]

As Bishop George recalled,

> After the Consecration we gathered at the Archbishop's house (Bishopscourt) for a light lunch and consecration cake. They gave half of the cake for us to take to Papua New Guinea.

Then followed a crowded garden party where George and Marcella, Simon Peter and Jennifer, shook hands with over four hundred people.[240]

The same evening, a Liturgical Welcome was arranged in St John's Cathedral, Brisbane, for people to meet the two new bishops. In a simple sung service, they were introduced and each gave a message to the congregation. Bishop George said,

> It is a very great joy to visit our mother Church in Australia. When I flew over two of your big cities and saw the lights, I thought the sky had turned upside down. I compared them with our little villages. I was touched when I thought that your sons and daughters had left their good, comfortable homes to work with us in New Guinea. Thank you for your support…We can't do our work without your support…I urge you to pray for me…So I give you my last word—pray for me always because I can't do my work without your prayers and support.

In this his first speech as bishop, he emphasised a message which he would continue to give throughout his future years. Stirrings of nationalism would soon flourish among the educated elite who were advocating 'no foreigners in our land'. Not so Bishop George! With commonsense and realism he faced his critics, claiming that the link with Australia could not yet be cut. Her support, money and prayers as well as the help of her sons and daughters would be urgently needed for many years to come.

After preaching at the cathedral in Brisbane on the Sunday, he left for Ipswich where he gave the sermon at Evensong. Having attended numerous receptions and greeted crowds of people, he finally left for his own country.

Early in the morning of Friday 4 November 1960, the party of three bishops, Philip Strong, David Hand and George Ambo, arrived in Papua New Guinea,

together with Marcella, his son Oliver, Simon Peter and Jennifer. They were officially welcomed at Jackson's Airport in Port Moresby. Fr Lashford had gathered together the two hundred or so Anglicans of the town as well as the Franciscan Friars to greet their new bishop. The government had arranged for the Papuan Police to form a guard-of-honour. After Fr Lashford's speech of welcome, the people, kneeling on the strip, received the blessing for the first time from their own Papuan Bishop. To the heartfelt singing of *Now thank we all our God*, he and Marcella were driven away.[241] Thus began their triumphal return to their own people of Papua New Guinea.

Bishop George blesses the people at Jackson's Airport. With him are Bishops Philip Strong and David Hand. (Photograph courtesy of Bishop David Hand)

More official occasions followed in Port Moresby. Having attended a reception at Government House, where a large mixed crowd of Papuan and white people were presented, they spent the next few days meeting various government officials and representatives of other denominations. Then they flew by seaplane to Samarai.

The official welcome had been planned by Fr Henry Kendall. Bishop George describes it:

> Government officials with the police force were at the wharf to represent their departments. The honour, respect and courtesy with which they greeted me were very well done. Deep in my heart, I felt that I was not worthy of that welcome.

But it was not all honour, respect and triumph which welcomed Bishop George on the return to his country. Already at Samarai, the prophetic words of Oliver Brady, written after the Consecration, were fulfilled:

> Now George must face it all. He will suffer. The older and very Wedauan Papuan Priests will resent him and North and South (the two parts of the Diocese) will flare up a little.[242]

During the following weeks, as he made his way up the coast on his visits to the missions, Bishop George would feel the truth of this prophecy:

> Although I was welcomed at Samarai by Government departments and the few Anglicans who were there, the people from the coastal missions of Wedau, Wamira, Boianai, Menapi, Mukawa and Wanigela stood some distance away from the jetty. They did not come later to greet us. I offered this sorrow to Jesus, asking Him for His Divine Grace.

Before leaving Samarai, Bishop George received a message from his uncle, Roland Dogi Somboba, who was at Dogura. He was planning a traditional welcome to show the respect, honour and love of the Somboba Clan (Bishop George's own clan from the Gona area). According to their custom, he would bring a live pig, its legs tied to a pole, and place it on the Wedau jetty for his nephew to walk over when he arrived. Having stepped over the pig, he would be expected to give a bishop's blessing on his clan. Bishop George saw that this would be divisive, and reacted appropriately.

> After one day, I sent my answer. 'My dear Uncle, thank you for wanting to receive me with respect and honour in our traditional way. But I will not accept it. If I did, it would be a bad show to all my people. They will think I am only the bishop of our own clan. Therefore, kill the pig for the people to eat and enjoy.'

Bishop George was never afraid to break with custom. This incident shows his early concern that the 'wantok system' (the system of social support for those of the same clan or tribe, speaking the same language) could easily divide the unity he sought to develop in the fellowship of Christ.

A large crowd had gathered at the Wedau jetty. '*Egualau — Egualau — Egualau*' (Welcome) shouted the students from St Aidan's College and the Holy Name School, as well as the children from St Paul's School and the white missionaries. All the southern stations of the Diocese had sent representatives to Dogura for the installation in the cathedral of the first Papuan bishop. It was an impressive occasion, full of joy for many people and well worth the wearying journeys, which meant they often arrived late at night, on foot or by boat.[243]

Bishop George continues,

> But a jealous and unchristian spirit had already spread from Wedau up and down the coast and across the border into the Northern District. At the Dogura Station, I experienced the ill-feeling of the Wedauans and Wamirans, especially the hostile attitudes and evil spirits of their ordained ministers. And I said, 'Father, forgive them, for they don't know what they are thinking'. But all the white missionaries gave me their support.

At this time, plans were being made for the new bishop's visits up the coast to the Northern District.

> We arrived at Wanigela, the first station over the border. There were not many people on the beach to welcome us. The same unchristian spirit had spread as far as here. Again, I offered their evil attitudes to Jesus. During the night I tried to pray with tears in my eyes. I said to God, 'I don't want to be a bishop. But You said, "I have chosen you". So, help me, Father, to carry my cross'.
>
> At Naniu Mission it was a different picture. The Station was full of people, all wearing new *tapa* cloths [traditional bark clothing] and decorated with traditional ornaments. Their shiny bodies and hair

had been smeared with coconut juice and their bodies painted. They were singing and dancing, even crying, full of joy and happiness. As the *St George* [mission boat] was slowly approaching the beach, five canoes, decorated with flowers and palms, were paddling out to meet us. Two pretty girls, also dressed in the customary way, were dancing on the platforms of the canoes. One of these [boats], especially decorated, picked up the bishops off the *St George* and the others followed it to the Station. The beach was covered with people full of joy. It was very moving and exciting. At Naniu, I was encouraged to go forward by the power of the Holy Spirit to minister and to help my people.

The next stop was Sefoa Mission. Spread out on a high plateau, it has views of mountains dropping steeply into the deep, turquoise water of the fjords below. It must be one of the loveliest places on the coast. In Bishop George's words,

Here again, we met a happy Christian Spirit. Six canoes came out to greet the *St George*. As we sailed into the Sefoa Fjord, two Church Councillors were swimming around us, crying and shouting full of joy, '*Oro, Oro, Oro Mama*' (Welcome, Welcome, Welcome Father). On the decorated canoes the crews were singing their ancestors' war song. It was a fine welcome and above all, the Spirit of the people was very encouraging for me.

Strengthened by the affectionate welcome of the people closer to his home, Bishop George sailed on towards Eroro, the last mission before Killerton and Gona. It was late when the *St George* dropped anchor off Eroro beach. The station itself was two miles inland but the mission tractor, beautifully decorated with flowers and palm branches, was waiting to provide transport for the bishops.

As we stepped off the canoes we climbed into the tractor and it then proceeded slowly towards the station. All the way, painted dancers wearing colourful feathers, *tapa* cloths and ornaments, were beating their drums, dancing and singing around the moving tractor.[244]

According to the mission doctor, Blanche Biggs, the whole parish of Eroro were gathered together at the station to greet their first Papuan bishop. Banners of welcome hung across the pathway, and electric lights were strung across the *deba-deba* (central oval) for the evening's traditional feast and dancing.[245] In front of the tractor danced two of the senior men of the district in feathers and paint, carrying their war-clubs… As the party arrived, all the children threw frangipani flowers at the tractor, and a little girl presented Marcella with a bouquet. As Dr Biggs recalled:

George was…unaware of it all, and occupied with the presence of God. He has an immense dignity. He gave us his blessing, using Bishop Strong's staff, and then a little speech of thanks.

Then [there was] a much-needed cuppa with various eats—and everyone was ready for it—then the liturgical welcome and

Evensong …Thank goodness our broken-down engine was repaired so we could have the lights in Church…I took Marcella over to the mission house where they were to sleep…and George caught us up. He thanked me with such natural courtesy beyond the usual Papuan courtesy.

Bishop George never forgot that they were given a room in the mission house, where they mixed with the white staff living there, and where Papuans never expected to stay. He wrote humbly,

That taught us and also our local Christians, very much about the attitude of the white missionaries. I strongly believed that they were committed and devoted Christians.

At the Eucharist on Sunday morning the two bishops concelebrated. In his sermon, Bishop George emphasised the need for the Papuan Church to work towards being self-supporting. He also said that he was a bishop of the Church of God, and that rivalry and jealousy between the northern and southern parts of the diocese should have no place in the minds of his people.

'He looked tired,' recalled Dr Biggs. He would have been sad, too, at the death of his beloved sister, Rachel. While still at Dogura, before setting out on his journey up the coast, he had received a radio message telling him that she had died in childbirth at the Gona Hospital. She left a newborn baby daughter, her tenth child. Cecil Uiari, the husband, was the brother of Jennifer (wife of Simon Peter), so it was a shared family sorrow. She died on the occasion of Bishop George's installation at the cathedral. Once more, he had lost a beloved family member at the time of an important occasion in his life in the Church.

After the service and communal breakfast, the two bishops went the short distance to Embi to see St Luke's Tuberculosis Hospital, recently established there by Dr Blanche Biggs. She was in charge of the hospital and recalled how glad she was that their distinguished guests allowed time for the patients to see them. 'The poor old T Bs miss out on so much,' she wrote, 'and they were all able to shake hands with the bishops'. Bishop George himself wrote of this visit, 'The white staff at Eroro and Embi hospital were very kind and their love and respect uplifted me. I had confidence in them'.[246]

The following day, Bishop George set off inland for Siai Mission. He had to dedicate a new church there and take a big confirmation. What would have been his thoughts and feelings, when, after a long and strenuous journey, partly on foot through the swamps, partly by canoe, he again saw the Siai Station? It was there, twenty-two years ago, that he had first arrived with Fr Benson. Then he was a schoolboy and they had been met by Isaac Tago, his wife and three sons—the only Christians in the large heathen area. In the evening the people had come together in the middle of the village, and Fr Benson had read aloud passages from the Bible which George had translated. That was the first time a white missionary had visited the area.

Later George had returned to Siai. In his last year at school, he had been in the party which set off from Gona with school equipment and medical supplies to open the new station. He had been at the first Holy Communion celebrated there in the modest bush chapel. Several times the chapel had been enlarged to hold the increasing number of Christians. Now, at the time of his first visit as bishop, the dedication of the new church at Siai and the large confirmation must have symbolised for him the rapid growth of the Church in Papua. It must also have made him deeply aware of his own part in that growth since his young days.

His triumphal journey was nearing its end. Before sailing back to Dogura, there were only two more stations to be called at: Holy Cross, Gona, Bishop George's home place; and All Saints', Manau, the northernmost mission before the border with New Guinea.[247]

Being welcomed by his own people in his homeland was the strongest and most moving experience:

> The Holy Cross beach was covered with girls and boys and men and women of all ages. A sea in glowing colours of gently moving feathers of the bird of paradise greeted us. Nearly everyone who came to give thanks, praise and honour to God was waving branches of palms, and the young girls were holding flowers and waving. There was great excitement and women were crying with tears of joy and gladness. Dancing groups were welcoming us with drums and songs. When we got off the canoe and I was standing on the sand, seeing the Holy Cross beach full of people and listening to their song in local words and tunes, the meaning of it all moved my spirit deeply. Then Bishop Strong handed me his pastoral staff. The people knelt down and I gave God's blessing on them all.

The next morning, at the Holy Eucharist — a great thanksgiving service — prayers were offered for the many blessings bestowed on this parish by God in His love and mercy. It was the largest parish in the diocese. Thoughts went back to its white mission priests, Frs James Benson, Alfred Clint and John Wardman, who, in turn, had devoted their lives to it. Fr Douglas Jones and Fr Edward Kelly, who followed, had also done their very best, being fully committed to the Church and Holy Cross Station. Many teacher-evangelists, medical health-workers and priests had sprouted forth out of the Gona soil. The Christians had remained faithful and devoted to their Church.

It had been a fine welcome at Gona, the highlight of the affectionate homage paid to the newly consecrated bishop on his return to his home country. He had been swept along by a wave of euphoria, being lifted up to immense heights before crashing down on the sandy shore of everyday life. After the last joyful reception at Manau, Bishop George sailed back to Dogura — back to the hard reality of having to learn to cope with his new position, often amongst people who felt mistrust and jealousy towards him. His words show his feelings.

> In the years 1961 and 1962 I was in charge of my old parish of Boianai. I served my people as an assistant bishop, headmaster of

All Saints' School, and parish priest. I soon discovered that I was trying to do three men's jobs, which meant that some of the work was left uncompleted. Often I had to let down some of my people.

They were not easy or happy years. I tried to carry on my ministry in the large area under my charge, but some people were hostile to me. These enemies interfered with my work and caused much trouble. However, I thanked God for the Christians who were on my side. They encouraged me and I completed my first two years.

A large and strenuous part of his work was to undertake pastoral visits in the rugged mountains of his area.

It was not easy to walk in the Dogura and Boianai districts, which are wild and mountainous. It was sometimes impossible to walk across the rivers of Wamira, Magawara, Mase and Kutu when they were in flood. Three times I had to spend cold and uncomfortable nights in a cave near the river. In these particular areas the cargo cults, witchcraft and sorcery were very bad. These superstitious beliefs were so evil and immoral. Many men and women were adulterers, especially the leaders of cargo cults. It was nearly like the ancient times of Israel when the people worshipped Baal and other false Gods.

During my patrols I learnt that being a bishop in the Church of God is not an easy job. It is a high and holy call from God, but, like Jesus Christ, you will have friends as well as enemies. My first patrols in 1961 were very hard and difficult. The clever and cunning Devil was working through some of the Church workers saying that I was not fit to be a bishop. Some of the local priests interfered with my patrols through their evil gossip and slander.

As I was trying my best to do the work of three men, priest, headmaster and bishop, I soon experienced that it was not a fair situation for the school and parish. Above all, it was too much for my family and my own health. It nearly killed me. Therefore, I went to Dogura and asked Bishop Strong to find a priest for Boianai, which he did. He put a married European priest in charge of the parish and transferred me to Wamira Village.

I was very happy to be at Wamira and to carry on my pastoral work as assistant bishop. But I soon found that there too was a lot of gossip about me and that many of the Christians, amongst them the teacher, George, and his wife, Mary, had ill-feelings against me. When, after a few months, I went on patrol to the north coast, there was a meeting of the people with their Church Councillors. It was on a Sunday after the Service and one of the subjects they discussed was about me. It was said that I was a bishop for the white people—not for Papuans.

The Cathedral of St Peter and St Paul, Dogura
(Photograph courtesy of Chris Luxton)

Bishops David Hand, Philip Strong and George Ambo, at
Dogura 1961, with Mt Pasi-Pasi in the background
(Photograph courtesy of John Wardman)

Staff Conference, Dogura 1961
(Photograph courtesy of Peter Robin)

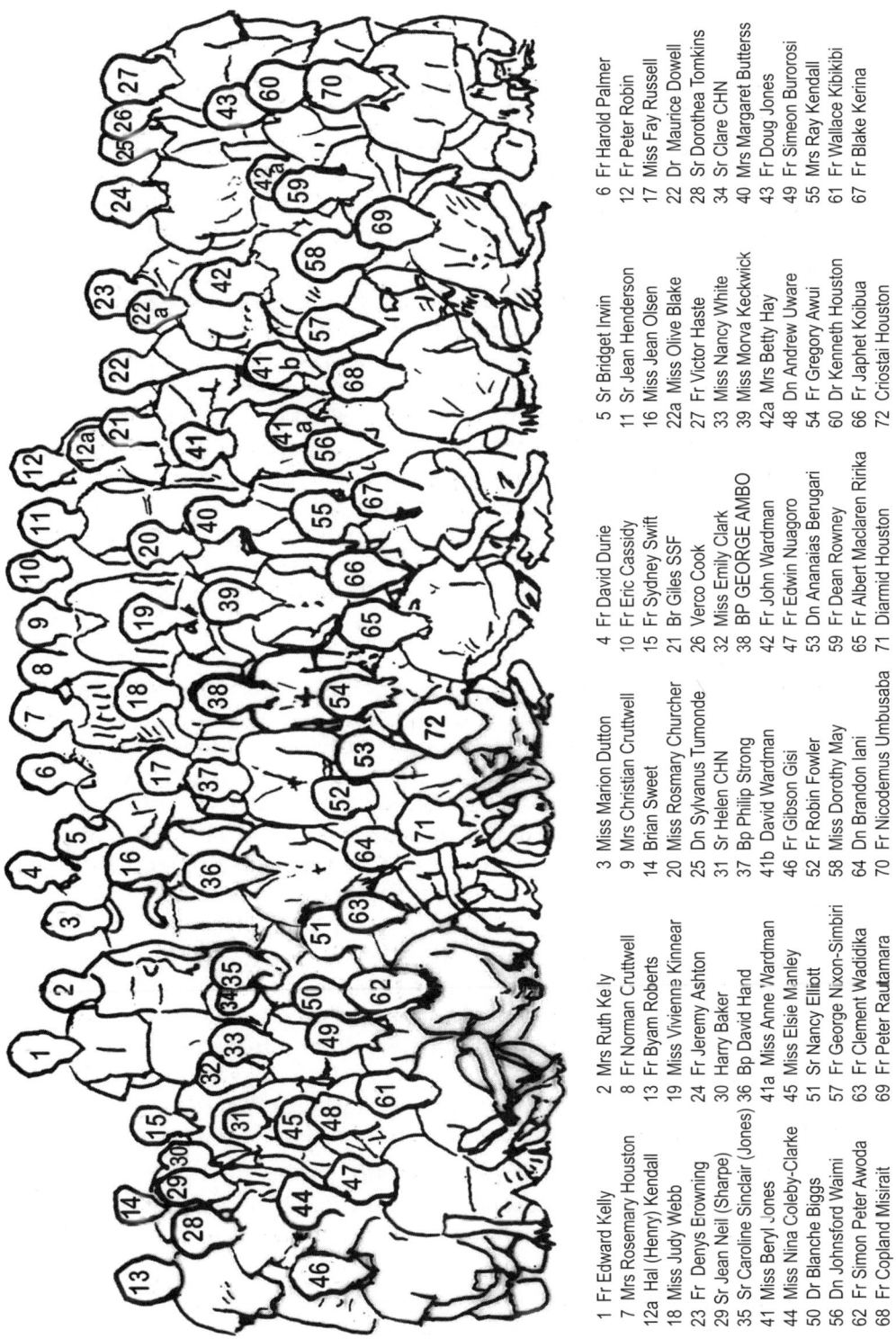

1 Fr Edward Kelly
2 Mrs Ruth Kely
3 Miss Marion Dutton
4 Fr David Durie
5 Sr Bridget Irwin
6 Fr Harold Palmer
7 Mrs Rosemary Houston
8 Fr Norman Cruttwell
9 Mrs Christian Cruttwell
10 Fr Eric Cassidy
11 Sr Jean Henderson
12 Fr Peter Robin
12a Hal (Henry) Kendall
13 Fr Byam Roberts
14 Brian Sweet
15 Fr Sydney Swift
16 Miss Jean Olsen
17 Miss Fay Russell
18 Miss Judy Webb
19 Miss Vivienne Kinnear
20 Miss Rosmary Churcher
21 Br Giles SSF
22a Miss Olive Blake
22a Dr Maurice Dowell
23 Fr Jeremy Ashton
24 Fr Jeremy Ashton
25 Dn Sylvanus Tumonde
26 Verco Cook
27 Fr Victor Haste
28 Sr Dorothea Tomkins
29 Sr Jean Neil (Sharpe)
30 Harry Baker
31 Sr Helen CHN
32 Miss Emily Clark
33 Miss Nancy White
34 Sr Clare CHN
35 Sr Caroline Sinclair (Jones)
36 Bp David Hand
37 Bp Philip Strong
38 BP GEORGE AMBO
39 Miss Morva Keckwick
40 Mrs Margaret Butterss
41 Miss Beryl Jones
41a Miss Anne Wardman
41b David Wardman
42 Fr John Wardman
42a Mrs Betty Hay
43 Fr Doug Jones
44 Miss Nina Coleby-Clarke
45 Miss Elsie Manley
46 Fr Gibson Gisi
47 Fr Edwin Nuagoro
48 Dn Andrew Uware
49 Fr Simeon Burorosi
50 Dr Blanche Biggs
51 Sr Nancy Elliott
52 Fr Robin Fowler
53 Dn Ananaias Berugari
54 Fr Gregory Awui
55 Mrs Ray Kendall
56 Dn Johnsford Waimi
57 Fr George Nixon-Simbiri
58 Miss Dorothy May
59 Fr Dean Rowney
60 Dr Kenneth Houston
61 Fr Wallace Kibikibi
62 Fr Simon Peter Awoda
63 Fr Clement Wadidika
64 Dn Brandon Iani
65 Fr Albert Maclaren Ririka
66 Fr Japhet Koibua
67 Fr Blake Kerina
68 Fr Copland Misirait
69 Fr Peter Rautamara
70 Fr Nicodemus Umbusaba
71 Fr Nicodemus Umbusaba
72 Criostai Houston

Although there were these critical feelings towards me, I tried to meet them with forgiveness and Christian love. I did not lose my faith in my people. I was always hoping and believing that one day, by God's Grace, I would win them back.

One Sunday I called a parish meeting after the Service. Only a few people turned up. I did not lose heart but after some time, I called again for a second meeting. This time we had a very difficult meeting and many people did not take my thoughts and ideas seriously.

Although my position was not easy amongst these proud, resentful people, I tried again after some time to get them to come to a third meeting. This time, I had put the matter of a new church on the agenda. St Matthew Church was not in good condition. The rain was coming through the roof and I asked them if we should build a new church. At first they did not know that I would help them build it and that I wanted to teach them through my actions. We had meeting after meeting but they still had no faith in me. Then some Church Councillors and parishioners came to see me in the bishop's house and again I explained my vision about the new church. At last we all agreed to go up in the hills to start cutting the timber for the new building.

It was not easy to build big churches in the Dogura District as you had to walk long distances to collect bush materials. On a certain day we went up in the mountains to cut bush timber. We stayed a week up there, cutting enough tree trunks for the building. We removed the bark and left the trunks to dry for eight days or so. Then we went up again and floated them down the Wamira River. That was very hard and difficult because of all the rocks, rapids and little islands in the winding watercourse. Eventually we managed to float all the timber to the beach at the mouth of the river and transport it to the station.

The spirit of the people had completely changed. By now, they had full confidence in me. Their true Christian spirit strengthened Marcella and myself and made us very happy. We thanked and praised God. We all started working together, putting up the first posts. After much hard work the church was completed. Bishop David Hand was invited to dedicate it. He came down from Dogura and dedicated the church in the name of St Matthew.

It was not only the people of Wamira who had been won over by Bishop George's positive personality and concern for them. The priests and teachers of the whole 'Eastern Side' of the diocese, as they used to call it, came to him to apologise and make their confessions:

'We are sorry we spoiled your Ministry by gossiping about you. We are seeing and experiencing that God has called you to be our

Bishop. Forgive our sins.' This Sacrament of Confession from my fellow workers of my own colour made me very, very happy. God poured out His Grace and I felt strong and brave to carry on my Ministry.[248]

Bishop George's main role was to assist Bishop Strong with the pastoral work in the large diocese. He frequently made long journeys to visit the various parishes to dedicate new churches, to confirm new Christians, and to help sort out many disciplinary cases such as the practice of sorcery. He was exceptionally wise with people. As a Papuan he understood, better than any European, the local culture and relationships. He knew the things which were hidden away in the undergrowth, and which were never made known to white people. He later said,

I have always wanted to be a good pastor. I hope, in future genera-tions, if I am remembered, it will be for being a good pastor.[249]

During my patrols I discovered that many Christians were still living in fear because of the practices of sorcery, cargo cults and magic, which were still alive and strong. The leaders of these cases often had two or three wives, some were very young girls. When I saw the power of sorcery, I prayed to God for guidance to save my people from Satan. I had now come to understand the great need of my people. I saw that God had called me to work together with my white brother bishops in their efforts to spread the Christian beliefs. I also realised that being a bishop is a very sacrificial call. By this I mean you have to sacrifice family life and separate yourself from your wife and children for the sake of God's Kingdom.

It would have been hard for Marcella during these first years as a bishop's wife. She had to get used to her husband's long absences when he was journeying on foot in the mountains on his patrols. Often the family were short of food. Great was their joy when he returned, sometimes bringing gifts of food with him from the villagers. She had a lot to learn about leadership in the community. Earlier in their life at Boianai there had been difficulties with the Mothers' Union. Being very quiet and shy, she said nothing at their meetings. One of the lady missionaries had said to Bishop George:

Fr George, we wonder if your wife will ever be able to support you? We know you will do your best to help your wife speak up!

His reply came quickly:

My wife, my love — to talk about my wife is not your business. You worry about your husband and your staff. My wife is a very shy woman but since I became a bishop I have always trusted in her wisdom. One day she will speak up.

Gradually, as her confidence developed, Marcella won the trust of the people. Later, when they had moved to Wamira, all the women came to love her from the bottom of their hearts.[250]

145

At the beginning of his work as bishop, George Ambo suffered the loss of yet another beloved Sister, Mavis Parkinson. She died of tuberculosis in the care of Dr Blanche Biggs at St Luke's Tuberculosis Hospital, Embi. All her six children needed treatment, too. Dr Biggs and her helpers were trying to work out who would look after the children.[251] Bishop George and Marcella adopted little George Junior after his mother's death. Two years later, they had a second daughter of their own, to whom they gave the name of Helen Anne, after Sr Helen of the Community of the Holy Name, later Community of Visitation (see photograph on page 153). Some years later they had another daughter, Jean Margaret, named after Sr Jean Henderson and St Margaret's Hospital at Oro Bay, founded by Sr Jean.

While he was at Wamira, a message came to Bishop George from his own people about an outbreak of sorcery, this time in the Gona district. In the message they said that the white priest in charge, Fr Edward Kelly, was unaware of the evil deeds carried out by some of the heathen villagers.[252] 'Fr Ted had recently come from England with his pretty wife, Ruth,' wrote Bishop George, 'to replace Fr John Wardman. This couple also worked hard to convert my own district for God'.[253]

Fr George travelled to Gona to see Fr Ted. Together they set off on their long and strenuous walk through the villages of Bakumbari and Katuna, right up to the north-west as far as Ambasi Station. From there they turned inland to Waietutu, the end of their patrol. Both men wrote accounts of this important journey in the fight against sorcery and superstition. As Bishop George recalled:

> We received a fine welcome at Katuna where we spent the first night. There was a big gathering of people at this place where one of the main sorcerers was located. During Evening Prayer the sick people came to see me and I gave them God's Blessing. Then I interviewed people involved in discipline cases such as the practice of sorcery, but made no decisions before I had discussed it all with the local priest.

At Ambasi they were also warmly welcomed by the large number of Christians. Having heard the reports of the Church Councillors from the various local areas on cases of sorcery, the two men set off for the end of their journey. Waietutu was an out-station of Holy Cross, Gona. It was due west from Ambasi, about four or five hours' walk inland. The Christian community had built a new church which Bishop George had been invited to dedicate. Bishop George recalls his visit:

> All the Church Councillors, whom we had met at Ambasi, had come to Waietutu to see me. After the big Mass the following morning, while the feasting and dancing were going on, I interviewed the people involved in the discipline cases. The Church Councillors brought the sorcerers, witchdoctors, leaders of cargo cults and dealers in magic to me. Fr Edward Kelly was with me witnessing it all. They were not easy cases to deal with, because the whole district

was living in fear of these sorcerers. My relations at Ambasi had warned me in the night to be careful of myself, so I prayed to God to give me Grace and guidance.

The following account written by Fr Kelly gives a clear picture of Bishop George's courage in facing the dreaded sorcerers:

At Waietutu was the gathering of all the sorcerers whom Bishop George had managed to find on his patrol, or who had been reported to him. There were about fourteen of them. These were very powerful men, because people really did believe in sorcery. It is a powerful thing which can kill a person if he believes it is directed against him. George confronted the whole lot of them. It was quite remarkable. It was very brave because he took away all their sorcery bits and pieces, bits of bark or people's hair, bits of toenail-cuttings, leaves and stones or whatever it was. They kept these things in little boxes in their bags and took them all out and showed them to George at his command.

Bishop George himself recalled how he had opened the meeting with prayer.

It was not easy. These sorcerers believed that sorcery was their all-powerful God. We were sitting in the open under the shade tree watched by villagers in the distance. First I dealt with the witchdoctors who went about giving so-called medicines to sick people. In return for their services they demanded pigs and other foods as well as valuable ornaments. They threatened to kill people if their demands were not met. I remembered once, as a schoolboy, I became very sick with malaria. My Dad invited the sorcerer 'Bana', the local man from Kurou, to come to our home. He played his sorcery tricks on me, and my father killed a very big pig and gave clay pots, ornaments and food to him. This memory from my childhood came to me when I was sitting there at Waietutu trying to deal with these evil and greedy people.

Then I warned them that my God and their God was the same Creator who had made them and me and the whole world. I told them that our God was asking me to eat some of their sorcery poison in front of them all. Then I ate a little of the dangerous poison, which was obtained from the roots of a special tree and which was used in suicide. They looked at each other, moving and bowing their heads. I said to them, 'If I die on the way down to Ambasi or in the night, you will believe in your sorcery. But if you hear news that I am still alive, believe and have faith in my God'. And I took away their sorcery pieces and burnt them.

At the same time I dealt with the cases of cargo cults and magic. After I had warned them strongly not to play any more tricks on their brothers and sisters, I asked them to come and see me individually later. I interviewed them in the church and asked them questions such as: 'Where did you learn this sorcery? Who taught you and helped you to be a sorcerer?' They all gave the names of the three brothers of the Ijiba family, Jarugaba being the leader. These three brothers of the Ijiba clan were cunning and evil devils who had killed many people.

I knew this sorcerer, Jarugaba, when I was a schoolboy. He was from the Ope River. We were warned by our parents not to go near him or to pass him on the path, if he was walking towards us. We were warned strongly to hide away in the bush, and let him pass by. Everyone knew that he was a great and dangerous sorcerer. Much later, when I had left St Aidan's College and was working at Holy Cross, Gona, I met him again. This time, in 1946, I tried to talk to him, but he walked away, warning me to be careful in what I was trying to do. After that, I met him a few times, but he did not want to see me. When I met him at Waietutu in 1963, I warned that I would come and see him in the near future. When I did visit him he was pleased to see me again and talk with me about his evil practices. After some time, he gave up sorcery.

As Fr Edward Kelly recalled this incident, he commented on the positive result of this patrol:

After that amazing confrontation at Waietutu, the most senior sorcerers recanted. They agreed to stop their evil deeds and some became Christians. It was all positive. They would never have a chance of doing anything against the wish of George when he was on the warpath in a case like that. He persuaded them to give up and repent. A good number of them were baptised.

George Ambo is a man of extraordinary breadth. Like a rainbow arching over the sea, his life spans the vast expanse of human experience between Stone-Age superstition and Western sophistication. Shortly after dealing with the sorcerers at Waietutu, he found himself at the Sydney Town Hall, attending a meeting of the Anglican General Synod.

There was an enormous crowd.[254] I was not asked to take part in the speeches because my English language was not good enough. Bishop Philip spoke and also Mr John Guise (later Sir John), the Papuan lay-representative for the Diocese of Papua New Guinea. Both spoke very well and I learnt a lot from them.

It was a busy time for the three bishops Philip, David and George in Australia, where they tried to encourage the Church in its efforts to raise funds and find new missionaries for the ever-expanding work of the Mission in Papua New Guinea. With the higher standards set by the Government in health and education, and with the opening up of new areas, especially in the Highlands, at least sixty-two qualified Anglican missionaries were urgently needed before the end of the year.[255]

After a second major gathering at the Brisbane Town Hall, organised by the Australian Board of Missions, at which Bishop George thanked ABM and the Anglican community for their efforts at his consecration, he set off on deputation work. He visited various parishes, widely scattered in Brisbane, Sydney and Newcastle: 'I stayed with many good Anglicans and made many new friends. Above all, some young men and women offered to serve in my country'.

During the deputation work, Bishop George made this appeal:

> We need: 1. More white priests; 2. more primary school teachers; 3. more doctors and nurses, please. There are hundreds of heathens who are living in fear of sorcery and witchcraft. Their minds are troubled with fear, just as their bodies are troubled with sickness and disease. So come over to Papua New Guinea and help us, so that the Papuan ministry, and Papuan teachers and medical workers, will be well educated to take over the good work which white missionaries have begun.

When he returned to Papua New Guinea, he heard rumours that Bishop Philip Strong had been called to be the next Archbishop of Brisbane.

> I was wondering and pondering this rumour. Deep in my heart I was worried because he had promised to help me be a good pastor for my people. I feared being left behind by myself. I was not an educated man but he had said, 'George, I will teach you to become a Bishop!' The rumour was true. When I told him of my fears, he said to me, 'George, when you go away Bishop David will carry you. He is a young man but he is tough'. This was all very worrying for me, especially because I felt I didn't know Bishop David very well.

In January 1963, Bishop Strong had the last conference with his staff at Dogura before his enthronement in Brisbane in March.[256] It was a sad occasion for all the 150 or so white missionaries and their hundreds of Papuan clerical brothers. They all knew that the work begun by their beloved Bishop twenty-six years previously must shortly be handed over to a new leader. They could only comfort themselves that, as Archbishop of Brisbane, Bishop Strong would also be the Metropolitan of the Province of Queensland, of which the Diocese of Papua New Guinea was a part. Thus he would be able to visit his former diocesan flock from time to time and maintain contact with the affairs of Papua New Guinea.

In the last letter to his staff, Bishop Strong expressed his love for them all and the happiness he had felt in his life with them, but he also accepted that a change in leadership might, in the end, prove to be for the best. For some time, together with many others, he had realised that a change in the status of the country would have to come. Many progressive changes, preparing the people for self-government, or independence, were already happening in Papua New Guinea. Bishop Strong wrote,

It is important that the Church should have a leader who can win confidence in these coming years and then, when the new way comes for the country, go on leading the Church into it.

Bishop David Hand had been appointed administrator of the diocese until a new bishop was elected. In January 1963, at the time of the diocesan conference, an election committee was formed at Dogura for which Bishop George was asked to be the chairman. Bishop George remembered the procedure:

> It happened in the Cathedral. Three names had been put forward as possible successors to Bishop Strong, one of which was that of Bishop David Hand. Our committee members, both white and brown, had assembled in the vestry where we waited to discuss the people's choice. During this hour, Bishop David was praying in front of the Tabernacle. He was lying flat on the floor on his chest, praying. He won the election. Although David was very tough in his young days, they voted for him. Why? Because he loves us. Wherever he goes, he sits with us, he talks with us, he eats with us. His humility was the sign we saw in him. Although tough, he is very humble.
>
> While we were in the Vestry, Bishop Philip was praying in his little chapel in his house. I went over to tell him the result of the election. 'Then give David this message,' he said. 'My brother, if you promise to try and control your temper, I will ask you to be our new Diocesan Bishop'. So I went to see him, as he was lying face down on the floor in the cathedral. I knelt down beside him and whispered the message. He was quiet for a few minutes. Then he said, 'Is that you George? My brother, I would like to be the next Bishop of Papua New Guinea. If you and your people pray for me, I will try and control my temper'. After that, he did control it.[257]

While Bishop Philip's relationship with Bishop George had been that of father and son, between Bishop David and George it was like that of brothers.

> At the time of the election, I worried because I did not know David well. So I asked Bishop Philip for his permission to step down as Assistant Bishop. I said that if David wanted me as his Assistant, he must invite me to take up that position. Shortly after, I received a letter from David, 'George, you are automatically my Assistant. I want to work with you'. After that, David and I were brothers. We love each other as brothers and he always turns to me for my answers in matters to do with the Papuan people.

During the later part of Bishop Strong's episcopacy, a growing sense of nationalism was emerging amongst some of the educated Papua New Guineans. Although, at this stage, there was no call for outright independence, demands were expressed that steps be taken towards self-government and more autonomy for local areas.[258]

New political ideas of national freedom for colonial dominions were formulated in the United Nations Charter which had appeared soon after the war. The administration in Port Moresby was influenced by the UN Charter, which stated, amongst other things, that the basic objectives of colonial governments should be 'to promote the political, economic, social and educational advancement of the inhabitants of trust territories, and to promote their progressive development towards self-government or independence'.

Guided by these ideas, in 1951 the administration had established a legislative council. The influence of the Church on the council was considerable, as most of the elected members had been educated by the various missions. Furthermore, the government had stipulated that three of the nominated members must be mission representatives. With Bishop Strong's election to the council in 1954, the predominance of Christian values within the political sphere was further strengthened.

The 1950s also saw the emergence of local government councils. They were welcomed by most missionaries, who regarded them as helpful institutions for the upholding of Christian principles. Some Europeans, holding entrenched paternalistic attitudes and a belief in the continuation of colonial rule, felt threatened by these new centres of local power. Whether of progressive or reactionary mind, the missionaries' involvement with the local councils was inevitable, as the Church had always been closely bound to local affairs.

Although most people believed that independence would eventually come, many feared, as did Bishop George, it would happen too quickly. They accepted the need for white people to remain in their land for yet a long time to come, preparing them and leading them towards their future nationhood. Only amongst some of the educated elite had a hope been aroused for a rapid end to colonialism and white man's rule.

The movement forward was slow but steady. In 1964, the House of Assembly replaced the old Legislative Council. By that time, the system of local government councils had only reached half the population of Papua New Guinea.

It was an exciting event when Papua New Guineans for the first time voted at the election of the House of Assembly in 1964. For the first time their own people would predominate in the government of the Territory. The elections brought some victories for the Anglicans. Such Papuan leaders as John (later Sir John) Guise won places in the House. He had been educated by the Mission and was several times a lay-representative at the Anglican Synod in Sydney. Together with four other Papua New Guineans, he was also elected to the Administrator's special Council, his 'Inner Cabinet', and so had the opportunity to uphold his Christian values when called upon to make decisions.[259]

Bishop George had the honour of being invited to give the address in Port Moresby on the occasion of the inauguration of the House of Assembly. At this, his first and so far most important opportunity to influence the future

151

leaders of his country, he emphasised the view of the Church: that the Christian leaders must lay the Christian foundations upon which the political structure would be built. For him, the movement towards independence was a religious as well as a political progression. He saw no separation between Church and State. Considering the missions' contribution to the building up of the colonial Territory, he saw it as a natural consequence that Christianity should blend with the new political aspirations. He believed it must be a gradual process, however. Stating that although Papua New Guineans had had many chances to learn new things from white people, he warned that time had not yet come for them to govern their country by themselves. They still had much to learn so that they would be able to judge what was good, and accept only things which were right for their people.

In his speech Bishop George said,

> We, as leaders of our people...must never suppose that all the things done in this world are right. Some of them are indeed quite all right...but some are very bad. They are against the Christian Way of Life. They war against the soul...We can see ourselves that our country is developing rapidly in our time. So we, as members of the Church, have a citizenship in Heaven; and as members of a village, town, city and country, we also have an earthly citizenship, and we have duties to both...We do not belong to this world but we must do our best for our country and our people while we are on our way through...especially, we the leaders must obey the Government and the laws of the land... So finally, to you my brothers, who will sit in the House of the Assembly tomorrow and become the leaders of our country and people, I would like to say this: It has been said that there are three steps along the Christian Way — 1. To know the Will of God. 2. To do it. 3. To love it. So we pray that God may bring our unruly wills ever nearer to His own perfect Will, so that we may build our country in the fear and love of the Lord, and our country will become a Christian country.

The year following Bishop Strong's departure from Papua New Guinea was very busy for Bishops David and George. It had been hard for the mission workers to cope with the loss of their leader, but his successor had risen to the call. He was soon accepted loyally by all the staff. 'Bishop David is trying to be another Philip,' wrote Dr Biggs, 'and along the line of organisation and correspondence it is nearly killing him'. Both he and Bishop George had been continually on the move for a year or so and were looking very tired and much older. Despite this, as Dr Biggs recalled, both of them had grown in grace and power.[260] During 1964, their burden was eased by the appointment of a second assistant bishop. John Chisholm was consecrated to provide much needed help in the leadership of the Church.

Bishop George had developed greatly since his consecration. He had matured spiritually and in other ways, and felt confident and secure in his relationship with white people. As Dr Biggs recalled,

> I saw him greet Bishop David a few weeks ago in Moresby—'Oh, my brother David, it is good to see you', with no trace of that submission that always seems to be present when Papuan greets European.

With the changes happening in the way of development and political government, it became necessary for Bishop David to plan for change within the organisation and leadership of the Anglican Church. As Bishop George put it,

> He divided the Diocese into five centres, Dogura, Popondota, Port Moresby, Aipo Rongo and the New Guinea Islands. Gradually, each of these regions would have their own Regional Bishop.
>
> I was asked to serve my own people in my own Northern District [later renamed Oro Province]. At first I did not want to accept it, but after a couple of months spent in prayer, I talked it over with my wife and both of us agreed to accept.

So Bishop George and Marcella left Wamira, for him to take up the position as Regional Bishop of Popondota Diocese.

Bishop George and Marcella with some of their children at Wamira
in 1964—from left, Helen Anne, George Junior and Gloria
(Photograph courtesy of Bishop George Ambo)

CHAPTER 15

Lambeth and Change

Popondetta in the Northern District, now Oro Province, was the place where Bishop George and Marcella were to have their home for the next twenty-three years — the base from where he would work until retirement. At the time of the eruption of Mt Lamington in 1951, Popondetta did not exist. By the time the Ambos arrived in late 1965, it had grown into quite a town. Offices had been established for the Department of District Administration (DDA), as well as the residency of the white District Comissioner, a post office, a bank and a number of stores. The local pub was the meeting place for the three dozen or so European owners of cocoa and rubber plantations in the district.[261]

On the outskirts of the township was Ururu Mission Station which had been established by Bishop David shortly after the eruption of Mt Lamington. Ururu was to replace Sangara, the old station on the slopes of the mountain, which had been completely destroyed.[262]

Originally, Ururu was a modest station comprising only a few buildings. There was the small Church of the Resurrection, built of bush materials and dedicated one year after the Lamington disaster (see photograph, page 155); the mission house for Fr Henry Kendall, priest-in-charge; and Bishop David's house. Ururu was the base for Bishop David's work of restoration and reorganisation of the devastated areas.

Across Ururu Creek, which flowed through the station, was the home of Rod Hart and his wife, Maddy, and St Christopher's Manual Training School which he had established. Being by trade a motor-mechanic, amongst other things Rod was able to teach local men to repair and maintain old war-time jeeps, an activity which proved very helpful for the mission. There was also a small primary school which was run by Maddy.

When Bishop George arrived, Ururu had grown into a large and well-organised parish. As it was the head-station of the Northern District, the work of the mission included the supervision of widely spread out-stations. While the numerous *popondo* trees surrounding the area gave name first to 'Popondo-ta Region', later to 'Popondo-ta Diocese' (literally 'the place of the *popondo* trees'), the township came to be called Popondetta. This was due to a spelling mistake made by expatriates, not realising the significance of the word. The Diocese has retained its original name of Popondota.

The building of a new Church of the Resurrection was well under way. Nearly two years before the Ambos came, the Administrator, Sir Donald Cleland, had unveiled the foundation stone for this large permanent building.

Traditional dancing at the dedication, Church of the Resurrection, Popondetta 1952. (Photograph courtesy of Ray Kendall)

The New Church of the Resurrection, later the Cathedral of the Resurrection, Popondetta, foundation stone laid in 1964. (Photograph: Donald Johnston)

Bishop George dedicating a church in the Northern District

Bishop George baptising newly converted Christians in Ururu Creek,
Popondetta 1967 (Photographs courtesy of Ray Kendall)

156

After twelve years of service, the old bush church had at last become inadequate for the increasing number of Christians.

With its steel trusses rising to an apex of forty feet, the new building provided a striking contrast to the coconut palms and surrounding bush. Later Bishop Kendall recalled how, with the help of 'a large volunteer labourline' during the construction work, the steel frames went up in four days. As he wrote,

> Putting the iron on the roof took a little longer. Then, week by week, we laid the cement floor…then we ran out of funds. However, roof and floor were the main consideration, it seldom blows at Popondetta…People grew to love the open church …the 'East End', with its view of jungly trees and the peaks of Mt Lamington has never been filled in except for the enormous carved *Risen Christ* which Bishop David gave (see the photograph, page 155).

For his first two years at Popondetta, Bishop George worked alongside Fr Henry Kendall and his wife, Ray, in charge of the Resurrection School.[263] While Fr Kendall mostly worked in the area around Popondetta, Bishop George was responsible for the Christians in the whole of the Northern District. He felt that he should try to visit all the parishes in his area and spend at least two or three days in each.

> First I must know and understand the particular conditions of every parish. Secondly, I will try, by God's Grace, to get to know the life and way of living of the different groups of people.[264]

Ray Kendall recalled how Bishop George travelled everywhere by canoe or on foot.

> He had no vehicle of his own. He walked a lot. Henry also did a lot of travelling but Rod Hart and his mechanics had provided him with a jeep which took him to some places, as long as the tracks were passable. Bishop George had to depend on whether Henry sometimes could give him a lift. I always felt, looking back, it wasn't fair, but that was how it was.[265]

Bishop George felt weighed down by the responsibility and trust placed upon him by the Church. He began to doubt his own abilities to cope with the pastoral work in the new situation. Besides, as happened so often in his life, he was seized by feelings of inferiority, especially because of his lack of formal education. As he puts it,

> My Region had no money and I, as the Bishop, was very poor. Above all, I was not a university graduate. Therefore I prayed to God to give me His Grace and wonderful wisdom to govern the Christians according to His Will. Every day, with tears in my eyes, I shared my worries with Jesus Christ. These worries were with me when I was posted to Popondota. I knew that Satan was working hard to bring me down and make me give up.

However, he was not a man to give up the Call which he felt had come to him, not from a human source but from God. Through prayer as well as through music he was able to strengthen his soul. The bishop's house had been built near the cathedral. A path, which led from the main road into the station, ran between the church and his house. Many a night, when he felt sad or depressed, overburdened by his heavy workload and responsibilities, Bishop George would cross that path and enter the empty cathedral. He remembers these times:

> There, in the silence of the night, I would beat my drum and sing away my own compositions. That lifted me up. I felt the Holy Spirit was lifting me up.[266]

Before long, it became clear to him that one of the most important parts of the work was to be with his people in the isolated areas.

> In the first year as Regional Bishop I managed to visit some of the parishes, and I began to grasp and understand how best to carry out my pastoral work. In my second year, I completed all the pastoral visits in my Region. I also sent out my yearly Bishop's Letter to all the parishes with the visitation program, warning them that I would try and keep up my schedule. I urged them to try and keep up their part of the preparations for my visits. Above all, the confirmation candidates must be properly and well trained. I warned them that I would interview the new candidates before I would confirm them.

Bishop George never forgot the advice to him by Bishop Philip, that he must always interview thoroughly every candidate before confirming.

> I learnt that he was right in asking me to follow his footsteps. By doing that, I got to know my candidates and they came to know me. I believe this is a very vital and important part of my work and that every bishop should try and do it.

1968 was the year of the Lambeth Conference. For the Diocese of New Guinea, history was being made by the participation of the first Papuan Bishop. Bishop George and Bishop David were planning to travel together to England via Jerusalem and Rome. The travels were not uneventful, and proved — in the case of Bishop George — to be a very significant experience for the development of his own personality and the growth of the Papuan Church. Through this experience he came to realise that his Church would have to change in order to be really meaningful for the Papuan people.

In early April the two bishops set off on their journey. The Dean of the Anglican College of St George in Jerusalem had invited them to stay during Holy Week in the precincts of St George's Cathedral. The only charge for staying was to give two sermons! 'I invite Bishop George to preach on Palm Sunday,' the Dean had said, 'and you, David, to preach at the three hour service on Good Friday'. So, they sang for their supper in the Holy City! [267]

Unexpected difficulties played havoc with their plans, however. Due to a strike by Qantas workers, their plane was re-routed via the Philippines. Having spent the night at St Andrew's Seminary, Manila, they left a day late for Jerusalem.

Bishop George recalled the anxious moments when, instead of arriving on Saturday as planned, they were circling over Jerusalem early on the morning of Palm Sunday when he was due to preach:

> The place was covered in fog. So we went round and round, trying to find a way through the thick cloud. Then the announcement was made that we were going to Cyprus to wait for the cloud to clear. Luckily the service wasn't until eleven o'clock and Cyprus was not very far away. We came back and landed at Tel Aviv airport about ten o'clock in the morning.
>
> When we arrived at St George's Cathedral, they were singing the last hymn before the sermon. I felt shaky. I felt nervous and afraid. I said to David, 'Excuse me, David. I had better not preach. It is too late'. He answered me, 'No, George. You prepared your sermon a long time ago, and now they are singing the last hymn. You've got to preach!' He opened my bag and put my priest's robes on me and he washed my face. Then the people saw the Bush-Kanaka Bishop climbing up into the pulpit. All my body was shaking. I was so nervous. 'In the Name of the Father and of the Son and of the Holy Spirit,' I said, praying that the Holy Spirit would come to my aid. I preached my sermon there. A copy of it was published in the newspaper. The collection taken at the service paid for my fare to England.

Bishop George was deeply moved by his experience of Jerusalem. 'It was too great and too wonderful to be there in reality—in the Holy City itself,' he said. It was a moving experience, but also revealing, at times perhaps disillusioning. After his visit there, he saw things more clearly and he never forgot the lessons he learnt.

As he walked with Bishop David through the old, narrow streets of the Holy City, they passed little stalls on the roadside where people haggled over prices and shouted at each other. It seemed that everybody was against everybody. Conflict ruled. As Bishop David recalls,

> You felt the difference between the traditional Jews and the modern Jews, between the Christian groups, the Roman Catholics against the Eastern Orthodox, let alone the Anglicans—a funny little group against others. There were people whacking the backsides of their donkeys loaded with things for sale, others whacking the backsides of their camels bringing travellers to town—the place smelling of camel and donkey dung and filled with dust, noise, shouting and haggling for prices.
>
> In the middle of all this commotion, Bishop George suddenly stopped and said to me, 'David, I have got it!' he said. 'I have got it!' I asked, 'You have got what, George?' He said, 'I can see now why our Lord had to suffer and die here. If he had to suffer and die for the reconciliation of men with men, and more importantly of men with God, then if any place in the world needs reconciliation it's this one—Jerusalem'.

Little did Bishop George know that, thirty-five years later, his statement would have far deeper poignancy.

Bishop George had gone to the Holy City thinking it was the home of peace, paved with gold, and that its houses and glorious temples were built of gold. Instead he found conflict and men fighting. He had learnt a lesson which he would later use in coping with his people's false beliefs.

The two bishops saw many of the places where Jesus had once been — where he was crucified, his (supposed) tomb, and the site of the Resurrection — but it was in Galilee that he felt at peace. They went down to the Lake of Galilee and saw the Hill of Beatitudes where according to tradition Jesus gave the Sermon on the Mount. He recalled the occasion:

> We sat in silence by the lake under one of the Olive trees, meditating for some hours. Then we spent the night at Nazareth at an Anglican Girls' High School built where Mary and Joseph were supposed to have lived. I had the privilege of saying Mass in the lovely chapel. It was right above the city looking out over all the buildings, away towards the distant hills and the plain of Esdraelon, the meeting place of all the trade routes in ancient times. The window behind the altar looked out over this glorious view and I felt completely at peace.

The flight to Rome went smoothly. They stayed with the rector of the American parish who had organised for them various tours of the major basilicas and catacombs. They were also invited to lunch with the Australian Ambassador to Italy when, according to Bishop David, they had a seven-course meal and met some distinguished people. Bishop David commented,

> But that wasn't the thing that struck Bishop George. He wanted to see the Vatican to see what makes this extraordinary organisation called the Roman Catholic Church tick.

Seeing the Vatican was a somewhat bewildering experience for Bishop George. The first building he saw as they entered the vast area was the Bank of the Holy Spirit. He wondered what money and the bank had to do with the Holy Spirit!

Bishop David recalls the reaction of his travelling companion to the Pope's own church:

> We went into St Peter's Cathedral where there are these tremendously big pillars all the way down the aisle with the statues of the twelve Apostles. And underneath the statues, in quite small printing graven into the stone, was the name of the Apostle, St Jude or St Philip or St Whoever...Below that in great big letters were inscribed the words: 'This was the gift of Pope So-and-So'. 'What's the good of that, David?' said Bishop George. 'Which is more important, the name of the Apostle or the name of the Pope? By the looks of that, the name of the Pope is made out to be more important.' So when we went out into the sunshine in St Peter's

Square afterwards, I said, 'Well, George, what did you make of that?' He said, 'David, too much glory of the Popes, not enough glory of God'. End of comment. It is worthwhile going round the world with a person like George. He immediately prods straight into the spiritual climate. He sees the essential. That's what matters.

No arrangements had been made for them to meet the Pope. Unexpectedly, however, they were able to join a large group of pilgrims from England travelling to Jerusalem who called at Rome for an Audience. As Bishop George recalled,

> The Pope has a lot of police, governing half of the kingdom of Rome. When we were climbing up the huge stairway in his large palace to see him, his bodyguards put their spears across the stairs so that we had to stop. They went through our bags and ordered us to leave them behind, as well as the contents of our pockets. They also took our cameras. Perhaps they feared there was a gun in the camera and that we wanted to shoot the Pope. Then we climbed more stairs and again we were stopped and searched by more guards with more spears.
>
> At last we were herded into a large room where we waited, over two hundred of us and David and myself. An announcement was made, 'Ladies and Gentlemen! Your Holy Father, the Pope'. We stood up. He went around amongst us. Then he made a speech and one of the group thanked him. We were introduced, one by one. I was the only coloured man, so he took me by the arm and said, 'Reverend Father!' That was all he said. I said nothing at all.

Bishop David's memory of the occasion slightly differed from that of his travelling companion:

> The Pope talked very concernedly with George and very humbly and simply. George was very impressed by that particular Pope, Paul the Sixth, as a man and as a Church leader. So he saw the difference between the individual occupants of the See of Rome and the machine, as it were, that sort of throws itself at you when you visit the Vatican.

After Italy they went to England and the Lambeth Conference. Many people were looking forward to Bishop George's arrival—returned missionaries who had worked with him in Papua New Guinea, church people keen to meet the first Papuan bishop, supporters of the mission and so on…So Bishop George felt he had to go. He could not then have foreseen the significance of his first Lambeth Conference for his future work in the Papuan Church.

As he recalled his time in England, a most dramatic event came to mind:

> I spent about six months over there and ended up with appendicitis. Oh dear! I had to go to hospital and they operated on me. Many people came to see me, bringing flowers, apples, cake and so on.

The other patients in the ward were amazed. 'This brown bishop,' they thought, 'how did all these white people know about him?' I explained that many of them were missionaries and some of them were my friends. They came to see me so that I would be encouraged and get better quickly. Everybody was very, very kind to me.

How could you be other than kind to Bishop George? He had that 'indefinable something' which drew people, white and brown, to him and which made them listen to his words and take note. This was the case with the nursing sister at the hospital who was on duty looking after him. Bishop David recalled the story:

> She came into the ward one day to see him and he said, 'Sister, are you a Christian?' She hesitantly replied, 'Well, I don't know'. Then he said, 'You would know if you are, because it makes all the difference to you'. She wasn't an acknowledging Christian. And so he asked, 'Do you say your prayers?' 'Oh well, no, no, not really,' she replied. Then he said, 'Sit down on my bed and I'll teach you'. So she did and he did!

Some time afterwards, Bishop David heard from somebody else that the sister had started saying her prayers and continued saying her prayers because the Bishop had told her to!

After the operation, he stayed at Gosport near the south coast with Fr Ted Kelly, who had been priest in charge of Gona, and his wife, Ruth.[268] According to Ruth, he was very concerned to do exactly what the doctor had said and to recuperate for exactly the number of days he had been told. 'As soon as that was at an end, he was up and about and full of beans and great fun. The children thought he was great.'

He visited the Kellys again when he came for the next two Lambeth Conferences, in 1978 and 1988. The last occasion was a year before his retirement. Ruth remembers these visits:

> He was always very warm. The children reacted very favourably to him. It was as if he was one of the family [see photograph, page 171]. He was an easy guest and helped with the washing up and things like that. He was making a point to show that Papuan men could and should help with the housework too!

Perhaps one of the most remarkable features of Bishop George's personality is his ability to fit in everywhere, be it amongst villagers in a remote jungle of Papua or with a white family in England. He was at home amongst traditional Papuans, dealing with magic and sorcery, as well as in Western society, as a patient in hospital or attending sessions at Lambeth. Somehow he coped with it all.

Some of the issues which were debated at the Lambeth Conference, such as the style of the English language in the Liturgy, were hard for Bishop George to follow. Other subjects, such as the ordination of women as deacons and priests, he had never heard about.

They debated it thoroughly. Some of the bishops disagreed and pulled out of the discussion. They asked questions of the two Bishops from PNG, but that is not an issue in our islands. My country is not ready yet. It is not in our culture to have women priests. We will wait and see. If that is God's will we will introduce it, but at the moment it is against our custom. God will tell us when the time is ready.[269]

However, other issues made a deep and lasting impression on Bishop George. As he recalled:

When I was at Lambeth, an Indian Bishop got up and said to the assembled bishops, 'Reverend Fathers! My people will only understand Christianity fully when they can accept Christ as an Indian and his mother, Mary, as an Indian. When the service and the hymns are in their own language, when Mass is in Indian with Indian music, then they will understand the message of the Gospel of Christ. Then our people will realise that the Church does not belong to other nations but their Church belongs to them'. [270]

Bishop George said,

His words opened my mind. I wanted to travel the world. [Following a thoughtful pause...] No, I didn't want to, because I was a simple bishop, but God gave me the opportunity to see and learn in other countries. I had to do it. Now I look back, I see it was good I did it, for God gave me these new ideas. They were important for Papua New Guinea.

In the 1960s, many leaders of the main Churches could see changes coming in the Christian worship of the Third World. Especially in Africa, where political independence was passionately, even violently pursued, the Churches were embracing local expressions of culture in traditional songs and dances. Liturgies were being rewritten, such as *The Liturgy for Africa of the Anglican Communion*. In April 1961, the Anglican Archbishops in Africa had met to discuss plans for composing a new Liturgy for a Holy Communion which could bring the chief Sunday service closer to the people. They hoped that such a Liturgy might form a bond of unity between Anglicans all over Africa.[271]

Perhaps one of the most notable features of the Second Vatican Council under the leadership of Pope Paul VI, was its emphasis on the fact that the Roman Catholic Church was not exclusively Roman. With a greater openness to non-European ways, it recognised the value of some aspects of local traditional culture in worship. Its new aspiration was to make the Church truly universal and meaningful to all people. That could be achieved, the Council believed, through a process of incorporating local languages and traditional elements into the Christian services—a process called 'inculturation'.[272]

Bishop George experienced these new ideas first-hand on his travels overseas. He talks of some of them:

We went to Africa for two weeks for a bishops' meeting at Nairobi. I talked with some African bishops and I attended their worship. I saw how the African Church had traditional elements in the service using traditional music and dancing with drums. I also saw it with the Indians in Canada and with the Maoris in New Zealand. I went to the Solomon Islands and other places in the Pacific where the Church had picked up these new ideas. Through their own music and dance the Christians were expressing joy and praise for God. That taught me a lot and I felt inspired. And the message came to me, 'Do the same thing in your own Church while you are a bishop before it is too late'.[273]

Back in his country, the message he had received was reinforced. He heard a voice inside himself saying:

If you do not use drums and your own traditional music in your worship, your Church will remain an imported Church. Bring guitars, *kundu*-drums and conch-shells into the service, and you will make it part of Papua New Guinea. Then it will belong to your country and to its people.[274]

So it was that Bishop George started composing. 'I was not born to be a composer,' he said, 'but God gave me this special gift with which to accomplish the task I had before me'. He had in his young days been leader of the dance in his clan. 'Dancing was in my blood,' he said. So it came naturally to him to start teaching his people who were keen to use their traditional dancing. Soon, the liturgy for the service at the church of his home area at Gona had been enriched with local words and music. *The Gona Mass*, as it was called, became an inspiration for other language groups in the Northern District.

I composed music for the Mass based on our own traditional music. The service was partly in the *Ewa-ge* language, the language of 'the sea-people' at Gona. It became a model. The Orokaiva people copied it, introducing the *Orokaiva* language and music into their service; the people from Tufi and Sefoa began using their own *Korafe* language and music; the Binandere people their *Binandere* language, songs and dance and so on. Ours was the first to adopt a local style of worship in a local language with traditional music and dancing. We felt that our Church really belonged to us.

Of course, there had been some attempts from early times to make the service more relevant to the Papuan people. This had been done mainly in terms of translation. Such pioneer missionaries as Fr Copland King and Fr Samuel Tomlinson had worked hard translating texts into local languages from the *Book of Common Prayer*, the Scriptures and some hymns from the English hymn book, *Hymns Ancient and Modern*.[275]

Other missionaries and some Papuan clergy continued the translation work. Fr Romney Gill, for much of his time in charge of the mission in the Mamba area, translated the liturgy into the *Wedau* language, which in his day, alongside English, was considered the *lingua franca* throughout the whole of the Anglican Mission.[276]

When Bishop George and Marcella arrived in the Popondota Region at the end of 1965, the *Orokaiva* language had been partly in use for over ten years in some services in the area. Bishop Henry Kendall recalled that, in the 1950s, when he was first in charge of the Resurrection Parish, they had the Liturgy, Matins and Evensong in *Orokaiva* as well as 'a few hymns to their original Western tunes in careless *Orokaiva* doggerel'.[277]

Some of the first *Orokaiva* translations were done several years before the war. In the early 1920s, Fr Henry Holland, an Australian missionary, later to be martyred, and Deacon Andrew Uware, his Papuan helper and friend, together founded the first inland station at Sangara. Fr Holland soon became an authority on the language, and both he and Deacon Andrew were engaged in translation work, which unfortunately was lost during the Japanese invasion.

Deacon Andrew Uware at Sasembata in the Northern District (now Oro Province). Photograph taken in 1955 when he had just finished the translation of St Mark's Gospel, *Mark Otohu*, into the *Orokaiva* language.
(Courtesy of the late Nancy White)

After the war, a few attempts were made at translating the Gospels into some of the languages of the Northern District. For example, the *Gospel of St Luke* was published in the *Binandere* language in 1949 by the British and Foreign Bible Society, Sydney. Bishop David Hand, for a time acting priest in charge of Sangara Station, encouraged interest in Bible translation. He himself was working with Fr John Rautamara, a Papuan priest and teacher, on translations into *Orokaiva* of the Collects, Epistles and Gospels from the *Book of Common Prayer*.

In 1948, Miss Margaret de Bibra, Headmistress of the Martyrs' School, with the help of some Orokaiva teachers and senior students, began to translate the *Gospel of St Mark*. After her death in the eruption of Mt Lamington in 1955[1], in which Fr John Rautamara and most of the teachers also lost their lives, some of Miss de Bibra's surviving young men started at St Aidan's College to train as teacher-evangelists. There they continued the translation work begun by Miss de Bibra.

After their training, they were helped by Nancy White, teacher for seven years in the Orokaiva district, who typed countless pages of the translation of St Mark for use by priests and teachers. According to her, the chief workers in this group of Orokaiva translators were Gilchrist Asimba, Lancelot Sangitari and Harold Heru. Their work was checked and revised by Andrew Uware, Neville Taune and Maxwell Hatopa, former Sangara teachers. But it was Andrew Uware upon whom Nancy White most heavily relied to complete the translation of *Mark Otohu* (*St Mark's Gospel*). She wrote to the British and Foreign Bible Society in Sydney:

> Andrew Uware has been our chief authority. The final revision was done by Andrew Uware, who has had many years experience as teacher, evangelist and interpreter in the Orokaiva and surrounding districts, and who knows well all the languages to which reference has been made.[278]

These Bible translations were important achievements in the Christian development of the Northern District. They were accompanied by literacy classes so that the local people could learn to read their Bible. It is not possible to mention all who worked so hard with the languages, but their efforts are not forgotten. *Mark Otohu* was published in Sydney in 1956. Over the years, it has been improved by other translations, but not until twenty-two years later would a complete *New Testament* in the *Orokaiva* language be published. In 1988, at Sui Village near Agenehambo, Bishop George dedicated and blessed this new translation completed by Bud Larsen, American missionary and translator with the SIL (Summer Institute of Linguistics).

Into this process of 'inculturation', Bishop George, as mentioned above, came back from overseas with fresh ideas for the liturgy.

> I began by writing music for the Procession into the church. Dancers in traditional costume, playing *kundu*-drums, sang and danced their way up the aisle. I taught them all this. Then, the *Kyrie*, 'Lord have Mercy' is sung in the local language to local tunes. The *Gloria* follows the Confession and Absolution. We used to say it in English, of course, but again I had a vision. I saw Angels with their musical instruments dancing and praising God and I heard a voice: 'You have a lot of music in your culture. Use some of it now'. So I wrote the words of the *Gloria* in our own *Ewa-ge* language and set it to our own music. It is one of the high points when we confess our sins and are forgiven. The dancers, erupting into praise with singing

and music, go bang in the dance — just dancing and drumming for the Glory of God. That is something joyful. It makes the service come alive. I believe in this. It moves the people — they feel joy in their hearts.

But the climax is the Eucharistic Meal itself. In our language we sing, 'Come with Faith, take the Bread of our Lord Jesus Christ. His blood was shed for you. Feed on Him with thanksgiving'. Then the dancers drum and sing straight from the heart, welcoming Jesus — '*Oro, Oro, Oro Kaiva*,' (welcome, welcome, welcome) — 'The feast is ready. Jesus is coming to the Divine Feast'. The people can all identify with this. It is part of their custom. In the past, at times of celebration, an Announcer would get up and sing the same sort of words, 'Welcome, the feast is ready, come to the feast'. And the people, full of joy, would beat their drums to welcome their guests. The people responded with their hearts in a way they could never do to the English liturgy and hymns in a foreign language imported from a foreign culture.

The hymn, sung during the Communion and printed at the end of this chapter, is an example of Bishop George's writing. In his own words, in the *Ewa-ge* language and set to music based on a traditional tune by himself, he expresses what he believes and feels about his relationship with God. Bishop George values highly the hymns he wrote:

These hymns are important to me. People must know what I believe about the message of Christ. I must try to write hymns in which my people feel they understand the meaning of the Holy Eucharist.

In the night, if feeling low, he sings the hymn *Bada Iesu Dubo — Bari Mamo* (see page 169) to himself while beating his drum. It strengthens and uplifts him.

Although some people had certain fears that the dancers might be carrying heretical beliefs into the Christian worship, there was, and still is, much support for the changes introduced by Bishop George. Bishop Denys Ririka, (son of Fr Albert Maclaren, ordained priest at Dogura with Bishop George), worries about his people's ancient belief in the influence of ancestral spirits:

For example, it is the custom that a dancer, before performing a dance, must call the spirits and say certain prayers to them. How do you control this sort of practice? Dancing encourages contact with the spirit world. How do you know the dancers are not under the spell of the spirits?

Despite seeing problems in certain situations, Bishop Denys acknowledges that Bishop George was the one person who had the power to teach and inspire his dancers to perform in the true Christian way.

Bishop George has enabled the Church of Papua New Guinea to express its own identity through unique, pure and genuine performances woven into the liturgy. Using traditional instruments and chants, composing hymns in his local language and setting them to his own music inspired by traditional tunes, he has made the worship more Melanesian — more meaningful for the people. I think Bishop George was the first to do this. It is his greatest contribution to our Church.[279]

Perhaps Bishop George was not the very first to see the value of traditional elements in worship. Such Anglicans as Stephen Tago, another friend, had already some ten years earlier experienced the first small beginnings of future changes. In Stephen's words,

I was a dancer too in my young days at Dogura, doing a lot of traditional dancing. One day Fr John Chisholm, the priest in charge, watching me, said, 'Stephen, you danced beautifully outside, now you must dance inside for God'. He made me practise for special occasions when we danced in the Procession in the Cathedral. He was influenced by those churches in Africa too, I think.

However it was Bishop George who really pushed for these changes. He was the first to fully realise the need for Papuan music and dancing to express wholeheartedly joy and praise for the Glory of God. Imported hymns and tunes could never, in the same way, touch the heart of the Papuan people. At Gona, he introduced *Ewa-ge* music and dances into the Mass. He composed and decided what music should enrich which parts of the liturgy in the *Ewa-ge* language. *The Gona Mass* was his creation — the first to be celebrated in the local words, songs and dance.[280]

We Papua New Guineans were religious and spiritual people before the missionaries came. But we were not allowed to express our spirituality according to our own traditions. All these things were put away.* It was Bishop George who brought back the expression of this religious feeling and spiritual quality. He christianised our cultural values like dancing and worshipping with drums and conch-shells, ornaments and chants.

It was Bishop George who brought about the full dawning of the new day.

---

* Stephen Tago's statement that 'All these (traditional) things were put away', did not apply to all places in Papua, expecially the Anglican areas. For example, at [the Anglican Mission Station at] Mukawa on Cape Vogel traditional drums were used since 1906 at church festivals. Also, a description of a Harvest Festival Service at the church at Boianai in 1929 gives a vivid picture of villagers taking part with decorated spears and drums. See David Wetherell, *Reluctant Mission*, pp 310, 311.

BADA IESU DUBO-BARI MAMO

1.   BADA IESU DUBO-BARI MAMO
   NA MAIN ITO MI BE DAO TENA
   JIDE GEGATA NATORE PIENA
   BADA GOROBA ARI PIE

2.   BADA IESU DUBO-BARI MAMO
   IMONDE TEDO BE GOTENA
   NANE ARI ATORE DANENA
   BADA KONDADE ARI PIE

3.   BADA IESU DUBO-BARI MAMO
   NANE BEIAE MI TA-NDODEIRI
   TO-REGARI NEIN AVE BE ITAE
   BADA IMO AKUTA BE

4.   BADA IESU DUBO-BARI MAMO
   JIDE ITO YAI DA GUPENA
   DO-WATO SATAN NA KUMBURE
   BADA NANE IMO TOPORA

5.   BADA IESU DUBO-BARI MAMO
   TO-RIWASI NATO DO BEDA
   EDO NATO DODA ANUMBE
   BADA NATO DODA BURO-E

6.   BADA IESU DUBO-BARI MAMO
   BEIAE NATORE TE-IEWASI
   EDO ITO GOROBA ARI MI
   BADA UTU DA BE AIMANA

Bada Iesu Dubo – Bari Mamo, the hymn written by Bishop George in the *Ewa-ge* language, and referred to on page 167. See overleaf for Bishop George Ambo's own English translation.

BADA IESU DUBO-BARI MAMO

(1) Lord Jesus, Father of True Love.
I am your adopted son calling you.
With tears offering my prayers to you
Lord, give me your strength to help me

(2) Lord Jesus, Father of True Love
Asking you, with all my heart
I am finding hard to help myself.
Lord, give your grace to help me.

(3) Lord, Jesus, Father of True Love
I am posessing greatly by evil spirit
There is no one to help and suppot me
But you are the only one to help me.

4 Lord Jesus, Father of True Love
Coming to you with great sorrow and tears
Do not let Satan will get me forever
Lord, I am belonging to you forever.

(5) Lord Jesus, Father of True Love.
Enter into my poor sinful heart
And stay always with me forever
Lord let your grace work in my heart

(6) Lord Jesus, Father of True Love
Wash my sinful heart with your mercy
And you will fell me with your strength
And with joy I shall enter into Heaven

Bishop George's translation into English of his own hymn *Bada Iesu Dubo –
Bari Mamo,* referred to on page 167 (size of handwriting slightly reduced).

Top: Bishop George with sorcerer in the
Northern District
(Photograph courtesy of Ray Kendall)

Left: Bishop George with Richard Kelly,
his godson, in the garden of the Kelly
family, UK 1968
(Photograph courtesy of Chris Luxton)

Traditional dancing in the Resurrection Cathedral, Diocese of Popondota
(Photograph courtesy of Chris Luxton)

CHAPTER 16

Independence, Church and State — Cults and Rebellions

The 1960s and '70s were most significant and critical decades in the history of Papua New Guinea. During these years a growing political awareness emerged in the towns, and to a lesser extent in the rural areas. This, together with an increasing concern with identity and national pride amongst educated Papua New Guineans, eventually contributed to the coming of self-government and political independence. Many people, especially the educated elite, were hopeful that the end was near of the colonial period and white domination.

Early in the 1970s, Michael Somare, the Chief Minister, wrote a message to his people reflecting the importance he placed upon traditional heritage as a basis for a strong and united nation. It is quoted here at length, as it expresses clearly the new awareness of the roots of Papua New Guineans, so symptomatic of the times:

> I firmly believe that the real strength of our nation lies in our traditional values and in the many good aspects of the traditional village life...Both son and daughter have learnt in the past from their parents about the spiritual life. They have heard the stories of great leaders of the clan who have died, or the legends that explain how the lakes, the mountains, the rivers and seas, have come about. They have also heard of the strange mythical forces which control our lives, of ghosts, of sacred objects and ritual and tradition which must be kept for a successful and happy life.
>
> Whether the legends and stories are true or not does not matter... they give us self-respect. If we are proud of the clan members who went before us, then we are proud to be a member of our own family unit. If we are not proud we would not remain with our family. There would be disunity among ourselves.
>
> I become angry when I think about the ways of some of the early missionaries...They told us our ways were wrong...I believe the Church should first have studied Papua New Guinean culture and tried to keep that which was clearly good. The Church has played its part in the past in some of the destruction of our values. I know that your own Church leaders will agree with me when I say that they can now play a very real part in rebuilding some of those values. I believe the Church and all Christians must seek a road towards nationhood which is not only Christian, but also Papua New Guinean.[281]

Bishop George, however, in an outspoken answer to the Chief Minister's article showed he was partly of a different opinion.

> It is true that we have lost some of our good customs. But I must disagree that the missionaries tried to destroy everything. This is not true, at least in the Anglican Church. In fact, the early missionaries tried to protect the culture of the country. Bishop Sharpe [an early bishop in the Anglican Mission] wrote a book in which he told the missionaries to take note of the old customs.[282] Our work is to bring back good customs and make them part of the life of the Church.

Bishop George claimed that the real strength of the nation lay not in its traditional values. Agreeing that traditional culture built up a strong and unified community, he argued that this was only within the tribal group. A unified nation could not be achieved by traditional culture being upheld within the different tribal groups as customs often varied from place to place.

> Unity within the country as a whole can only come when the love of God is alive in the heart of every person—when Papua New Guinea becomes a truly Christian country.

It was during these decades that, for the first time, a national 'Black Writing' emerged, reflecting the newly found pride in Papua New Guinea heritage. Young writers, mostly students at the University of Papua New Guinea, felt that with their writing they could contribute to the awakening of a national identity. With a sense of urgency, they recorded village life and traditional legends and customs, believing these to be in danger of being lost. These writers included John Waiko, later a Minister in the Government of Papua New Guinea, who wrote his doctoral thesis on the history of his own Binandere people: *Be Jijimo: A History According to the (Oral) Tradition of the Binandere People of Papua New Guinea.*[283]

Albert Maori Kiki, another of these young writers, was the first Papua New Guinean to raise his voice and write about his own life. His autobiography, *Ten Thousand Years in a Lifetime*, was published in 1968. Asserting his own identity, he described what it was like to grow up in a traditional Papuan village. Later, studying Political Science at the Administrative College at Waigani in Port Moresby, he met Michael Somare, one of his fellow students. Together with others, in 1967 they founded the Pangu Party, the first effective political party in Papua New Guinea. As well he became Secretary of the Port Moresby Trade Union Congress, and so was in the forefront of those who demanded the right to control their own affairs. Some found his book agressive and bitter, but it represented the currents of the time.[284]

Racial intolerance in Papua New Guinea generally was not a dominant feature during these decades. This was proved by the smoothness of the path to independence. However, the rapid changes in society brought for some anguish and frustration. *Reluctant Flame*, a poem written in the early 1970s, reflects this anguish, also a bitterness of suppressed emotions against the colonial regime.[285] Strongly rejecting white domination, John Kasaipwalova vents his feelings against foreign rule:

> This is the white cradle, this is the white pool
> This is the white ocean chasm in which we float steerless and
>   captured
> Black destination with villages of joyful living seems impossible
> Made unreal and distant by the thick white fog
>
> The fog blankets over, it pierces — no black density withstands the
>   flood
> I tremble in fear, the cold westerly chills my flesh and bones
> Memory of past warmth swims in my heart like stone
> What is this chill, where is that flame to warm and melt me?
>
> The chill is killing the flame, it is everywhere...
> Every turn of my head sees your tentacles strangling innocent
>   kanakas
> You have trampled the whole world over
> Here your boot is on our necks, your spear into our intestines
> Your history and your size makes me cry violently for air to breathe.

The colonial regime in PNG was nearing its end. In the early 1960s, a United Nations Mission had emphasised to the Australian Government the urgency of preparing the country for independence. According to their report, this could mainly be achieved through economic development and the expansion of education into secondary and tertiary levels. An exploitation of resources by overseas companies which invested in such financial ventures as the Bougainville Copper Mine and commercial timber projects began to occur. The increasing involvement by indigenous people in the growing of cash crops such as copra, coffee and cocoa further stimulated the rapidly growing cash economy.[286]

Within the field of education an equally rapid development occurred. The Australian Minister for Territories, Mr CE Barnes, together with Les Johnson, the Director of Education in Papua New Guinea, supported the expansion of both secondary and tertiary education. By 1966, the University of Papua New Guinea had been established in Port Moresby, together with the Institute of Technology (later the University of Technology) in Lae. With the increasing number of literate Papua New Guineans, the ranks of the public service swelled. Furthermore, with the government's encouragement of urban business, a group emerged amongst the educated elite having both commercial and political interests.

During the 1960s, increasing pressure was put on the Australian Government to promote early self-government and independence from various groups such as The United Nations, the Labour Opposition in the Australian Parliament, and sections within Papua New Guinea society. When in 1972

Gough Whitlam and his Labour Party came to power in Australia, the colonial regime was doomed. Michael Somare, leader of Pangu, the most influential party, was assisted by the new Australian Prime Minister in his efforts to obtain early independence. He succeeded in persuading the House of Assembly to support the plan to achieve self-government by December 1973, and complete independence from Australian control in September 1975.

Opinions in Papua New Guinea were divided as to an early date for independence, however. Some expatriates with commercial interests were concerned for the future viability of their businesses should they lose the protection of the Australian Government. Groups of Highlanders, fearing the possible domination of people from the Lowlands, sought to delay the coming of political change. Some Members of the House of Assembly working in the Constitutional Planning Committee claimed more time was needed to formulate a truly Papua New Guinean Constitution.

Bishop David Hand was amongst the supporters of early independence. At a Synod of the Diocese of Papua New Guinea held near Port Moresby in 1971, the delegates debated the question of 'localisation' (meaning the handing over of leadership and responsible positions to Papua New Guineans). In his presidential address, Bishop David declared that the colonial era was finishing:

> The sooner the hand-over to at least complete self-government, the better. That will remove all kinds of misunderstandings and bitternesses which otherwise will poison our nation.

Bishop George was of a different view. For the first time since becoming a bishop, his opinion seriously conflicted with that of Bishop David. Facing his senior bishop and the delegates, most of whom agreed that self-government and localisation should happen quickly, he firmly claimed that his people were not yet ready to take control of either Church or State. They still lacked the necessary sense of responsibility and dedication. He said that he hoped and prayed that national independence and complete localisation in the Church would not come in his lifetime.[287]

In 1972, national elections were held throughout the country for the third House of Assembly, in which elected Papua New Guineans made decisions about the running of their country. In Bishop George's Northern District (later Oro Province), there was uncertainty and confusion concerning the elections and the political future of the country. According to a report written by Arthur Jawodimbari, one of the young writers from the University of Port Moresby, the people were generally bewildered. Most had heard about the concepts of self-government and independence, but they did not understand their meaning. They feared the consequences of political change. Concerned that the white people might leave, they foresaw the breakdown of economic enterprises and organisations, conflicts, fighting and bloodshed. How would self-government affect their lives, they wondered? Uncertain and anxious, the villagers, mostly illiterate, felt they could get no answers to their questions. A political education officer had been appointed to travel around the district, talking to the local government councillors, but generally the councillors themselves were of low education and politically ignorant, unable to offer clear explanations to the people.[288]

In Bishop George's region, several candidates were standing. Some of these were well known Anglican teachers such as Stephen Tago and Mackenzie Daugi. The area had been divided into three electoral divisions: Northern Regional (contested by Daugi), Ijivitari Open (contested by Edric Eupu, an Administration Clerk and President of Higaturu Local Government Council), and Sohe Open (for which Stephen Tago was standing). Both Eupu and Daugi had joined the United Party, recently established and with a moderate platform stating that independence should be delayed until the people wanted it. A fourth influential candidate was Paulus Arek, also contesting the Ijivitari Open in opposition to Eupu. Arek was a teacher from Wanigela on Collingwood Bay. Amongst his many public responsibilities he was the President of The Federation of Papua New Guinea Workers' Associations and, most notably of all, the Chairman of the Select Committee on Constitutional Development in the Second House of Assembly. As such, he often spoke in the House on nationalist themes, feeling close to Michael Somare's *Pangu Pati* and advocating its policy of early independence by 1975.

Bishop George was actively involved with this election in his district, backing the candidates who favoured delayed independence. According to Jawodimbari's report, he campaigned 'in the name of God' against Paulus Arek in the Ijivitari Open. Strongly supporting Mackenzie Daugi, he travelled widely, urging people to vote for a good Anglican, 'a man of God'. Warning of the bad effects and possible disasters likely to be the consequences of early independence, he reminded the villagers that only God and his Church could save them. He stressed that Daugi had promised to work for delayed self-government should he win the election.

Victory in this political contest did not so much depend on party politics as on having influential contacts within the Church. As well as the support from Bishop George, Mackenzie Daugi received backing from Bishop David, who spoke in his favour at Gona during the campaign. Likewise, Fr Simon Peter, Bishop George's brother, in charge of the churches in the Kokoda area, openly encouraged his people to vote for Daugi. And so did many of the mission teachers.

Bishop George's influence in his region was widespread and highly significant. Together with David Marsh, the District Commissioner and Anglican Church Councillor, he was seen by the people as a man of the highest wisdom, holding God-given authority. They wondered if perhaps these two men would be choosing the future national leader of their country. In the meantime, they believed that they must vote for Daugi. The support for him by Bishop George and other Church leaders was to them the clearest indication that Daugi had been chosen by God to represent them in the House of Assembly. Daugi won the contest for the Northern Regional Electorate by a very large majority!

Cults and Rebellions

Early in 1972, at the time of the campaigning for the election, Bishop George became involved in a cargo cult case. Rumours had reached him that a man, Matthias Emumu Anide, living on an oil-palm block at Sorovi on the way to Gona, had for some time been spreading false information in the area. He was going out to villages, urging people to join the 'Totoima Society' which he himself had started. He told them if they paid an amount of money for membership, at a certain time they would in turn be paid a very large sum, with which they could buy cars, ships, planes and goods from the stores!

The promised date for payment was Tuesday 8 February. On that day, according to Matthias, three strange ancestor creatures, Eripa, a deceased female, Totoima (or Dodoima), a mythical Orokaiva monster after whom the society was named, and Banu, an eagle, would appear at Sorovi with Matthias.[289] Somehow being involved with banking affairs, these supernatural creatures would enable him to produce a cheque which would be cashed. The money would then be paid out to the members, according to how much each had originally given.[290]

Bishop George recalls that some Church Councillors and community leaders came to his home and told him about Matthias and his false prophecies. They said that Matthias had great influence amongst the people, who flocked to him from faraway areas such as Tufi on Cape Nelson. He was believed to have supernatural powers, as he claimed to possess one of the poisonous teeth from the monster Totoima with which, according to legend, the monster killed people. Furthermore, it was thought he was in touch with the spirits, as he was able to produce from a small tape-recorder the voice of a spirit! He maintained that Bishop George and David Marsh, the District Commissioner, were members of his society and so guaranteed its validity. Bishop George wanted to go down to Sorovi and see for himself what was happening. As he described it,

> There were hundreds of people crowding around. I couldn't see Matthias. A second time I went, I warned him strongly not to carry on with his work. I told the villagers the money they gave him would never earn money for them. A few with commonsense believed me but most did not. The third time, I nearly lost my temper. 'You must stop these lies or you will find yourself in the hands of the police,' I said. Matthias went on. The police came and took him to Popondetta jail.[291]

On 25 February 1972, according to the Assistant District Officer's report, Matthias was brought before the Court. Some thousand people had surrounded the Courthouse. As the case proceeded, the crowds outside became increasingly angry. At one time, it seemed they were about to break into the building and remove Matthias by force. Bishop George recalled the occasion:

They were very angry. I said they must calm down. 'The government has power over you and me,' I told them. 'If you are not careful, they will put you in jail. Then you will miss your wife and children.' But they were furious, flew into a wild rage. 'If you try to kill the Court officials, you will kill your Bishop too, for I am ready to stand for what is right. You will see that someone has to give up his life for the truth and I am going to do that. My sons and daughters, be careful.'

Somehow he managed to calm the crowds. Martin Chittleborough, an Australian priest assisting Bishop George as archdeacon, was by chance in town. He recalled seeing Bishop George standing up in the middle of the road and taking control of the masses. He was directing government officials and government vehicles like a traffic policeman, telling them to take people back to their villages. Who else but Bishop George would have had the authority and stature to take control, not only of the crowds but of the government as well? Martin later remarked, 'It was the biggest tingle down my spine that anything or anyone had ever caused me'.[292]

When the hearing resumed on 28 February, the crowds outside were orderly, patiently waiting for the case to be closed. As the official report has it,

At 4.15pm the Court adjourned...The Assistant District Commissioner addressed the people outside. They were reminded that Bishop George Ambo is the first Papua New Guinean to be consecrated Bishop; that Simon Kaumi (a local man from Buna) is a man who holds a particularly responsible position within the Administration; they were reminded that the name of Orokaiva is known and honoured throughout Papua New Guinea. They were asked not to besmirch the names of their leaders and of their people.[293]

Bishop George calming the crowd outside Popondetta Courthouse, 25 February 1972

(Photograph courtesy of Martin Chittleborough)

The report further states that a spokesman for the Totoima Society then got up and requested that Matthias be given one more chance to produce the cheque. That request was refused. Then, according to the report,

> Bishop Ambo stood up and slated the spokesman in the strongest terms and finally hurled at him the deadly insult — 'You are a man who eats the excreta of dogs'. Complete silence for five minutes! Then the crowd melted away.

The movement was broken. Matthias was sentenced to six months jail. He had collected thousands of dollars but much of the money was never retrieved. Asked by a news reporter what he felt about it all, Bishop George said that he had believed that cargo cults had been got rid of in the Northern District.

> I have been impressing on my people that their first and main gift is their land and they must use their eyes and brains and reason on how to use this land for their own benefit. They must not listen to such impossible schemes as this. Wealth comes from human labour, not from stupid ideas of easy money.

Bishop George added that he had often reminded his people of the example from the war, when some Orokaiva villagers had thought the invading Japanese were their dead ancestors. In the belief that they would be rewarded with goods and money by these 'ancestral spirits', they had betrayed the white missionaries to the Japanese. These Orokaiva traitors were publicly and brutally hanged by the Australian military authorities at the Higaturu Government Station on Mt Lamington. Bishop George went on,

> It was God's will to teach us a lesson, not to believe in the power of ancestral spirits, that they can bring rewards to the living human beings.[294]

During the 1960s and '70s, decades of restless change and ideas of independence, secessionist movements were sprouting in widespread areas. Groups such as 'The Papua Besena', led by Miss Josephine Abijah, actively campaigned for Papuan independence and separation from the former Territory of New Guinea. On the island of Bougainville, voices were heard protesting against the National Government; angry at not gaining a fair share of the wealth from the Panguna Copper Mine, islanders were discussing the possibility of forming a separate nation.

In Bishop George's own region, similar stirrings for control of an independent Oro Province emerged in the Buna area. Simon Kaumi, referred to during the court case of Matthias, was a respected and responsible Administration official. Having for ten years been a trusted Member of the House of Assembly and an Electoral Officer, Kaumi suddenly turned against Michael Somare and his newly-formed government. After passionate speeches against their policies, he was finally sacked from the House of Assembly. Shortly after the election in 1972 he formed his own rebel army, intending to break away from government control.[295]

Having heard rumours of 'The Papuan Republic Fighters' Army' at Buna, Bishop George did his utmost to avert what could have been an ugly situation. The crisis began with the rebel army taking and occupying the neighbouring Joropa Plantation. Stephen Tago and Mackenzie Daugi, members of the Oro Provincial Government, were sent down to investigate the situation. They were insulted and stopped on the way by the rebels. According to their report, they were spat on and threatened with death should they dare come down again. Fearlessly, Bishop George decided to go himself.

> I sent a message: 'My Christian people, your Father in God is coming to see you'. I didn't want to take my wife and said, 'I'm going myself,' but as I started off she jumped in the car, so I didn't stop her.
>
> The first entrance to Kaumi's area was at Dobuduru Village. Large petrol drums blocked the road. Soldiers were standing by with homemade guns, made from black palm, and bayonets. They stopped my truck. 'My sons, take the drums away. I am your Father in Christ. I came to see my people.' They let us through. I saw several hundred men marching. It would have been a big, powerful army. Had they all carried guns, there would have been a war. As it was, real guns had been ordered from somewhere, but they hadn't turned up. Stopped by several more roadblocks, eventually we reached Kaumi's headquarters on the coast at Buna. I couldn't see him but I spoke to the crowd in the village. They were hostile. 'Do not support this,' I warned them strongly. 'The government is more powerful than you. You will be very sad, like the Israelites who went against God's will and had to suffer in Babylonia.' Some people understood my warning, and I returned home.

Bishop George made several trips to Buna to see the rebel leader. 'If anyone wants to kill me when I enter into Kaumi's area, that's up to you', he told the guards, 'but I am visiting Kaumi'. The rebel leader avoided him. Finally, Bishop George warned a large gathering of people that police and soldiers were about to arrive.

> You, my sons and daughters, be careful! They have real guns. Do not stop them or you will be sad. They will form a line, the police followed by soldiers, and I will come with them. If you resist them, they will kill you in front of me and I will bury you. I told them the simple truth. Soon after, the special task force, led by a Sergeant-Major, came from Port Moresby. 'You little boys, playing with guns,' the Sergeant said. 'What are you trying to do? Take their guns away, and throw them in the cars. This time we came to warn you, next time we come to kill!'

In Bishop George's words,

> That opened their eyes. The Sergeant saw Kaumi. What he said to his people, I wouldn't know. I hope he learnt a lesson.

At the next election in 1977, Simon Kaumi returned to the National Government as a Member for the Ijivitari Electorate. One morning he came to see us before the election. My wife was cooking scones for breakfast. 'Father, I am a newborn Christian,' he said. 'I was a sinner. Now I am a born-again man. I want to stand for the coming election. Father, I cannot do it without your support.' I was very pleased indeed. 'These scones came from the fire to the plate,' I said. 'I am giving you new scones straight from the fire to the plate and into your tummy. You have become like them, new fire, newborn scones. If you have become like them, you will do well in the new government.'

I went up and down the coast in my dinghy, right up to Iwaye and down to Baku, campaigning for him. He got two thousand votes because of me, not because of himself. In Popondetta, I won for him six hundred more votes, which made him win the election. I knew he was a born political leader. He had a clever brain. That was why I supported him. He wanted to have his own military force and used force to take land from others and to demand illegal taxes.

In his usual readiness to be positive and to think the best of others, George added, 'But I think he has changed. Now, he is a good man'.[296]

Martin Chittleborough wrote an account which illustrates the courage and influence of Bishop George. During the rebels' occupation of the Joropa Plantation, the land disputes increased. Rumours spread that the Buna people wished to take over all the nearby lands, owned by the people of Killerton. According to Martin, thousands of warriors, coming in their canoes from distant places, assembled near Buna, threatening to attack the villagers:

Honour must be given to Bishop George and his clergy, to Mr MacKenzie Daugi, the regional member, and to a lot of fine Christian men and women who worked for peace at considerable personal risk. Bishop George, a man from Gona, was visiting the Buna area weekly, trying to bring peace.[297]

By early 1975, the results of the work of the Constitutional Planning Committee were still being debated in the House of Assembly, but by September they had been passed as law. The *Preamble to the Constitution*, combining the elements of both traditional culture and Christianity, expresses a broad view, lending equal importance to the past and to the future of the newborn state:

We, the people of Papua New Guinea — united in one nation; pay homage to the memory of our ancestors — the source of our strength and origin of our combined heritage; acknowledge the worthy customs and traditional wisdoms of our people — which have come down to us from generation to generation; pledge ourselves to guard and pass on to those who come after us our noble traditions and the Christian principles that are ours now.

By authority of our inherent right as ancient, free and independent
peoples, we the people, do now establish this sovereign nation and
declare ourselves, under the guiding hand of God, to be the
Independent State of Papua New Guinea.

It is notable that references to the ancestors and the ancient heritage of
the Papua New Guinea people should be linked with the idea of a future for
the Christian nation under God's guidance. In traditional Papua New Guinea
societies there was no sharp distinction between the secular and the sacred
spheres. Everything was seen as part of the whole spiritual realm.[298] With the
coming of the Christian Mission, an added commitment to education, health
and social welfare became the basis for the functioning of the local societies
within its sphere. The Christian Church was involved with both the religious
and the secular affairs in the lives of the people. As the political development
began to evolve, the Church continued to play its vital role in society. Hence,
it was natural that Bishop George should be actively involved in the politics of
his own region and outspoken in his political views.

It must have been with sadness and disappointment that Bishop George,
on 16 September 1975, took part in the celebrations of the National
Independence Day. Later he wrote:

Many people were in favour of Independence but others were not
happy. I myself was not happy to have Independence too early. I
suggested waiting one hundred years or so, but they didn't listen
to me. Leaders in politics and in the Public Service desired very
much to have it, but I personally disagreed with them because I
knew my people were not yet ready. Being a full-blooded Papua
New Guinean, I fought for Independence to be delayed for one
hundred years. But what I believed in and hoped for was lost.

According to Bishop George, the celebrations on 16 September 1975, the
National Independence Day, were generally well planned and organised.
Sir John Guise, the newly appointed Governor-General, solemnly declared in
a speech in Port Moresby: 'Papua New Guinea is now independent. The
constitution...is now in effect. We have, at this point of time, broken with our
colonial past...'. In a speech at St John's Cathedral in Port Moresby, the Prime
Minister, Michael Somare, pledged that he and his leaders would uphold the
Christian values, declaring their loyalty to God and to the guidance of their
Church leaders.

At the Eucharist in the Resurrection Cathedral at Popondetta, Bishop
George produced special prayers:

We have brought our gifts and money to the Lord...In the same
way, we now bring forward our chief men to stand before the altar
of God. We, the Church, will ask God's blessing and strength to be
with them to follow the right path of duty and service before God
and men.[299]

At the birth of the young nation, the Western concept of separation between Church and State did not apply. The independent country of Papua New Guinea had a sound foundation of Christian ideals.

After the service at the Resurrection Cathedral, there was traditional dancing on the oval near the market place in Popondetta. According to Bishop George, nearly all the districts in his region attended the celebrations to play their part and to show their gratitude to God. They all brought dancing groups as well as gifts of *taro*, bananas, yams, sweet potato etc. Bishop George wrote,

> I was invited to attend the celebration and all went well to start with. The dancers started to go to the dancing oval and the great crowd moved to watch the dancing. People were all happy and full of joy. But at this point, things went radically wrong.
>
> During these years, Papua New Guinea had problems with crime. Some silly young men formed gangs of so-called rascals [young criminals]. During our Oro Province Independence Day celebrations, some rascals were amongst the people. They had come from Kerema in the Gulf Province. Some of our young men suddenly shouted in loud voices that the Kerema rascals were amongst us. The rascals ran through the crowds, two of them running straight towards me. One of them was taken to a policeman's house. The other one escaped. The Orokaiva men flew into a wild rage, running to and fro shouting, 'All join! Let's kill them! Let's kill them!' It nearly turned into bloodshed.
>
> Mrs Marcella Ambo (my wife) was with me together with Mrs Maureen Ambo, who had just married my second son, Mr Alban J Ambo. The young Oro men were throwing stones here and there with pride and anger. I took my wife and daughter-in-law to the Mt Lamington Hotel. Then I met Bishop David Hand. I urged him to go back to the Resurrection Mission Station as the young men had completely lost their commonsense.
>
> I walked back to the new radio station near the market place. People were running in all directions. When I saw the situation was out of hand, I shouted to the people to hurry up to the Resurrection Station. Then the Police Commander went down to pick up the Kerema rascal in the police house. The young men, shouting and yelling, picked up stones to break his car. I feared there would be bloodshed and many would be killed. They followed him to the police station, wanting the rascal to be brought out. As he was kept under guard, they lost their temper and broke down the police office with stones.
>
> While the Police were waiting for the task force from Port Moresby, I shouted with worried spirit for my people to move quickly to Resurrection Station. Through God's Grace they started to move away.

For a second time within a few years, Bishop George again bravely took control of enraged crowds of people. Having to find means of moving them away, he sent a message to the Government Department for Transport. He wrote about it:

> Two big trucks arrived. With another church truck and a bus, and with help from Christian spirits, we were able to send many back to their own places.

> When the police task force arrived, Popondetta town was quiet. Hearing that crowds had gathered at the Mission Station, the task force came with their guns. I was standing in front of my house. They asked, 'Where are the troublemakers hiding?' I said I didn't know. I said that these people were innocent. They had come to enjoy the Independence Day Celebrations. After the police force had gone away, I was wondering and pondering over it all. Why did the loving and merciful God let these troubles happen on this important day of celebration? I concluded He let this happen to teach us all a lesson.

As political independence evolved, the Anglican Church of Papua New Guinea was preparing for its own independence. At the General Synod in Sydney, as early as 1973, Bishop David foretold that 'by 1977, at the very latest, we will have our own Archbishop and five dioceses...'.[300]

Bishop David's prophecy was to be fulfilled, and he himself was elected as the first Archbishop of Papua New Guinea. 27 February 1977 was the day decided for the celebration of the independence of the Anglican Church of Papua New Guinea. On that day, the Diocese of Papua New Guinea would become an Independent Anglican Province, no longer a part of the Province of Queensland but standing alone in its own right. On that date, the five Regions of the Church would become Dioceses of the new Province, their five assistant regional bishops gaining the full status of diocesan bishops. (They were Bishop Bevan Meredith of New Guinea Islands; Bishop Jeremy Ashton of Aipo Rongo, the former NG Mainland; Bishop George Ambo of Popondota; Bishop Rhynold Sanana of Dogura; Bishop David Hand of Southern Papua and Port Moresby.)

Although most Anglicans throughout Papua New Guinea looked forward with enthusiasm to the independence of their Church, some did not. Bishop George was one of these. Once again, his view conflicted with that of Bishop David. As he recalled:

> When my Brother in Christ, David Geoffrey Hand, was considering independence for our Church, a couple of times he came to see me personally, asking me for my view on the matter. But I did not share my thoughts with him. I was pondering it over and over again, praying to God to reveal His Will to me.

> Then it came to me that I must share my views with a gathering of my brother bishops. I said to them, 'I, as the first national bishop,

want to share my opinion with you that we must be careful and patient. As a Papua New Guinean, living with my people and doing pastoral work amongst them, I know they have not yet reached the true Christian standard. Although they are full members of Christ's Church, they are still practising some evil habits. At this stage, we have not produced true, committed national leaders in the priesthood. Most of our clergy do not speak the truth. They do not teach in the Christian spirit nor do they make decisions according to the Divine Will for the best of their people. They do not stop fighting and bloodshed. Furthermore, let us not have localisation for localisation's sake. I believe the Church is universal. It belongs to all people no matter of what colour, race or land. When we chose our leaders, it is not a question of localisation, of having all Papua New Guinea leaders. No, irrespective of colour, let us have the right man for the right job. I hope one day we will have an Independent Church but it must be in God's Good Time'.

At a final Conference of Bishops in Port Moresby the matter again was debated at length. Then the chairman, Bishop David, asked for the voting papers to be given out. First we remained silent for ten to fifteen minutes. Then the voting began. Most voted for independence. I voted against and lost. I told a news reporter who came after the meeting that I was totally against my Brother Bishop David who was pushing for independence now — which was far too early for us!

For most Anglicans 27 February 1977 was a day of joy and celebration. At Dogura Cathedral hundreds of people had gathered to celebrate the inauguration of the new Province. Dr Donald Coggan, the spiritual head of the universal Anglican Church had arrived for the occasion. His visit to PNG was the first ever by an Archbishop of Canterbury. During the service, the five new diocesan bishops were installed and the new Province entrusted into the hands of its first Archbishop, David Hand.[301]

Shortly after the celebration at Dogura, the Archbishop of Canterbury was welcomed by Bishop George and hundreds of his people at the Church of the Resurrection — from then on to be the Cathedral of the Diocese of Popondota. Such were the numbers of happy worshippers that many had to sit on the grass outside the large building.

In Popondetta town, Dr Coggan officially opened the new Christian bookshop, part of the community centre which had been recently built by the Anglican Church at the instigation of Bishop George.

Bishop George had been greatly impressed by the words of Dr Coggan, spoken at a press conference at Government House shortly after his arrival in Port Moresby. Asked about the impact of Christianity on traditional culture, a subject very close to Bishop George's heart, the Archbishop replied that he believed Christianity was a universal faith and that we should not apologise for bringing it to the people of PNG. He said, however, 'We should not impose our Western patterns, for example of worship, on the people to whom we come'. He said he hoped to see national worship and national patterns of music during his time in the country. That hope was amply fulfilled, largely because of the efforts over the last ten years or so of Bishop George: attending services in various places, the Archbishop found the worship was permeated by traditional music and culture.

Asked if it was right for a European to be the first Archbishop of Papua New Guinea, Dr Coggan said, 'All I'd say is hurrah, you've got a good man… The Church here has gone for the right man for the job, rather than [choosing] on racial lines'. His answer brings to mind the tenet of Bishop George: 'Do not localise for the sake of localisation, but find the right man for the right job, irrespective of colour and race'.

There was joy and excitement in Oro Province when, a few weeks after the inauguration of the Province, it was announced, that Queen Elizabeth and Prince Philip would spend two hours at Popondetta during their forthcoming visit to PNG. Bishop George wrote,

> It was her first visit to our town. Pictures of the Queen and the Prince were put up around the town and many people saw them and heard about the royal couple. There was great excitement when, on the 25th March, the Queen and Prince Philip landed at Girua Airport. They were welcomed by the Environment Minister Stephen Tago and his wife with groups of dancers, all wearing traditional costumes. As they were driven round the streets of Popondetta, about 12,000 happy people, waving palm leaves and colourful croton branches, shouted '*Oro! Oro! Oro Kaiva!*' (Welcome, Welcome, Welcome) as they greeted the royal visitors.[302]

> Then Marcella and I were given a chance to meet the Queen and Prince Philip. We took them around the Memorial Park for fifteen minutes. Meeting the royal guests was a great honour for us both. Above all, the fact that they were talking with simple people like us for fifteen minutes was a very great honour indeed. We often shared our memories of that wonderful occasion with our friends and especially with our own family and the young children.

The rather forced coming of independence for his country and his Church, together with the conflict with Bishop David whom he regarded as his real brother, must have caused great pain for Bishop George. He began to doubt his own judgement. He asked himself, pondering if he was right,

> Was I following the guidance of the Holy Spirit? Or was I fighting against the Holy Spirit?

At last he concluded,

> Anyway, I followed my conscience and my belief in the best for my Church. As a bishop I had stayed in villages with Church

Councillors to meet and talk with my people. I had learnt a lot about their minds and thoughts. Especially their secrets. They were not yet fully Christian people. This knowledge was in my heart and mind. Therefore I voted against independence for our Church.[303]

They had been turbulent years preceding independence. Uncertainty as to the effects of the political change and fear of the future had made people restless and unstable. With social change had come an increase in crime and violence. Unemployment in towns had brought lawlessness, poverty and social problems, such as drunkenness and gambling.

At the time Archdeacon Chittleborough wrote,

> What is the cause of all this? Perhaps the biggest thing is the increase in fear…The Church, as probably the most influential power at the moment, has a vital part to play in trying to reduce all these factors, and under Bishop George's leadership it is doing remarkable work.[304]

In the years leading up to independence, Bishop George had been keenly involved in politics and in trying to deal with such social ills as cargo cults, rebellions and rascal gangs—some of the rumblings of the end of an era and birth pangs of the new one to come.

Bishop George with Queen Elizabeth and Prince Philip at Popondetta, 1977
(Photograph courtesy of Chris Luxton)

CHAPTER 17

Diocesan Bishop of Popondota

Trinity Sunday in early June 1977 was a special day for Bishop George. On that day, as Diocesan Bishop, he took over the full responsibilities for his own, newly-created Diocese of Popondota.

In a letter of congratulation, Archbishop Philip Strong of Brisbane wrote to Bishop George:

> May the Love and Power of the Holy and Blessed Trinity overshadow, surround and envelop you and the Church in your Diocese, and its special gift of Wisdom be given you through its Holy Spirit for your added responsibilities. You are never alone—He will be ever with you and within you…[305]

Bishop George soon felt the weight of his new responsibilities. Although it seemed to him that God during the last twelve years in his life as Regional Bishop had been teaching and preparing him for this higher position, more than ever before he needed God's wisdom and power to guide him. One of the foremost problems facing him was the lack of adequate staff. In his answer to Archbishop Strong, he wrote,

> As you know, we have only a few white missionaries working among us and nowadays, we are finding it very hard in getting missionaries. We would be very grateful if some of them offered, as it used to be.[306]

In another letter, this time to his former Archdeacon, Martin Chittleborough, he expresses the same problem.

> At present I am hoping to get a Diocesan Secretary for our Diocese. Other Dioceses have their Secretaries but Popondota Diocese has none so I am looking for one, so I am asking you to give the message to your people that I need a Diocesan Secretary very much. We have written to England and other parts of the world but there was no answer. I am not lost in heart but I hope and pray that some day God will give us the right man to help us.[307]

Trying to run the Diocese, as well as coping with correspondence and administrative work, was not easy for Bishop George who, first and foremost, was a pastor at heart. Keeping up with his programme of yearly visits to all the many and widespread parishes in his care, he was often away for long periods of time. His family suffered. As he wrote,

This is a very high, holy and important position in the Church, but also a very hard and self-sacrificing life. By this I mean you have no time for yourself and your family. I discovered my own family missed their father. I often remembered Bishop Strong's words to me: 'Never, never turn your back on people who come for your help. Your time is for people, not for yourself'.[308]

Bishop George felt strongly that God had entrusted him as well as Marcella with this high position in the Church. As far as he could, he shared his problems with her. 'My dear wife Marcella and I prayed together in our few private moments for God's Grace,' he wrote. He believed that if they were to try to help people live Christian lives, both he and Marcella must set an example by putting their words into action. 'Our people must see that what we say and preach is proved in our own home and in our lives.' His motto since college days was foremost in his mind: 'Do as you preach' or 'Site-Eité' in his native Ewa-ge language.[309]

He felt perhaps more deeply than ever before the importance of his own family. He recalled how he had seen great significance in St Paul's First Letter to Timothy, Chapter 3, Verses 1–7:

God revealed to me this passage as my special text for prayer and meditation: 'If a man is eager to be a church leader, he desires an excellent work. A church leader must be without fault...he must be able to manage his own family well and make his children obey him with all respect. For if a man does not know how to manage his own family, how can he take care of the Church of God?'

Letters which he wrote during this year to two of his daughters reveal his love and concern for them and the warm relationship within the family. Helen was doing her Grade 3 at the Holy Name School, Dogura, and Gloria was at the Balop Teachers' College in Lae:

My dearest daughter [Helen],

Thank you very much for your letters. Our apologies for not writing to you so often. The things you asked for, the comb, we got it. I am bringing it down on the 29th June. Later on I would like to talk to you about your future but the other things you asked for, I lost the letter you wrote to me, so please answer my letter and let me know as soon as possible before I go down to Dogura for the inauguration of your Diocese...

We are very sad that you are not having enough food. But my dear daughter, do not grumble or lose your temper and be rude about it. Offer this to Jesus and you will succeed.

At present, you must work hard, pray hard, and play hard. As a motto I have been telling you over these past years: 'Let others see that Jesus is in you'...

Your dearest Dad...

On the same day, he wrote to Gloria in Lae:

My dear daughter,

I hope you are doing well in your last year at College…I shall get the radio you asked for but let me know clearly which type you want.

As I have been telling you over these past years, there are many temptations in the world and no doubt you have been facing and experiencing it but you as a bishop's daughter and God's daughter as well, take care of yourself. You can't overcome temptations by your own power but you can always do it with the help of God. Therefore, my dear daughter, work hard, pray hard and play hard. All these are good, if you do them with Jesus…everything will be according to God's plan and you will find joy, peace and a happy home.

You are receiving many letters from boys but do not let them carry you anywhere…Offer these letters to Jesus and he will give you the true partner and the right one who will help you when you get old. True love really comes from God. Pleasure of this world comes from any human young boy. Look and pray for the true love, do not look for pleasure. As I always told you in the past…let others see that Jesus is in you…

Your dearest Dad…[310]

By 1977 Popondetta had become the centre of a widespread, active Anglican area. According to Bishop George, his new diocese had a population of over 60,000 people and nearly all of them were Anglicans.[311] Many of the former large 'Mission districts', such as Gona, Eroro, Manau and Agenehambo, had each been divided into several smaller parishes, so that Popondota Diocese had more parishes than any of the other dioceses. The population of the town itself had almost doubled, with nearly 8,000 inhabitants. Many recent developments had gone ahead, such as the building of the Christian Community Centre next to the market. The Centre included a chapel and a Christian bookshop and was supervised by an expatriate Archdeacon, Francis Cumberlege.

Also within the last year or so, some institutions of the Anglican Province had been established near the town area, such as the centre at Hetune for the Sisters of the Community of the Visitation, the friary at Haruru for the Franciscan Brothers, Newton Theological College at Jonita, the Christian Training Centre, and the Rural Life Development Centre. Bishop George had, and still has in his retirement, close contact with the Sisters and Friars of the two religious communities. As he wrote,

I like to go to the Friary for a time to feel the prayer. We in PNG need some people who are always offering prayer as the most important thing in their lives — prayer for the spiritual needs of the Church. When I go to Mass at the Sisters', I feel a different atmosphere.

He would have been inspired by the beauty of their chapel, set in the loveliest garden.

A large oil-palm project was being developed by the National Government at Higaturu, a few miles from Popondetta along the road towards Agenehambo. Within a short time, this project attracted a large number of people from all over Papua New Guinea. The Anglican Church was urgently seeking a priest and community workers to minister to the newcomers. With the growth of the town and the advent of the oil-palm project, urban problems such as immorality, gambling, drinking and juvenile crime increased.

With such rapid growth and development in his large diocese, the demands on Bishop George were heavy. All the parishes were now run by Papuan clergy, which, in his own words,

> was a great joy to us all but we need some experts from overseas to be our archdeacons, teachers at theological colleges and high schools, tutors in nursing departments, diocesan secretaries, etc. Our standard of education is not high enough for us to handle this, so my personal belief is that we have a long way to go.

This had been his message to the Western world from pre-independence years and still continued to be so. Even now, in his retirement, it is one of his main concerns that expatriates come to give advice to Papua New Guineans in areas where help is needed. He wants us to remember that the question of responsibility for assistance to his young country, reared by the West, will continue to lie with the West far into the future.

This lack of expatriate skills was a great worry for Bishop George who tried to deal with his many responsibilities as best he could. No wonder that a report from 1977 stated, 'The Bishop is always on the move, and there is evidence everywhere of his frequent and impressive presence'.[312] Wanting to share his problems of staffing with Bishop David, especially the urgent need for a diocesan secretary, he went to see him in Port Moresby. He was advised to write to the Australian Board of Missions (ABM). Great was Bishop George's relief when, soon afterwards, an invitation came from ABM for him to visit the Diocese of Brisbane. During his deputation work in Australia, he stressed the urgent need for expatriates to go to Papua New Guinea.

It was on this occasion that he first met Fr Gordon Guy and his wife Peggy, who were to be of such great assistance to him with the running of the diocese.

> They were very devoted and committed Christians. Their love for the Church was so real and true in them. I stayed with them in Cairns and when Fr Gordon saw that I was having troubles with my eye, he arranged for me to have an eye operation in Brisbane. The eye specialist was a friend of his. It took him ten minutes to operate on my left eye. Afterwards he told me the operation was free!

When he later heard that the Guys had offered to start work for the Mission in early 1980, he was glad and relieved to accept them for his own diocese.

193

'They were very efficient,' he wrote, 'and they knew how to run a diocese and to help a bishop in his work'.

Just over a year or so before, Bishop George had a refreshing break. In the middle of 1978, he attended the Lambeth Conference in the UK. Great changes had occurred in his country and his Church since the last Lambeth Conference ten years previously. Then he had travelled to England as the only national Papua New Guinean bishop with his senior expatriate bishop, David. The two of them had represented the Papua New Guinean Church which then was part of the Province of Queensland. Now, ten years later, he travelled with Bishop Rhynold, his fellow countryman. For the first time, two Papua New Guinean Bishops, together with Archbishop David and two white bishops, represented an independent Church of Papua New Guinea (see photo, page 201).

While in England, Bishop George travelled extensively, visiting parishes in many parts of the country. He even went by fast inter-city train to Glasgow, a most impressive experience. Wherever he went, he felt deeply moved by the warm welcome he received. It was reported that he made a great impact on the many people who gathered to meet him and hear him speak.[313] This was a refreshing and encouraging time for Bishop George — a time of gaining new insights and sharing ideas and experiences with the other bishops at the conference and with the people he met in the parishes.

19 July was a specially happy day for him. Together with Archbishop David and Bishop Rhynold, he was invited to the home of Maurice Wood, the Bishop of Norwich and his wife, to meet the friends of the Norwich Link. Through this organisation, the people of that Diocese had the opportunity to support their companion Diocese of Papua New Guinea with gifts and prayers. The Link had been established largely through contact with Bishop David, whose father had been a Canon of Norwich Cathedral, and through the personal interest of Bishop Wood.

On this occasion a new Land Rover was presented to Bishop George by his host on behalf of the Diocese of Norwich. Bishop Wood explained how, the previous year during his visit to PNG, he had ridden with Bishop George in his old vehicle to a service in a village near Popondetta. After that ride along the rough, bumpy bush track, he had decided that the old car must be replaced! The very generous sum of £3,953 had been collected by the people of the Norwich Diocese. On receiving the keys, Bishop George jumped into the car and drove round the garden with Bishop Maurice, his wife and Archbishop David on board. Little did he know that summer's day, as he drove round the beautiful English garden, that in some years' time this vehicle would be the beacon for many young criminals, 'rascals' as they are called. Their spies on the road to Gona and Kokoda would signal to the hidden gangs that the bishop's car was approaching their lonely hide-outs in the jungle.

During 1978, Bishop George was awarded an OBE. With typical humility, he did not have much to say or write about this event although it was greeted with joy in many parts of Papua New Guinea. Bishop George said,

I had a message from the Governor-General, Sir Kingsford Dibela, to come to Port Moresby to be invested with the award. They booked me and Marcella into a very expensive hotel by the beach. I was not happy about it. I am a simple bishop. I like to be with my people and spent my time with Fr Isaac Gadebo [a Papuan priest from Tufi, later to be consecrated Bishop of Port Moresby]. Then the ceremony took place at Government House. I was invested with the award by the British High Commissioner.[314]

Twice Bishop George went to Government House to receive honours from the Queen. Ten years later, in 1988, he was again invited to Port Moresby, this time as Archbishop of the Anglican Church in Papua New Guinea. As he writes:

When I was archbishop, another Governor-General, this one from Kerema, I have forgotten his name, invited me to Port Moresby. Again they booked us into the expensive hotel, but I refused. I stayed with Bishop Isaac. I was given the honour of KBE, but I don't wear the medals. They are from this world and from the Queen. I believe in the Queen of England, therefore I accepted. But it is all for the glory of God, not for the glory of me.

After the event in 1978, he wrote the following short letter to his sons:

My dear sons,

It was kind of you all to take thoughts on me and congratulate me for this honour which the Queen awarded to me. I know there are other people who did a far more better job than myself in this country. And I feel that I am unworthy of this honour.

May God bless you all.

Your father in Christ.

When Fr Gordon and Peggy Guy first arrived in Popondetta early in 1980, they were posted to Siroga Parish, an oil-palm settlement near Popondetta. Archdeacon Francis Cumberlege was assisting Bishop George with finance as well as running the Christian Community Centre. When Francis returned to England, Fr Gordon took over the management of the financial affairs. As Bishop George told it,

I brought Gordon and Peggy to the diocesan office. He became the diocesan secretary and the administrator and she became—a treasure! She was wonderful—very clever, efficient and working hard as my secretary. It made all the difference in the world. Fr Gordon is a very hard working man, his mind is on the job. But he has a very hot and short temper. I didn't argue with him. In the end he cooled down and saw my point of view. He can be very tough and abrupt but I didn't care about that. That was his way. He loved the people and he wanted the bishop to help them go ahead. That's the thing I was looking for and I found it.

I told them the diocese had no money and that we had to look for ways of making money and that it was in my mind to establish a shop with second-hand clothing. After a month or so, the Guys had collected from their friends a small sum with which to start the second-hand clothing store at Siroga.

During the first part of the 1980s, Bishop George was encouraged and excited by the progress of the building programme in and around Popondetta. More businesses with second-hand clothing were started in different places and they produced money. Bishop George tells of this:

The first house Fr Gordon built was Sangara Mission House. Then followed three new chapels for the oil-palm settlements of Siroga, Isivini and Sorovi. All with money from the second-hand clothing as well as from the Community Centre.

During these developments, Bishop George was still concerned to establish proper headquarters for his diocese. Fr Gordon agreed. Bishop George said,

I would like to set up a more dignified Diocesan Centre. First we must build a new Bishop's House, then a new Diocesan Secretary's house and office as well as a diocesan workshop.

The projects went ahead and the plans were completed. Bishop George moved into his new house, which stands today.

As the building programme had been carried out in and around Popondetta, Bishop George was keen to build houses of permanent materials for his priests in some of the out-stations. But he had to be careful not to favour his own home area.

If we do it at Gona or Eroro, people will say, 'Oh, Bishop is helping his *Wantoks* [relations, people of the 'one-talk']. So I planned to expand the building programme, following the order in which Copland King [one of the two founding fathers of the mission in 1891] 'put his pig on the ground' [ie established his parishes]! Therefore we started at Ambasi, where in 1900 Fr King started his first station in the Northern Papua. I gave K10,000 for the priest's house to be built of permanent materials. We did the same in other parishes.

Having the Guys to cope with the administrative and financial affairs of the diocese, Bishop George had the opportunity to be involved with the work closest to his heart. As he wrote, 'As a Diocesan Bishop, my pastoral care for my people became very vital and important in my life'. He undertook long, strenuous walks to isolated villages, being away for several weeks at a time.

My pastoral visits gave the people a chance to meet me, their Bishop, and to express their little weaknesses or successes to me. That was why I did it, not to increase my own importance, but Jesus was working in me.

One of his first pastoral patrols as Diocesan Bishop was into the Managalas, to the people on the south and south-eastern sides of Mt Lamington and the Hydrographers Range. They lived in isolated mountainous country with a culture and languages quite different from those of the Orokaiva people. In the mid-1950s, Bishop Henry Kendall, in charge of the Resurrection Parish in Popondetta, had arranged an expedition to make contact with these (as he wrote) 'completely heathen people'.[315] At Gora Village, Fr Kendall's first stop, they had been asked a question, which was repeated wherever they went in the Managalas: 'When can we have a mission?' A young teacher was asked by Bishop Kendall to go to Gora as the first step towards establishing a Christian station in the Managalas. As late as 1965, the first baptism took place in the Managalas at Gora Village.

Bishop George recalls how, on his first patrol into this area in 1967, he had visited Sakarina Station before going into the Musa River district (see maps, pp xii, xiii). He had confirmed the first Christians in that large, heathen area — at Domara Station near Safia and at Ai'ari, a mission further up the river.

Later in the 1980s when he returned, the number of missions in these isolated areas had greatly increased. The strenuous walk he undertook in this wild and rugged environment bears witness to Bishop George's physical strength and stamina. As he writes,

> It is not easy patrolling in this country with steep mountainsides, deep valleys and rivers. There were no truck roads. We walked through miles of dense jungle, following rocky riverbeds. Beside these obstacles, there were many leeches. They will get on your two feet and suck your blood.[316]

He visited several Christian communities in the Managalas where Fr Bill Houghton was in charge. The account of his visit to Sakarina, the main mission station, and its out-stations is typical of these patrols:

> A big crowd had gathered to greet us when at last we reached Sakarina where we stayed two nights with Fr Bill Houghton. Then on a fine day, Fr Bill came with me and also Sr Nancy Vesperman, an Australian nurse, and others on a long walk around his out-stations. Wherever we went, we were greeted warmly by crowds of excited people. I blessed and dedicated new chapels, interviewed confirmation candidates and took confirmations and services. We spent a week together walking around his large, mountainous parish. After visiting the last of his out-stations, I set off towards Safia and the others returned back home.

> Safia is a large parish in the upper regions of the Musa River. Fr Rhynold Sangai was in charge of Safia. The bush in the district is covered with gum trees and is teeming with wallabies and kangaroos. When the dry season comes to this particular area, the villagers live on wallabies and kangaroos. As I was walking, Fr Rhynold Sangai came to meet me at his last out-station where we spent the night. Then we walked to Namundi, had a drink of

coconut juice and pieces of pineapple before continuing together to Awala.

People from Namundi and the villages in the hills and mountains gathered together at Awala to welcome their Bishop. It was a fine welcome with feasting and dancing. I spent two nights with them, dedicating the new church and celebrating the Holy Eucharist. After one night on the way, we arrived at Safia head-station. There was another fine welcome. Mrs Lashmar Sangai, Fr Rhynold's wife, was my schoolgirl when I was a very young teacher. I felt greatly encouraged by this couple when I saw what they were trying to do for God's Kingdom. It was not an easy parish as the station was on the other side of Safia airstrip. People's homes and villages were three or four miles away from the station. They had to walk there to fetch water every morning and evening. But Fr Sangai and his wife did much to help their people and showed me that their love for God was really true.

On a second patrol, Bishop George undertook the long walk through the large area of jungle, from Safia in the mountains right down to Uiaku Mission on the coast on Collingwood Bay. Bishop George recalled this journey:

In these areas, there were no villages, only occasional rest-huts in the jungle for the Government Patrol Officer who came through. No church leaders had ever come this way. I had three police carriers of my own and two carriers from the Safia people, as they thought it was not a safe walk. There were wild pigs, kangaroos, cassowaries and big snakes around there. At night, when we made camp, we lit the Tilley lamps and fires all around. We had three guns, so we were prepared for visits by wild pigs or snakes or who knows! But, oh, it was very frightening because of all sorts of noises and because it was all untouched by human beings. On the last morning, we started walking at five o'clock and arrived at Uiaku at five in the evening. The following morning I celebrated Sunday Mass. Monday morning, the *St George*, our mission boat, picked me up and took me back to Popondetta.[317]

It was during his pastoral patrols that Bishop George experienced what he believed to be many wonders and miracles. From his early days as a young teacher-evangelist at Gomberu, he had experienced the power of faith-healing. Later, as a bishop, when he was praying and laying his hands on sick people he witnessed several seemingly miraculous healings. As he said himself,

I thank God that I was called by Him to be a bishop because He used me to do some miracles. He used me to bring blessing and healing to pregnant mothers who could not deliver their baby, and to barren women who could not have a child. They came to me for the Grace of God to help them. Many died in childbirth but many were blessed with children. Sick people, who could not be cured by doctors, came to see me. I heard their confession and gave them God's blessing and they recovered. But some of them died because God knows the heart of people by their faith. If it is strong they will get well, if their faith is weak and they depend on other people, who are weak, they can't get better.[318]

One example of such a healing occurred as he was returning home from several weeks of patrolling in the Mamba River area. He recalled the occasion.

As I was coming back along the Togaho road, I saw a woman standing by the roadside. Her husband was lying in the shade under a tree, nearly dead. His relations were sitting with him with small piles of *betel* nut and coconuts nearby. I sat down on the grass. They offered me a coconut drink. 'Why have you stopped me,' I asked. 'You tell me and I will have the drink later.' They told me his story.

The sick man was a sergeant-major in the Port Moresby police force and his wife was from Port Moresby. Because of his sickness, the police had asked him to leave the force. The doctors could do no more for him. He had come back with his pretty wife to die in his own village of Togaho. Then his wife said to me, 'Father Bishop, I am a foreigner to this community, if my husband dies I will have no one to look after me. I heard of you doing miracles and wonders, so I brought my husband out by the road. I ask you for God's blessing, please.' I did what she asked for. 'My dear daughter,' I said, 'you must have faith in God that your husband will be healed. His relations must also have faith in his recovery'. I asked them to kneel in silence and privately make their confessions. Laying my hand on the sick man, I prayed and gave him my blessing. Then I left for Popondetta. Later, he recovered. He came to my office to thank me for his healing. I said to him, 'Our Lord is mercy and love. He gives power and authority to His Church. That power was passed on to me at my Consecration, by the laying on of hands by the bishops. With that power, which I believe is in me, I pass on God's blessing'.[319]

A different aspect of his pastoral work is expressed in a message which he sent out to the people of his Diocese in the early part of his time as Diocesan Bishop. In this message he states some of the aims to be tackled by the Church during the following five years. One of the most important of these, he felt, was to upgrade the knowledge of the Scriptures of his evangelists, deacons and priests, so that they would have a deeper understanding of the teachings of the Church. In this way, they would be better prepared to run Bible Studies for the people, prayer meetings and a Christian education programme for adults and children.

Although since the time of his first Lambeth Conference in 1968, Bishop George had made great efforts to introduce traditional elements into the services, he found that many Papua New Guineans still felt they belonged to a foreign Church. As he said in his message, 'Many people in my Diocese still think and believe that the Church belongs to European society or is imported from overseas'. According to him, the only way to make the worship more meaningful was through educating the people in the teachings of the Church and through including traditional elements in the services. 'In that way, our people will feel and believe that the Church belongs to them.'

Bishop George continued right through his time as Bishop and Archbishop to work hard at marrying the Western English culture of religion with Papua New Guinea tradition. For example, he always encouraged the use of local language, music and dancing in services, as he had first done ten years ago when he composed *The Gona Mass* for the Holy Cross Church at Gona. He encouraged his own daughters to wear traditional costumes when they took part as his cope-bearers in the celebration of the Eucharist at the Resurrection Cathedral (see photograph, page 202). Martin Chittleborough spoke of Bishop George's belief in the value of the good traditional customs:

> He also worked very much on the marriage service. I remember him talking about how he wanted to see a traditional wedding mat and the bride and bridegroom, dressed in the customary way, exchanging traditional gifts. This was very important to him.[320]

Bishop George encouraged his own sons Alban and Oliver and their wives to keep the good traditions, saying he would be very proud to see them in traditional dress at their weddings (see photograph, page 202). Asked recently if he had regrets about anything in his life, he said,

> I regret very much that I did not wear traditional dress for my own wedding. Marcella's family were ready to help dressing her. She dressed up very, very well indeed. When she put on the traditional costume, she attracted me very much. A relative from Garara Village had everything ready for me to put on, but I said, 'I would like to dress up but my brother is not here'. He was away at college. According to custom, he had to decorate his younger brother. My wife was so keen for me to wear traditional costume but I said, 'I cannot do it. Please, forgive me'. I hurt her very much and I was very sorry. At that time, I would dress up for traditional dancing but not for our own special event. Later, I have felt really regretful. I was too hard. I should have worn traditional costume for my wife's sake.[321]

The five bishops from Papua New Guinea at Canterbury Cathedral,
Lambeth Conference 1978
From left: Bishops Jeremy Ashton, Rhynold Sanana, Bevan Meredith,
Archbishop David Hand and George Ambo
(Photograph courtesy of Blanche Biggs)

Bishop George with his daughters Helen Anne and Jean Margaret at the
Resurrection Cathedral, Popondetta. Wearing the single girls' costume,
they were his cope bearers during the service.

Wedding of Oliver Ambo and
Naomi, wearing traditional
costume at Bishop George's
special request.

(Photographs courtesy of
Bishop George Ambo)

CHAPTER 18

Archbishop of the Anglican Church of Papua New Guinea

The year 1983 was one of great change in the leadership of the Church. Archbishop David Hand, having reached 65, the constitutional age of retirement for PNG bishops, stood down. After thirty-seven years of devoted service to the Anglican Church of PNG (during which he brought Christianity to completely unexplored areas of the Highlands) he left the highest position vacant in the Church hierarchy. Before a new archbishop could be elected, a new Bishop of Port Moresby had to be consecrated. Each diocese had to have its own bishop before the election could take place. Fr Isaac Gadebo, a Papuan priest from Tufi, was consecrated to fill the position. Later, in November that year, the Provincial Council was to chose one of the five Diocesan Bishops to be the next Primate.[322]

Bishop George recalls the important event:

> The election took place during the meeting of the Provincial Council at the Christian Training Centre in Popondetta. According to the agenda, it was to happen after the morning-tea break. As the Senior Bishop I was chairing the meeting. Moving out of the Chairman's seat, I gave it to the Provincial Secretary who chaired the election. The first person nominated Bishop George Ambo. All the members supported him. There was no opposition. When I knew the result, my first reaction was to say, 'No, not at this stage. I won't accept it'. But Bishop Bevan said, 'George, you have to accept it'. So I agreed. Bevan Meredith was elected Senior Bishop after me and he became Archbishop when I retired. It all happened in a good spirit.[323]

In simple words, he announces an event the significance of which underlined the truth that the Church of Papua New Guinea had truly come of age.

Bishop George continued,

> From 1983–1989, I served my people as best I could. One of the things I learnt was that my prayer life and meditations became most important. My main duty as Archbishop was to make decisions. Some of these were in very serious cases and I tried to make my decisions according to God's Will. I felt this would bring peace to my people and unity in the Church. I was always aware that my fellow workers, both white and brown, had greater knowledge and a higher education than myself. But I prayed to God for guidance and I felt very strongly that the Holy Spirit was with me. Sometimes, during our meetings, I did not agree with them and there were not happy feelings among them.

The relationship between Bishop David and Bishop George had been special because it was mutual. Often they depended on each other. According to George, Bishop David was different from the other white bishops:

> In most matters concerning Papua New Guinea he trusted me for the final decision. I am not praising myself. I depended on him, but he always said, 'George, this is your country, I want you to make the final decision'.

In a recent interview in Port Moresby, Bishop David said,

> When I was thinking of becoming nationalised, it was George Ambo's opinion for which I asked. I will always get his advice.

With Bishop David's retirement from the leadership of the Church, the new archbishop had to form a different relationship with his white bishops. He said himself that generally it was good; only at the end of his official life did something happen which hurt him deeply. This will be clarified later.

Some decisions which he had to make were upsetting for Bishop George: for example, when he had to ask one of his senior clergy to resign because of his involvement in the misappropriation of Church funds. While Bishop George was overseas, attending his last Lambeth Conference in 1988, the matter of misappropriation had been investigated by the Church. When he returned, he was presented with a letter of resignation which he had to sign before the senior priest in question could resign from his position. Bishop George tells of this affair:

> When I came back from overseas, I found in my office the letter of resignation and another letter stating the details of the case and the resolution passed by the Council. It said: 'It's the Church's money. The man in question has agreed he is implicated in the affair and must step down'. But I said, 'No. Give me a week so that I can pray about it and think it over carefully'. After that, with heavy heart, I signed my signature and the senior priest resigned. But I warned that our decision would provoke division and an angry reaction.[324]

Bishop George was right. Soon afterwards, the whole congregation from the senior church leader's own place gathered under the large tree outside the Diocesan Office in Popondetta. Bishop George warned his staff not to go outside the office—the people had come to show their angry feelings against him. Fr Tom Williams, the Popondota Diocesan Secretary, recalls seeing the Archbishop going outside and talking to the enraged crowd as he tried to explain the reason for his decision.

> He was resolute about the matter and remained firm and uncompromising. He simply rode out the storm until it settled down.

A Papuan priest, Fr Lancelot Sangitari, also present at this disturbing event, recalled how brave Bishop George had been:

All by himself he faced the very thick and angry crowd. Due to his influence, their heart cooled down. Quietly they ended their demonstration and started to leave Ururu Station. Some people apologised to the Archbishop.

His period as Archbishop was to be the most troubled time in his official work for the Church. In 1985, in an address given at St John's Cathedral in Brisbane on the occasion of the silver jubilee of his consecration, he spoke about some of the current problems facing his Church and country. He spoke about families suffering, especially in towns where social ills such as alcohol, gambling and immorality had increased since the coming of independence. He mentioned that many people, unable to cope with modern Western ways, had reverted to the ways of the past, indulging in sorcery, witchcraft and payback. Unemployed young men were forming gangs. 'The break-ins, stealing, gun and knife-pointing are all on the increase in the bigger towns…' He spoke about the many religious sects infiltrating the country, adding to the confusion of the people.[325]

Bishop George was deeply concerned about the increasing influx of religious sects and movements such as the Assemblies of God and other Pentecostal groups. He saw these as posing one of the greatest threats to the survival of the Anglican Church in Papua New Guinea. In an interview with an Australian priest in 1986, he emphasised the need for help from Australia in combating this problem. He thought that a more thorough and enlightened way of teaching his people about their Anglican faith would enable them to distinguish more clearly between the values of the Anglican Church and those of the incoming sects. As he said,

> At present I need more specialist missionaries, teachers for our theological college and high schools, as well as doctors and nurses for the hospitals…but, most importantly, qualified people must come to teach our young priests to be real, committed pastors. At the moment only Fr Tom Williams, my Diocesan Secretary, is doing so. He is doing a tremendous job.

Bishop George continued,

> I need these people to convert our Anglicans from the hundreds of sects invading our country. They are far worse than cannibals! Our forefathers were cannibals and we thought it was hard for the missionaries to convert them…but it is far harder now to draw our flock back into the Anglican fold.[326]

To understand some of the reasons for Archbishop George's fears about the future survival of his Church, it is perhaps helpful to consider some of the background and teachings of the Pentecostal Movement. The first glimmer of Pentecostalism emerged in the 1890s in Kansas, USA, where a former Methodist Episcopal minister, Charles Fox Parham, established the Bethel Healing Home and the Bethel Bible School. He was inspired by the Book of Acts (2: 1-4) where Luke gives a colourful account of the early

Christians' Pentecostal experience, describing how they were filled with the Holy Spirit and broke into speech in 'other languages'. Parham saw this as being the form of a true 'Baptism in the Holy Spirit', required of all adult Christians. By insisting on this second baptism, marked by an emotional experience such as 'speaking in tongues', fainting etc., and demanding complete immersion in water, the Pentecostal teaching totally denies the validity of any previous baptism. By the rejection of any earlier baptism, this teaching radically differs from the rest of mainstream Christianity.[327]

Further afield, in Los Angeles, California, these new ideas were taken up by an Afro-American minister, William Seymour. Leading the regular worship for a congregation mainly of black Americans, he encouraged the 'speaking in tongues', a highly emotional response to his preaching, and the singing and praying 'in the spirit', all of which were seen by the worshippers as signs of a 'special anointing by the Holy Spirit'. Such were the beginnings of the new Pentecostal Movement. During the early decades of the 20th Century, the Pentecostal message flourished through the efforts of missionary organisations such as the Assemblies of God, formed in 1914 in Arkansas, USA, spreading through America and Canada into Europe, eventually reaching Papua New Guinea.

Many years later, in 1960, Pentecostal ideas entered the mainstream churches in the USA, and so began what is called the 'Charismatic Revival'. During a Sunday service in California, an episcopal (as the Anglican Church is called in America) priest announced that he had experienced the 'Baptism in the Holy Spirit' and the 'speaking in tongues'. The fact that such spiritual empowerment and revival was possible for a priest in one of the established Churches, encouraged Pentecostal evangelists to spread the Pentecostal-Charismatic Revival amongst mainstream Christians throughout the world. This development was to cause much anxiety for conservative Church leaders such as Bishop George.

In Papua New Guinea, in the late 1960s and early '70s, many Pentecostal evangelists appeared in Port Moresby, amongst them members of such Pentecostal groups as the Christian Revival Crusade and the Assemblies of God. Youth with a Mission, another of these groups, especially seeking to win adherents from the University of Papua New Guinea (UPNG) and other tertiary institutions, sparked off a Charismatic Revival amongst the students which soon spread throughout the country. Furthermore, Pentecostal-Charismatic Crusades were conducted in the major towns which drew thousands of people, clergy and laity alike.[328] Experiencing a spiritual renewal in the Baptism in the Holy Spirit, many were filled with a burning zeal to spread the Charismatic Revival movement and draw people to the Pentecostal Churches. As well, they formed Charismatic-Revivalist groups within the established Church communities, thus causing division and eroding the strength of the main conservative United, Roman Catholic and Anglican Churches.

Bishop George's fears for the survival of his Church were and still are justified by the Pentecostal 'poaching' of his people throughout the traditionally Anglican territories. Many indigenous Papua New Guineans are led to believe that the answers to their problems are found in the Pentecostal-Charismatic movement. With the growth of social ills such as immorality, violence, criminal activity, corruption, gambling and alcoholism, they hope for God's intervention in such evil times. This hope they come to expect from the teachings of Pentecostalism.

The emphasis on the divine truth of all teachings in the Bible, being the Word of God and sole authority for Christian living (a point of view also shared by fundamentalist Christians within the established Churches), gave Pentecostal converts a sense of absolute certainty and guidance in their lives. The prohibition on social evils such as alcoholic drinks enabled many Papua New Guineans to take a stand against the temptations of the Western world.

Being naturally open to spiritual influences, the indigenous people easily embraced the clear Pentecostal-Charismatic message of accepting Jesus as their personal Saviour. Finding in the simple and informal kind of service, joy, freedom and spiritual empowerment, they would break into spontaneous worship. Making confessions and responding with strong emotional reactions to the concept of divine forgiveness, they enthusiastically began 'speaking in tongues', crying, clapping and praying in the Spirit. The singing of easy-to-learn hymns and repetitive choruses added to their sense of joyful ecstasy and spiritual fellowship. Often distrustful of Western medicine they valued the Pentecostal-Charismatic emphasis on miracles and the faith-healing of physical illnesses, or the exorcism of evil spirits from their minds.

Empowered by such strong spiritual and emotional experiences, a burning desire to evangelise was ignited in the hearts of many adherents. Often using excessive emotional persuasion, they threatened potential converts with hell after death if they did not reject the validity of their previous baptism, as outlined above, and experience the 'Baptism in the Spirit'. Accused of being opponents of Christ, many conventional Christians defected from their own Churches. Such was (and still is) the fearful onslaught of the sects which Bishop George had to combat, to keep his people within the Anglican fold.

It seemed to him that the Australian Church was not trying hard enough to find trained expatriates willing to assist the young Church of Papua New Guinea, not just in its fight against the sects, but generally with its increasing social and economic problems. Added financial assistance was urgently needed for its future growth. He asked,

> Are they blind? Do they not see the hard work done by those missionaries who gave their lives for the Anglican Church in this country? Will all their efforts now be wasted?[329]

He pleaded for more money from the Australian Church. His five Dioceses needed help to stand on their own feet.

We don't want to ask for money, but the need for money at this critical stage is very great. If the Australian Church will not give us any more, we will be in big trouble. Yes, I believe we ought to stand on our own feet. At the moment we are trying to do so, but we can't do it by ourselves.

Archbishop George did his part to ease the financial burden for his Diocese. One of his major concerns was to assist his retiring priests 'who had served God for ages'. A superannuation fund, or Staff Retirement Fund (SRR), had already been established, which was controlled by the Provincial Office. 'But it is not enough,' said Bishop George. 'A retired priest could not live on that money. It is pocket money!' He wanted to help his priests build a home for their retirement. With the increasing amount of traditional land and gardens being subdivided into blocks for oil-palm cultivation, less land was available for subsistence farming. A retiring priest would often find, when he came back to his own village, that his relatives had left no land for him and his family. Nor could he find bush materials to build his home, as the bush had all been replaced by oil-palm trees. As Bishop George put it,

So I was looking for money. I was wondering about the future running of the Diocese. I had the idea of establishing a Priests' Retirement Fund.

In 1986 he undertook a long walk all around his parishes to raise funds.

I walked and walked, along the beaches and in and out of the hills and mountains, to the villages and the parishes. It took me one whole year to do my pastoral visits and the fundraising. I was well supported by the people because they trusted me and I raised K42,000 which was invested for future use by the Provincial Office in Lae.

According to Fr Tom Williams, Archbishop George launched the new Retirement Fund at a meeting of the Synod. It had been established for the retired Clergy of Popondota Diocese and was intended to be additional to the SRF. After Bishop George had retired, he reminded the priests of Popondota and the bishops coming after him about this fund. He wondered,

Had they discovered this money, and how much interest had it generated? But they seemed to know little about it. And I didn't have a clue. I hope the money is still there. It is not my business to check. But I have done my part. I started it all.[330]

Some time after his fundraising walk, a situation occurred in which Archbishop George demonstrated that he could be ruthless and uncompromising if he felt he was right, even if it meant standing up to his white bishops. At a Provincial Council meeting, he discovered that, long before, another sum of K46,000 had been put aside. It had been designated for Retired Clergy. He recalled that Bishop Henry Kendall once had told him of this sum of money:

When I was at school, the money was raised by Edward Guise, [a mission sea captain and] father of Sir John Guise, first Governor-General of the independent Papua New Guinea. My mother told me how, during his voyages, the captain went round to the various villages and homes along the coast asking for sixpence. That money was later kept in the Provincial Office for the retirement of priests. When I was a schoolboy, it was invested and the interest had built it up to K46,000. At the meeting, I said to Bishop Rhynold Sanana, then Bishop of Dogura, that we must take this money out and share it because it had been given by the people of our two areas. But we had to fight the white bishops for the right to that money. I said to the white bishops that it was not their money. Their dioceses had not contributed to this fund. It belonged to our people.

According to Fr Tom Williams, Archbishop George fought for this money with the National Secretary, the Bishop's Conference and the Provincial Council until at last they gave in. He had been 'quite uncompromising' about not sharing with the other dioceses despite the white bishops' insistence on his doing so.

Oh, we had a meeting at Popondetta. I stood firm and stuck to my view. Finally, the white bishops gave in and the money was given to me and Bishop Rhynold for the help of retired clergy in our dioceses.

At this stage, Bishop George was feeling more and more disappointed with the state of his country and his Church. Although in his leadership of the Church he was still strong and uncompromising, in political matters he was less active and vocal than he had been at the time of independence. Some people felt that he was not sufficiently outspoken regarding public issues. Stephen Tago, the former Minister for Defence who knew him well, was one of these. He thought the Archbishop should have been more definite in his criticism of the political leaders of the nation, and of Oro Province. Perhaps a growing disillusionment with the moral standards and behaviour of the politicians made him quiet. According to Stephen, such malpractices as embezzlement of government funds, misuse of time, bribery and corruption had grown increasingly worse in the years after Independence. Immorality flourished amongst the national and provincial government leaders. The principles of Christian marriage were often ignored, especially amongst politicians who frequently indulged in having more than one wife. As Stephen Tago said,

The Archbishop should have spoken out more openly, denouncing the evil doers living in sin and proclaiming the Christian principles.

Arthur Jawodimbari, one of the young writers of the early '70s, agreed:

Some of the leaders of the other main Churches have been very outspoken in criticising the Government and certain of their policies. But that was not Bishop George's way. I can't remember him being outspoken in any issues to do with the Government or in any political issues as such. When asked questions to do with matters in the Church or in the community, he expressed his personal views, but his leadership was of the quiet kind. I don't think he ever spoke out against the Government.[331]

During the 1980s, the problem of crime amongst the unemployed youth in and around urban centres was fast increasing. Bishop George was deeply concerned for these young law-breakers, 'rascals', as they were called. He thought one of the main causes for rascal activity, apart from unemployment, was the showing of violent Western films and videos depicting rape, robbery and fighting. They set a bad example for the young Papua New Guineans, who learnt from these films and tried to copy them. Bishop George recalls discussing the problem of crime at a Diocesan Council meeting. Thinking the Church might be able to influence the Government in this matter, he said, 'Haven't we the authority to make a law to stop the printing and showing of the wrong sort of pictures?' They all agreed, and a public statement from the Church appeared in the newspapers. The Government took no notice. The influence of the Church on the State was no longer strong and important as it had been at the time of Independence. Few politicians now had been influenced by Christian teaching. It seemed the Western way of separation between Church and State had been adopted by the Government of the young nation. The people depended increasingly on the wrong sort of politicians coming into power. Bishop George spent much time preaching in the churches and talking to his people about social problems, warning them of the unhappy consequences of crime. He encouraged his priests to do the same.

> We did our share as a Church but, sad to say, the young people did not listen to us. Some of the priests' sons joined the criminals and formed rascal gangs. I was so disappointed.[332]

He felt deeply concerned for these lost young people under his spiritual care. Perhaps the main part of his work as archbishop was taken up with trying to persuade them to come back to the fold. He recalls many cases of close contact with the criminals and of some successes, such as the following one:

> Once I was going down to Keoje, where my own place is, on part of my ancestors' land (see map, page xiii). I was going down to make a garden for our living. In those days we didn't have enough food to feed ourselves. I didn't have enough land in Popondetta to grow my own *taro* and bananas. Some days I would leave in my Land Rover at five in the morning and start work at seven in my garden at Keoje. I would drive back in time for Evensong. It was very tough but I did it for my family's sake.
>
> Once, on the trip back to Popondetta, some rascals were hiding in the bush by the roadside, between Gona and Beuru Village. Seeing me alone in my Land Rover, they jumped out. 'Father, have mercy on us, we are your bad children,' they said. I stopped. They

wanted me to take two of their leaders to town to buy food and kerosene for their Fellowship the coming Friday. I said, 'The shops are closed. Where will you buy it?' 'From our Wantoks,' they said. Although I thought they would steal it, I felt it was their need if they were going to have joy with other people. So I dropped them at the Chinese store in town.

On the Saturday, they came to see me. 'Father, we would like to thank you for giving our two men a lift. They got the kerosene and we enjoyed our social gathering.' 'I will try my best to visit you in the jungle,' I said. One day I sent a message, 'Your Father in God will visit you'. My wife didn't like it. I went alone. Their two leaders came out to meet me on the road. Their spies had seen I was alone in my Land Rover. The others were hidden in the jungle, ready with their guns in case I had brought the police. I walked into their camp. They go bush, like little fawns. Their sleeping nets were tied to the trees. 'Father, we will give you some money,' they said. 'Your money is dirty money,' I answered. 'I do not want it. I came here to meet you and talk to you. I want you to change your life'.

Oh, I struggled for one year. I went down by myself to talk to them often, to the ones who were available. One of the leaders was my own cousin of the Somboba Clan at Garara. 'Come home,' I said. 'Be with your clan; use your strength to build a canoe, get married, make a home and be full of joy with wife and children'. I pleaded for hours. At the next visit I said, 'I think time has come. I don't want you to stay in hiding any longer'. They said, 'Father, we will surrender. Take us to the police'. First they made their confession at the Holy Cross Church. Then I went back to notify the police. A couple of priests went down in a vehicle with me. The two leaders and twelve followers were waiting. 'My sons, are you ready?' I asked. 'Yes, Father, we are ready.' 'Do not worry about your life. I will be with you. Your life is in my care'. All the armed police met us at the station in Popondetta. I wore my cassock. The rascals walked with me, side by side, close to me.

Bishop George's influence amongst the young criminals was very significant. Quietly they handed over their guns. Trying to calm the police, he recalled what he said to them and what happened subsequently.

'I am bringing to you converted Papua New Guineans. I have heard their confessions and they are born-again men. I warn you not to beat them or mistreat them. If you do we will lose them'. The police accepted what I said. After one week they released them to their homes. Later, one of the two leaders, Philip, who lived at Jegarata Village on the outskirts of Popondetta, played up again. He was shot dead by the police. He left a good wife and two or three children. The other one at Beuru is now a good man. I think the other rascals down there are converted.

But there were other young criminals in the area in those years. Many would come in the night to Bishop George's house when they were hungry. Bishop George recalled one of these visits:

> They knocked on my door. 'Who are you?' 'Father, your bad sons.' I didn't wake my wife. I came out. 'Are you hungry only in your body, or is your spirit hungry too?' I fed them. Some came back. They were later killed by police. Among them was one of my own Somboba Clan. He was killed too.
>
> Another gang was operating in the Kokoda area. They stopped me many times on the Kokoda Road. I talked to them and prayed for them. I thought they must know that someone still cares for them, that I still loved them, although they were sinners. Their circumstances had made them hard. Sometimes they told me lies, but they never attacked me. They knew I respected them as human beings; that I was not frightened. That was the main thing. Wherever I was, walking or driving around, trying to do my job, taking confirmations, visiting depressed and downhearted communities where some people were victims of crime, the rascals let me through. I felt I must be with them. If I was not, they would all go down, down the hill. Nobody else would go into the rascal areas, so I carried on during those years as Archbishop, driving alone in my Land Rover from Kokoda down to the coast, beyond Oro Bay and all the way to Bareji. It was a dangerous time.

Tragic events unfolded during 1989, the Archbishop's last year before retirement. Four people in Oro Province—an oil-palm worker, a health officer and a villager, as well as an expatriate missionary—were killed by rascals. The author, who was living at that time near Agenehambo Village at the Martyrs' School where her husband was headmaster, wrote of the situation to a friend. Having herself been held up some months before by hooded gunmen, she had first-hand experience of the chaotic conditions:

> We have all been through a most worrying time with the outbreak of lawlessness all around us. For several weeks, four armed gangs have been operating in different areas of Oro Province. The police have been unable to cope with this exceptional situation. This latest spate of violence began at the end of March with the escape of seven prisoners from Biru Prison in Popondetta. One of these prisoners was responsible for the killing of Athol Smith, our Manager at Awala. [Awala was a plantation about seven kilometres up the road from the main school. It had been acquired during the time of a previous headmaster, to teach the students agricultural management and cultivation of crops such as cocoa, coffee, rubber, pineapples and so on. It was a most innovative and inspirational experiment, which sadly could not continue.]

Elin Johnston's letter went on:

The attack seemed inspired purely by the lure of money. The criminals were after the takings from the plantation cocoa fermentary and trade store. Athol Smith was murdered because he disturbed the thieves in the middle of breaking into the safe. They feared he might give evidence.[333]

Following the murder and subsequent trouble with the traditional landowners, Bishop George, as Chairman of the Board of Governors of the school, together with the members of the Board, decided to close Awala. In a message to the staff and students he wrote:

> Just now we are going through a very critical stage of our country and nation and I, as Archbishop of the Anglican Church and Chairman of the Board of Governors, am not happy with the recent event that took place at Awala. The spirit behind the killing of Athol Smith, our missionary manager, was evil...when the killing happened and the sad news of our Anglican Church was brought to the whole world, I felt deeply sorry. Later, I met his daughter in Sydney. She came and saw me at the ABM office, forgiving us and challenging our Church, Martyrs', and the person who killed her father. 'I hope that boy's future won't be spoilt,' she said. 'He especially must not lose hope completely by having chosen the wrong way...' Her father came to help us grow in a Christian way and the school must carry on in that spirit, forgiving each other, loving each other, helping each other and taking his spirit to the communities nearby, so that people will get rid of their evil thoughts...

True to Archbishop George's compassionate nature, he preached forgiveness and reconciliation even in a case of murder.

Towards the end of 1989, if you drove along the Kokoda Road towards Popondetta, it could happen that you would be stuck behind a truck. On its back, you would see young men standing up, singing hymns and waving guns in the air. They were on their way to the police to surrender their weapons. Gradually the rascals dispersed from the area, some going by boat to Lae, others walking the Kokoda Track to Port Moresby, while most settled down in their villages. Mainly due to Archbishop George's amazing efforts, relative peace came back to Oro Province.

But other conflicts occurred which demanded the Archbishop's attention and which also illustrate his capacity for forgiveness. A year or so before his retirement, a long-simmering land dispute erupted which caused him one of the greatest sadnesses of his life. It involved Fr Albert Maclaren Ririka, his friend and relation by marriage. Fr Albert and Marcella were cousins. According to Bishop George, their parents had divided the ancestral land near Kausada Village (formerly Old Gona), giving each of the cousins their share. Ever since the time of their marriage, Marcella's land had adjoined George's land, but Albert Maclaren had never felt the division had been right and fair. After all those years, the question of land ownership suddenly came to a head. At one point, Fr Albert's people provoked a fight with the family and friends of George and Marcella. Bishop George tells of it:

> When I had a message about the disturbance, I went down to protect my home. It was going up in flames. They were singing and dancing the local war dance. All my banana and coconut palms had been cut down and my dinghy was broken into pieces. I was open to revenge. Satan was in my spirit. It seemed as if he said to me, 'Come on, George, you have the manpower, you take revenge'. As soon as I stood up, my sons and my people were behind me. They blew the conch-shell for fighting. At that moment, the words from the Bible came into my mind: 'Father, forgive them, for they do not know what they are doing'. In front of them all, I sat down. We did not take revenge.

The following day, the police came to investigate the case, and a day later Archbishop George and Marcella were to leave for Australia and New Zealand to say their farewells before retirement. Before leaving, George warned his sons,

> 'Do not give any permission for revenge while I am away. People from Garara Village, Katuna and many other places from my side will want to come and damage Fr Albert's property but don't give permission.' When I came back from New Zealand, I thanked my sons for following my advice. Then Fr Albert came to Bishop's House to apologise to me and Marcella for what he and his people had done to their Bishop. He offered me a sum of money. I said, 'Fr Albert, customarily you are my brother-in-law, spiritually you are my brother in Christ because we were ordained together, but I will not accept your money. I will be happy if you make your confession and put yourself right with God. If you are truly sorry His blessing will come upon you'. After this I forgave him and my wife's people at Kausada and we tried our best to return their actions with good. Gradually, I am happy to say, we won them back. This event taught me that as a Christian we must try to carry our troubles with Jesus, and in the end we shall receive many blessings.[334]

Before retiring, Bishop George tried to visit every parish in his diocese. In the end he ran out of time. With sadness he recalls that three parishes, Ako, Sefoa and Ajoa, had made all the preparations to welcome him and Marcella, but they could not complete their program of farewell visits.

> I was very, very sad indeed to let them down and apologised to them. But all the other parishes welcomed us with great warmth. My people entertained us wonderfully and presented us with many valuable gifts, with kisses and tears falling from their eyes. We felt strongly that they loved, respected and honoured us, showing full confidence in us. As well, we visited the other dioceses and were thankful for their feelings of gratitude to us.

Only his own parish of Holy Cross, Gona, did not show appreciation for what he and Marcella had done for them. They had a negative attitude towards him. Bishop George was very unhappy about this:

> We felt very, very sad, that my own brothers and sisters, aunts, uncles and many with whom I went to school or whom I had taught had evil spirits in their hearts. This reminded me that when Jesus visited his home town of Nazareth, his own people went against Him and tried to kill Him (St Luke 4: 16-30). This happened to me at Gona. However, soon after my retirement, the new co-ordinator of the Mothers' Union apologised to me on behalf of the members.

Also, while overseas, George and Marcella tried for the last time to visit all their friends. The year before, in 1988, on the occasion of the Lambeth Conference, they had made their farewells in the UK. They spent one month travelling around England.

> In every home we visited we were received with joy and gratitude of hearts. When we entered the palace of the Archbishop of Canterbury, Robert Runcie, he himself came out to meet us, kissing us both. He put his hands on our shoulders, and as we sat together he talked to us both. Having received his blessing in his private chapel, we felt so thankful for his love and for the respect he showed to us two simple people.

During the final trip to Australia in 1989, they met many friends and ex-missionaries. As Bishop George wrote,

> It was Marcella's second visit, and she was grateful to ABM for inviting us. This time she realised it had not been easy for the missionaries from overseas to offer for service in Papua. She understood it was a great sacrifice for them, leaving parents, friends and beautiful homes behind. They had to adjust to a living standard much lower than their own. Reflecting on these things in her heart, she also saw that many Papua New Guinean Christians did not fully understand the missionaries from overseas.

> At home in Popondetta, I was trying to bring up to date the records at the diocesan office and put them into order for my successor as Diocesan Bishop of Popondota. I thank Fr Tom Williams, my Diocesan Secretary, for his committed and devoted service. At the same time I was thinking about and praying that the right person would be elected to follow me. I must reveal in the sight of God that I disagreed with the choice of my successor and the one who followed him. I blame myself for not advising the Bishops' Electoral Committee to be careful in choosing the right person for the right job. Especially regarding the election of a bishop, it is important that we all do away with the influence of the 'One-Talk' [*wantok*] System, ie the tendency to favour our own relatives. We must let the Holy Spirit guide us in the choice of the right spiritual Father for us all.

The years as Archbishop had been a mixture of joy and sadness. Perhaps the greatest disappointment was the Provincial Council's decision not to extend George's term as Archbishop. As we read his own account of the end of his official life, his sadness and resentment at this decision are clear:

> The date for my Retirement at the end of the year was drawing near. The year for our Centenary of our Anglican Church was also coming close. The Centenary celebrations would begin a year or so after I was due to retire. These celebrations were especially important because they marked the arrival of our first Anglican missionaries. On August 10th 1891, Albert Maclaren and Copland King stepped ashore at Kaieta near Wamira Village. During the year 1989, when I was 67 years old and my retirement was slightly overdue, we had a Provincial Council meeting at Port Moresby. At that meeting, they talked about my retirement at the end of the year. Bishop Isaac Gadebo asked the Council to allow me to stay in Office for one more year and a bit to celebrate the Centenary with them as their Archbishop. The other bishops were silent, but the Senior Bishop, an Australian who succeeded me as Archbishop, said that according to the rules of the Church I must go. I was sad, but I received his decision in a Christian spirit. After the meeting I was thinking and pondering it over and over again. I strongly felt that my Church should have allowed me to be with them as their own Papua New Guinean Archbishop on this very big and important day in the history of our Anglican Church of Papua New Guinea.[335]

Despite disappointments and difficulties, Archbishop George at his retirement was able to look back on a successful fulfilment of his Call to be his country's first Papua New Guinean Bishop. In an interview, he said,

> Looking back on twenty-nine years, I see that God has blessed us very much. During these twenty-nine years, my wife, brothers and sisters who came to help me, were all of my own colour. They were my own and they were first-class people. But missionaries also came from overseas to help me and my Bishop's home was always open to them. All these things happened by the Grace of God. Thank you from the bottom of my heart, for the support in money, gifts, manpower and prayer from overseas and especially for the Martyrs. Because of their prayers in Heaven, and because of prayers and support in Australia, England and other parts of the world, the Papua New Guinean Church was established. As I have experienced, it is not easy to be a bishop. It is hard work, but I have tried to stand up for what I believed to be right. At times, people went against me but in the end they saw my point and they repented. I thank God that I was called by Him to be a bishop. God used me to do miracles and pastoral care for His people. He called me to do things for Him.[336]

Farewell celebration at Agenehambo Village on the occasion of Archbishop
George's retirement at the end of 1989 (Photographs: Elin Johnston)

Bishop George at the Consecration of Fr Walter Siba, his successor as
Diocesan Bishop of Popondota, at The Resurrection Cathedral, Popondetta
(Photograph courtesy of Chris Luxton)

It is undeniable that the end of his full-time ministry was on a low note. His life in retirement was to be filled with work, however, and work for Bishop George, however hard, has been a joy. Perhaps this quality of joy, which radiates from his whole being, is best illustrated by the following story told by his former Archdeacon, Martin Chittleborough:

> I remember once walking up to a small village behind Eiwo to help them prepare for baptism, confirmation and the blessing of a new church and all sorts of celebrations. I went up the day before to ensure that it was all going to happen. George came up at night. He used to walk a lot at night. I remember he arrived about nine o'clock. We were just having tea and we were talking to the candidates and I said to him, 'Bishop, I think everything is organised now'. And he said, 'But Martin, that's all very well, but is it joyful?' He had that belief that worship must be joyful. He sat up that night, probably all night, I certainly weakened and went to bed, and with great enthusiasm he played music and taught the people. He taught them new songs so that when the next day's celebrations came, they knew how to sing, they knew how to dance and they knew the new songs.[337]

Taking with him into retirement the qualities of strength, joy and enthusiasm, Bishop George's radiant personality continues to have a deep impact upon his people.

CHAPTER 19

Retirement

After Bishop George's official retirement at the end of 1989, he and Marcella moved from Popondetta to live on their own land near the sea. Their place is between Kausada and Kurou, the villages of their birth. The address is as follows: 'Toumo and Waragi Nati (village), Keoje'. Bishop George explains,

> Toumo and Waragi are the names of the orchids which grow in our garden—they are the ancient totem for my Somboba Clan. Keoje is the name of a creek which flows near our house. It is also the name of the red flowers which grow all along its banks.

Thus the address means 'the village of orchids by the creek of red flowers'—a beautiful name indicating the importance for Bishop George of the ancestral tradition of the orchid totem of his clan.[338]

As you visit Bishop George and Marcella at Keoje, you will see several buildings in the large garden. Their simple house is of fibro-cement sheets with a corrugated-iron roof, while his private chapel nearby is of traditional bush materials. Close to the house stands a small bush hut with a cross on the roof. Set in its own carefully tended garden, this is Fr Simon Peter's 'tomb-house' above his grave. Some years into retirement, in 1997, Bishop George had to bury his beloved brother:

> He is in his little grave and I will keep him close to my home. I wanted to bury him near me so that I can look after him. One day, the children will decide where to put the bones of him and of others in the family.

It had been a small funeral for Fr Simon Peter, with just his close relations and some clergy who lived nearby. Contrary to custom, Bishop George is against the traditional, long period of mourning followed by a death feast. As he said,

> I wanted to bury him quickly, so that a lot of people didn't have time to come. If they wanted to see him they should see his wife instead. I did not want to keep him for a long time in the morgue.

Stephen Tago, an old friend of the family, was assisting at the funeral. He recalls the occasion:

> After the body had been for one day in the morgue, we took it down to Keoje. We went by ambulance and when we arrived Bishop George came out in his purple gown. The vehicle reversed close to the grave. The hole had been dug already. As they took the body

Bishop George and Marcella by their home at Keoje, 1998
(Photographs: Elin Johnston)

Bishop George's chapel in his garden at Keoje, 1998

Simon Peter Awoda's 'tomb-house' set above his grave. It is close to
Bishop George's house, seen at the back to the right.
(Photographs: Elin Johnston)

out, he said, 'I welcome you, Fr Simon Peter'. Then calling him by the clan name he continued, 'Somboba, God called you and me to serve Him. He has now called you to rest. I welcome you to our home'. His body was taken to the shelter where a small gathering prayed together. Soon after, he was laid in the ground inside the little 'tomb-house.[339]

According to Stephen Tago and to Oliver Ambo, who was also at the funeral, Bishop George did not break down. He is a man of strong feelings, but he keeps them deep down in his heart. He did not show any emotion although he had loved his brother dearly, so much so that he had given him his own son. And so much, that in death he wanted him to rest close to his own house. Believing that at death the Christian soul goes to the Lord, he preaches that we must not cry for long but thank God for the life of somebody who has died. Stephen Tago said,

> He did not consider other people's feelings in that. He believed he was right and that others must follow his example. He lives what he preaches.

Although many people from different places in Oro Province felt upset that they were not given time to attend the burial of Fr Simon Peter and pay him their last respects, Bishop George's ideas about mourning for the dead have generally been accepted by the Christian communities in his province. According to Bishop Denys Ririka, Fr Albert Maclaren's son, the normal practice nowadays is to keep the body in the morgue for one or two days, followed by a short period of mourning.

> You can always tell if people are still mourning after burial. If the shelters built for the mourners are still standing, then the mourning is still going on. Usually they are pulled down within a week, whereas in the old days they would stand for months. Bishop George is an influential man and not afraid to break with local custom. His new ideas on mourning have spread throughout this Province.[340]

In his retirement Bishop George is still much concerned with making the Church really meaningful for the indigenous people. He continues to work with the translation of the liturgy from English into *Ewa-ge* and *Binandere*, two of the major local languages. This work he had already started in his early years as bishop. As discussed previously, at that time he was inspired by his experiences at the Lambeth Conference in 1968 and also by what he saw on his travels which followed. He came back and started work on a liturgy for the Holy Eucharist in *Ewa-ge*, his own language. This eventually led to his creation of *The Gona Mass*, which became a model for other Christians, inspiring them to use their own languages and music in worship.

His life is as active and full of purpose as ever before. He is now working on putting together a new prayer book, which will be in both the *Ewa-ge* and

Binandere languages. Having recently completed the *Binandere Liturgy*, he is still translating the services of Matins and Evensong into his mother tongue. When this work is finished, he plans to combine the two local liturgies in one prayer book for the coastal people. As well, he hopes to include hymns in these languages. He says,

> I am writing new hymns. I would like to put my own hymns in *Ewa-ge* together with those of Fr Copland King, the early missionary, who translated English hymns into *Binandere*. My aim is to complete and have published a new prayer book containing the two liturgies as well as Fr Copland's and my own hymns, all in *Binandere* and *Ewa-ge*. Such a prayer book will make the coastal people of Oro Province feel that their Church is not imported but [that] it is their own and it belongs to them.[341]

Bishop George also sees it as a major part of his work to combat the influence of other religious groups, drawing the straying Anglicans back to their own Church. As he says,

> Oro Province is now full of sects and they build their little chapels and divide the whole Anglican community into many different groups.

The present Archbishop, James Ayong, has licensed him to help with this particular work, allowing him to preach and talk to different groups of Christians, explaining to them the Anglican Faith. He frequently travels to Christian communities in the diocese when invited to preach or take Bible Studies. In his words,

> I pray with them and run workshops, teaching the meaning of 'The One Holy Catholick and Apostolick Church'.[342]

The following incident illustrates how important this task is for Bishop George. According to his son Oliver, living in Port Moresby, George was severely ill in 1998 with malaria and pneumonia. A message was sent to Oliver to come quickly to Keoje. He recalled what he found:

> When I arrived on Holy Cross Day, to my surprise Mum was preparing buns for Dad to take to the Holy Cross Station. Dad said he was all right and went off to attend the celebrations. That night he told Marcella to get his things ready because the next morning he was travelling with Bishop Rhynold Sanana to Nindewari Village. It was a long way by boat, past the mouth of the Kumusi up to the Gira River and then a good distance inland up the river.
>
> I was angry. I said, 'Do you mean to say you are going to Nindewari when I came all the way here to visit you in bed! God knows you are sick'. 'I know,' said my father. 'This has been planned for a year. I have promised to preach the sermon. Bishop Sanana is going to celebrate. I can't miss this occasion of the annual gathering of the members of the St Francis Order.'

He was very ill with fever. He shouldn't have gone. He was not strong enough to travel that long way by small dinghy but he couldn't let them down. He couldn't break his word.[343]

His dedication to the work of deepening the faith of isolated communities was all-important.

Just as Bishop George expects much of himself, so he has always expected self-discipline from others, even his young sons. Oliver recalls an incident from his childhood which, as we shall see, in a rather remote way can be linked to another important aspect of Bishop George's work, namely his fight against the belief in cargo cult. As Oliver recounted,

When I grew up my father was very strict and very severe with me and my brothers. He would never tolerate any wrongdoings. When I was about eight or nine, we lived at Dogura. I was a Cathedral Boy, which meant I had jobs to do before and after the service. On this particular occasion it was my turn to take the collection plate over to the rector's house. My father had ordered a wooden box for me from Samarai for the collection. He had paid for part of it but four shillings was owing. As I walked across the playing field I put my hand in the box and took out four shillings. I thought I would give them to my father to pay the money owing for the box. I was wearing a *bo*, originally a strip of bark cloth, but in my time a piece of material tied around my waist, and I hid the money in my *bo*. In those days you wore a white one on Sundays for Church and other colours for ordinary days. When I was changing in the house the four shillings fell out. My father said, 'Where did you get that money?' I said nothing. 'So you stole from God. What was given to Him, you took back. I cannot accept this. You will have punishment.' He took me down the gully and beat me with a piece of timber. Then he left me. I weakly walked to my aunt's home nearby.

Later, he came to take me home. He sat down with me and said, 'I beat you because I love you'. He then told me the story of a man who had never had people teaching him to do the right thing. He grew up doing wrong things and eventually got into real trouble doing evil things. The authorities decided to hang him. As he stood at the gallows he was asked if he had anything to say to his parents, relatives, or teachers before his death. This is what he said: 'Who are my parents? Who are my relatives and my teachers? I had none. If I had those, they would have taught me not to do wrong things. They would have corrected me'.

'My son', said my father, 'I don't want you to have to talk like that man. That's why I beat you'. After I grew up I realised my father loved me. [344]

The background for this story can be traced to the widespread belief in cargo cult, which is still a big problem for Bishop George today; as he says,

Many people in this province are still believing in cargo cult. I don't know how I will do it, and how other bishops cope with it, but I as an old, retired man am still trying to get rid of that false belief.

The background for Oliver's story is as follows. The man sentenced to death, of whom George Ambo spoke to his son when he had stolen the four shillings, was Embogi, a former village constable from a place on Mt Lamington. Early in 1943, during the Pacific War, when the Japanese occupation of the Buna area had ended, Embogi, together with some of his compatriots, had been arrested by officials of ANGAU (Australian New Guinea Administrative Unit). Suspected of having assisted the enemy forces, they were charged with the betrayal of several Europeans, including May Hayman and Mavis Parkinson (two of the Anglican Martyrs), and with the murders of Allied servicemen. They were sentenced to death by hanging.[345]

Many investigations were made at that time of Papuan men who were suspected of treason or murder. Tom Grahamslaw, an Australian District Officer in Northern Papua, was involved in these investigations, and wrote an account of two hangings which he witnessed near the recently-established Higaturu Government Station on Mt Lamington. Embogi was amongst the group of men to be executed in the first hangings. (Records held by ANGAU verified that twenty-two Papuan men were executed by hanging at Higaturu Station in 1943. The following year, more hangings were carried out by the Australian military authorities, bringing the total to 34 deaths).[346]

According to Tom Grahamslaw, thousands of people from nearby villages gathered to watch the executions. Before the start of the grim proceedings, a government interpreter explained to them in their own language why their fellow Papuans had to die. Then each one of the five condemned men was given a last chance to speak to his people. Tom Grahamslaw later wrote,

> Embogi's speech had a profound effect on all of us. The gist of his speech was that he went wrong because he was uneducated and did not know any better. He freely admitted his crimes and said that the punishment he was about to receive was just. He concluded by enjoining his people to heed what the government said and to obey its laws.

According to Grahamslaw, it was further reported that Embogi attributed his wrongdoings to the lack of teachers and his inadequate knowledge of the Christian faith. He entreated his people, especially the village councillors, to ensure that in future their children would all go to school and would all be brought up as Christians in a Christian community. So ended the life of Embogi and his fellow Papuan transgressors, suffering a punishment at the hands of a white Government acting according to the ancient tribal code of 'an eye for an eye and a tooth for a tooth…'.

When Bishop George was asked if he thought that the hangings at Higaturu had been a just punishment for the traitors, he did not give a direct answer. Deeply sad about the whole affair, he did not offer blame or judgment, saying,

> I strongly believe it was part of God's purpose for my people. He
> let it happen to teach them a lesson.

Generally it was thought that the reason for the crimes was the fact that a
number of Papuan men had seen the enemy arriving in their thousands, so
they thought the Japanese would be their future masters. They saw the few
Europeans in the district as the losing party, not worthy of cooperation.

Bishop George and the villagers of the Mt Lamington area knew the real
reason behind the behaviour of the traitors: the teachings of the local cargo
cult. As Bishop George said,

> Many of my people believed then, and are still believing today,
> that their ancestor spirits are giving them food and other things
> needed for a good life. They believe they must serve the spirits in
> return. Some time before the Japanese invaded, certain villagers
> were teaching the people that their ancestors would be coming from
> overseas in a big boat bringing cargo for them all. The missionaries,
> both white and brown, were not told of these false ideas. When the
> Japanese soldiers came, the villagers walked up to meet them,
> saying, 'Aye, our ancestors are coming'. Therefore they served the
> Japanese. Their own spiritual belief made them do the wrong things.
> They had not been under the influence of a Christian Mission. My
> personal conviction is that God let the hangings happen to teach
> these people, because they strongly believed in the cargo cult. Also
> it is God's lesson for future generations. But these false ideas are
> persisting. Even today as an old man in my retirement, I am still
> spending much time trying to get rid of that belief.[347]

In 1997 an incident occurred which was to have a sad outcome for Bishop
George. Ever since the destruction of his place shortly before his retirement, ill
feelings had been simmering amongst some of the people at Kausada,
Marcella's village, and certain members of his own clan at Kurou. Although
he had long since forgiven them all, occasional arguments and disagreements
had been going on between the two clans, especially between the young people.
Suddenly the hostility came to a head. According to Bishop George, they
quarrelled about the rape of a Kausada girl. Although some young men from
her own village were guilty, they falsely accused some Kurou men of the crime.
One Sunday morning trouble flared up. As the guilty men were walking back
from service at Holy Cross Station, they were attacked and beaten by members
of Bishop George's clan. The wounded victims retaliated by burning down
some Kurou garden-houses. One of the owners of the burnt houses, an ex-
convict, then walked to Kausada carrying his gun. He demanded that the
perpetrators of the fire own up. As nobody did, he walked back to the beach.
There a group of Kausada men were waiting to spear him. Having successfully
avoided three spears, the ex-convict knelt down and fired his gun. One Kausada
man was killed.

Realising the situation was beyond control, Bishop George sent Marcella and the family to Popondetta. He was staying in his house by himself. He recalls his feelings at that time.

> My bones are old bones and I don't care if I am killed. But I wanted to stay and guard my home. Before long, an angry crowd eager for revenge came with their guns close to my house. I went out into the middle of them. 'Don't touch my chapel, it belongs to God. Kill me instead.' They went away but their intention was to burn my chapel. Having heard about the trouble, the police in Popondetta sent a message for me to come and tell them the real story behind the fighting. The Kausada men thought I was reporting them to the police, which I never did. They didn't realise that I am a neutral man and that this affair originally had nothing to do with me. Just as I was arriving home with Marcella, they burnt my chapel.[348]

Helen Ambo, Bishop George's daughter, recalls the details as she heard them:

> We were all here in Popondetta. Only Mum and Dad went back. They were brave. The chapel was still burning when they arrived. They watched the flames. Mum was crying on the ground. The altar, his bishop's throne, Uncle Simon Peter's tin trunk with his vestments which had been left there, books with prayers, everything was destroyed.

One reason why Bishop George and Marcella had been anxious to get back to their house was to protect the traditional family treasures which they kept there. According to Helen Ambo, the feathered headdresses and ornaments which one day will be passed on to one of her brothers are still with her father. As she said,

> If they were burnt, too, it would mean that we have nothing. Feathers and traditional costumes mean everything for a person in this Province. You have to own these in order to become a man.

According to Helen and to Oliver Ambo her brother, the old feathers, necklaces and armbands had been handed down to the family from Bishop George's father. Oliver described their importance:

> They are all old and very precious and they are still in the house. If he gives them to me, I will hand them over to one of my sons. There are enough for my brothers to wear but only one son will be responsible for keeping them.

For a second time Bishop George fully forgave the people of Kausada. The next year, with the help of people from overseas and various communities and groups in Papua New Guinea such as the Mothers' Union at Holy Cross Station Gona and the Mothers' Union at Killerton, he and his family were able to build a new altar and chapel. As he said,

> I am going to build it with native materials. The mangroves are the best ones for uprights and rafters. My sons and daughters must

help me collect the mangroves from the area between Ambasi and Gona, mostly from the mouth of the Kumusi River. Because of the oil-palm in my area, there is no timber left. It is now a very poor place.

By late 1998, his new chapel was ready. It naturally holds a most important place in his life and in the life of the communities around him. Every day he says Matins and Evensong there, and on Wednesdays and Sundays, when not involved in services at the Holy Cross Church, he celebrates the Holy Eucharist for the people in his area. His chapel is the meeting place for bible study groups and often the place of retreats, taken by him for such groups as the Sisters of the Community of the Visitation at Hetune, or for the Franciscan Brothers. Sometimes he leads retreats there before ordaining men to the priesthood. As Chaplain for the Mothers' Union at Holy Cross, he has responsibilities for pastoral care, and his chapel is sometimes the centre for prayer and healing of the sick.

From time to time, Bishop George is invited by the Diocesan Bishop to take retreats and ordinations in other parishes. One of the men ordained by Bishop George in the early part of his retirement is Archdeacon Denny Bray Guka, born at Ambasi and presently in charge of Hohola Parish in Port Moresby. At the end of his course at Newton Theological College, Fr Denny had specially requested that Bishop George take his retreat and ordination. For one week the two of them stayed near Ambasi on the hill where Fr Copland King, one of the founders of the Anglican Mission, had built the first church in the area.[349]

Fr Denny felt deeply enlightened by the whole experience. According to him, his retreat exemplified Bishop's George's ability to inspire and communicate with others, imparting to them what he considered to be the essential values to be upheld in life. Their day had started early. Before Morning Prayer, they would spend some time together. At breakfast Bishop George would continue talking before giving three addresses during the day. As Fr Denny recalled, 'The times for eating were also times for talking as part of the retreat'. According to him, in the addresses Bishop George would talk about all sorts of subjects to do with the priesthood and the Church as a whole, about commitment and prayer. Mostly, however, he would draw on his own personal experience as a priest and a bishop. Mentioning problems and different situations involving his clergy, Bishop George explained how he had tried to deal with them. He reflected on some of the Anglican Martyrs and Christian leaders and on their deep influence on his life and work.

Bishop George's own influence on people throughout his work for the Church has been, and still is, deep and long-lasting. Many with whom he has had contact, both indigenous people and expatriates, have expressed their views on this remarkable man. As Fr Denny said,

> Above all he emphasised that people will not only listen to you, to what you say and preach, but they will also look to see how you

live your life. The depth of his spirituality is clear for all to see as well as his special way of relating to people. 'Especially as a leader and as a priest you must live as you preach.' That was the main thing he taught me in my retreat.

Although now at the age of eighty and well into his retirement, Bishop George still leads a very active life. By his present way of living he sends a message to his fellow priests that retirement is not the end of their ministry. By his example he has shown that the call to the priesthood is for life. Fr Denny continued,

I think that his life is an encouragement and a challenge not just for retired clergy but for all Christians to continue being active in retirement.

Top: Bishop George and Marcella
with some of their grandchildren in
the garden at Keoje

Right: Bishop George making music
in his chapel at Keoje, 1998

(Photographs: Elin Johnston)

Bishop George in his chapel after celebrating the Eucharist, on the 38th Anniversary of his Consecration, at Keoje, 1998

Bishop George – in retirement, still the mediator on behalf of his people (Photogaphs: Elin Johnston)

CHAPTER 20

Reflections

The story of George Ambo's life now having been told, it would be meaningful to review some of the main influences and circumstances which have shaped him into the man he is. Likewise we should consider the impact he has had on others and his main contribution to the Anglican Church of Papua New Guinea.

Bishop George is a transitional man, his life spanning the vast gap between two very different worlds. Rooted in the traditional wisdom and spirituality of his tribe, his experience reaches far into the Western Technological Age. Being influenced by many people, Papua New Guineans as well as expatriates, his development has been affected by both the traditional and the Western cultures. As a child he absorbed the receding currents of a Stone Age culture, listening to his grandfather's stories of cannibalism and watching his father using stone tools. The earliest influences in his life were his father and his brother. As he reflects,

> My father was a pagan then, but he taught me by word and example
> the traditional ways of my people. My eldest brother Simon Peter,
> a 'mission boy,' gave me a vision of the Christian life...and
> encouraged me to go to school.[350]

George Ambo's first white teacher Mavis Eather, by her mature personality and great commitment to her work, left a deep and lasting impression on her student. He equally admired Fr James Benson, the priest at Gona, for his warmth, encouragement and devotion to the Christian life. At St Aidan's College, while studying to be a teacher-evangelist and later at the time of his consecration, Fr Oliver Brady, with his deep spirituality, played an important part in his development.

Most deeply, however, was he affected by the lives and deaths of the missionaries in his home region who became the Anglican Martyrs. Dedicated to their Christian faith and vocation and committed to the care of their people, they disregarded personal safety. During the war, fearlessly facing the possibility of death at the hands of the invading Japanese, they refused to leave their posts. So they paid the ultimate price through martyrdom.

Inspired and moved by the witness and dedication of the Martyrs, Bishop George has attempted to follow their example. As he states,

> They were living examples of their faith. In the same way, we must
> live out in our lives what we teach and believe. As they say in my

language, '*Site-Eite*'— 'Do as you preach.' I have tried to be a living example of what I saw in others as a young man.

At mission school he gained his first impressions of another world, far from his own. He recalls the new things he saw for the first time there:

> In the early 1930s, an announcement was made at our school that the first truck was coming to Gona beach. Thousands of villagers crowded on the beach, never having seen such a thing before. Anxious to see the truck, we young boys climbed up the trees. But it stuck on the beach. Some people pushed it out of the sand while others ran away in fear. Then the driver drove it through the station. Such very exciting and very frightening things did we experience at school.
>
> On another occasion our headmistress, Miss Eather, announced that a horse was coming to All Souls' Station. 'The children must be careful,' she warned, 'it is bigger than a pig'. Many of us ran away to hide behind the bushes. A man rode on top of the horse steering it with a string in his hand. Then he tied him up under a tree and gave him food. It was amazing and wonderful. The horse knew its master and did what he told it to do. We had never seen our pigs behave in that way. We were amazed and marvelled and couldn't talk. We thought it was an incredible creature.
>
> Then we saw our first plane. Our headmistress said, 'Children, go out and look up'. We saw something like a big bird flying and making a noise. Our teacher tried to teach us about the plane, how it was invented and so on. That's another new and exciting thing we experienced at school. Gradually, our experience of the wider world was increasing.[351]

Little did he know, that many years later, after completing his priestly training, he was to travel for the first time to 'the wider world' for his consecration as the first Papua New Guinean Bishop. As he reflected,

> I was a newcomer to the civilised world. Before my first trip overseas for my consecration in Australia, I had to learn how to wear shoes. I had never worn shoes in my life before. As our plane was approaching Sydney, I saw thousands of twinkling lights. I couldn't believe it. I couldn't talk. I thought the sky was upside down and that we were approaching paradise.

Bishop George was convinced that his Call came from God as part of God's purpose. He saw it as not of his own, nor any other human being's doing.

> At first when Bishop Philip asked me to be a bishop, I refused. I just didn't feel worthy. Then God spoke to me in a vision, calling me to this high position. At my consecration I was shaking, but during the laying-on-of-hands the shaking went. Spiritually I changed altogether. I had courage. I felt the power of God in my heart urging me to go out and do my work as a bishop.[352]

The text on which the Primate of Australia preached the consecration sermon became Bishop George's tenet for life: God dwelleth in us so we can do all things... (2 Phil. 4:13).

Bishop George's influence on people as leader of the Anglican Church has been, and still is deep and long-lasting. Many with whom he has had contact, both brown and white, have expressed their thoughts on the unique power and authority radiating from his personality. Amongst these are such people— referred to above—as Lancelot Sangitari (priest), Stephen Tago (former Minister of the Crown), Arthur Jawodimbari (writer), Martin Chittleborough (Archdeacon) and Bishop David Hand.[353] From their statements emerges a clear picture of a remarkable person of deep spirituality and faith in God. His confidence in his own position as Church leader, as being chosen by God, gives him the authority and power which are such noticeable features of his strong personality.

Yet simplicity and humility were equally the marks of this spiritually powerful man. He often said, 'I am a simple bishop without higher education and university degrees'. As far as his limited knowledge of the English language is concerned, he humbly expresses his regret:

> My English is very poor. I have written about my life, but it was not me writing. It was the Holy Spirit, to whom I continuously prayed for guidance.

Then he added:

> Wisdom is mine—but bear in mind that the early Apostles were simple uneducated fishermen. They were given wisdom to carry out their work for Jesus.

In the early part of his life as a bishop, some people had doubt in his ability to lead the Church mainly because of his low academic standing. It soon became clear however, that this deeply spiritual man had in him 'something indefinable', first referred to by Bishop Strong shortly before the consecration. That 'indefinable' quality, together with those of charisma and maturity of mind, far outweighed any factual knowledge—which, after all, in the life of the Church could only be of secondary importance.

For those who worked with Bishop George, Papua New Guineans or expatriates, his leadership and personal qualities were a continuous source of encouragement and inspiration. His compassion and pastoral care for his flock made a deep impact on all who knew him. So did his warmth and ability to communicate and make friendships with most of the people he met, irrespective of nationality or race. His own house in Popondetta was always full of people. Limited by financial considerations, he would say, 'You are all welcome but you must all bring food'. And so people brought food to his house, sharing the joyful fellowship and spiritual support which he imparted to all by his radiant personality.

His relationship with most white people was of great importance to them. Their feelings can be exemplified by Martin Chittleborough's statement:

> I think his understanding of Europeans was unique. He was a great counsellor for white people. His strength lay in being able to put a very simple analysis of what could be to white people's Western mind a quite complex situation. I think all his white staff very much appreciated the kind of things he said — the simplicity with which he clarified quite complex moral and political questions.

Although Bishop George himself always felt inadequate to handle white people's problems, it was to him most of them would turn for answers and advice. He said,

> The majority of my white fellow-workers, oh…they loved me, they trusted me and respected me as their Father in God. Our relationship was first-class. This was made clear at my retirement when we were in Australia to say good-bye. In every city we went to, I saw their respect and love for us. It was almost too great to bear.

Considering his cultural background and the conservative attitude of his Church to the position of women, indigenous or expatriate, Bishop George has a broader view than most of his fellow countrymen. He puts it thus:

> Time has come for the women to take part in reading, preaching and taking the religious offices. I encourage them to do these things. I would like my members of the Mothers' Union to preach but they are not doing it at Holy Cross. That is my aim now. Maybe they have started in other parishes; I always encourage parish priests to allow women to take part. In our culture we look down on women because we men have superior strength. But regarding the brain and in education we are all equal in the sight of God. It is my view that the cleverest brain, however, God gave to the ladies!

A small incident which happened on one of the occasions when the author and her husband Donald visited George Ambo at Keoje, demonstrates his openness to change in the question of equality for women. It was the Feast of St Simon and St Jude, the 38th Anniversary of his Consecration. His people had come together for the celebration of the Holy Eucharist in his own chapel. It was to be followed by a feast in the garden. The small bush chapel had been beautifully decorated with colourful hibiscus, bougainvillea and frangipani flowers. In the sanctuary stood an armchair specially brought in for Donald. Gradually, the chapel filled with people, sitting on mats on the floor and quietly waiting for the service to begin. As an expatriate, I was asked to sit on an upright chair at the back. Dressed in his episcopal robes, Bishop George entered and moved with great dignity to the sanctuary. To everybody's surprise, he turned around, saw me and asked in the *Ewa-ge* language for an armchair to be brought from his house and placed next to Donald's chair in the sanctuary. His request fulfilled in silence, he beckoned me to move up and sit next to Donald. Most likely this would have been the first time a woman had been asked to sit near the altar, a position usually reserved for priests. Bishop George was never afraid to break with custom, however. Even if his radical views, such as those on the importance of women, were bound to cause a stir amongst traditional village people, he did not shy from facing the consequences of his actions. Though at present he believes that his country is not yet ready for the ordination of women as priests, he views with sympathy the possibility of this occurring some time in the future.

Bishop George is a deeply feeling man, yet he never allows his judgment to be swayed by sentiment. He has a clear and critical mind. For example, at the time of Independence of his country and Church there was a great patriotic feeling for nationals to replace expatriates, but he said,

> Even if Papua New Guinea were to become economically completely self-supporting, and able to supply PNG experts sufficient for all her needs, we would still not want to forget that the Church is Catholic, that means universal, and to make this clear we need people to serve here from other parts of the world for it is in bearing one another's burdens that we fulfil Christ's law to love each other.[354]

Seeing through outward appearances, he has the ability to grasp the essential things, to get to the heart of the matter. This was already noticed by Bishop David at the Vatican (see Chapter 15, particularly page 160). Having seen statues of the Apostles and pictures of Popes and famous families, Bishop George had exclaimed, 'David—too much glory of man, but not enough glory of God!' He was not confused by grandiose expressions of pomp and power, but saw straight through to the spiritual core of things.

With his innate understanding of what is right and wrong, and the courage and strength of character to stand up for his beliefs, he could at times appear ruthless and be blamed for seeing things in black and white. This was the case when he, in an uncompromising and rather abrupt way, introduced a change to the traditional custom of mourning for the dead (see Chapter 19). By curtailing the time of mourning for people to express their grief, he initially hurt the feelings of many. So great was his influence, however, that they soon accepted his reform of their custom, and followed his judgment.

He was widely regarded as 'a man of truth', having great concern for the value of his word. He meant what he said. He would never break an engagement, allowing the weather, sickness or any other thing stop him from fulfilling his promise. As he said himself,

> I think keeping your word is important. Only once or twice did I fail to reach one of my 23 parishes when I had said that I would.

Many are the examples which illustrate his self-discipline and commitment. Arthur Jawodimbari recalls one of these instances:

> Bishop George had been asked to preach at a Mothers' Union meeting at Kurereda Village up the coast. Just before the meeting

he became ill, vomiting blood, and was advised not to go. But he said, 'Well, if the Lord takes me when I am in the field, that's OK for I know the women are gathering and I must be there'. Most of the women thought he would not last to the end of their workshop, but miraculously he recovered while he was there. Such was his dedication to his work. As a man of integrity and truth, his influence is strong amongst his people. They trust him and take his words as truth.

Reflecting on his life which has been rich in significant events, joys and sorrows, he admits that some of the latter have left deep marks upon his soul. As a young man he experienced two devastating tragedies. As previously described, the first of these was the Japanese invasion with the ensuing destruction of missions and the killing of the Anglican Martyrs, some of whom he had known and loved. Nine years later followed the devastating eruption of Mt Lamington. Amongst the four thousand or so people killed by the volcano were some of his dearest friends and family. Furthermore (as also referred to earlier), such painful experiences as the conflicts with some of Marcella's people at Kausada and the hostility of some of the Gona people at the time of retirement have caused him much sorrow. These happenings are, however, long since forgiven by his compassionate and understanding heart.

With a radiant smile, he tells about the greatest joy of his life:

> The greatest joy for me is and always has been that I am married to a person who loves and honours me so dearly. I am very, very happy that I was married to the right person. At Boianai, when I told Marcella that God wanted me as a bishop, she didn't say anything. Tears were falling from her eyes. After a time of silence she said, 'I know that you will do it. If it's God's will, you must be a bishop. But me, your wife, I lost my education…!' [this was interrupted by the war]. When she said this, her tears were falling. After the visit to Australia at my consecration, she changed altogether. Although at times frightened and bewildered by her new position, she gave all she had to support me. Because of her great help in our young years, I was able to do whatever I could to help and teach our people so that some of my schoolchildren became leaders in the community. That was another great joy to me.[355]

Other regrets come to mind as Bishop George ponders his life. Reflecting on his happiness with Marcella, he recalls sadly that only once did he manage to dance with her after his ordination. This was a time when she was dressed in traditional costume, though he just wore his ordinary clothes. As he recalls:

> She was a wonderful dancer, amongst the best in her village. As a bishop I went with her to Ajoa Village, between Tufi and Wanigela Stations. After the service, the Mothers' Union decorated her in traditional dress. I said to the priest, Fr Wesley, 'Excuse me, have you got a drum?' Then I danced towards her, starting to sing and

drum and we danced together. At times, when by ourselves and she is feeling sad, I pick up my drum and dance for her to make her laugh. Feeling better, she says, 'Oh, my dear darling'. It's a private thing.

He has regretted deeply that after his ordination as deacon, he never danced in traditional dress again. When told by Fr Cassidy, his principal, to put away his feathers and ornaments and to stop dancing, he did as he was told. He never took part in traditional dancing again. As George Ambo said, 'I obeyed him because he was my teacher, but I was very, very sad. I was born to be a dancer'.

His traditional background emerges in the fact that, right through his life, George Ambo has picked up his drum and danced by himself. When he was attempting to introduce traditional dancing into worship, he would teach the dancers by dancing for them the particular steps they must perform in the service. At other times, when he is low and all by himself, he drums and sings his favourite composition, *Bada Jesu*...Father Jesus, you died and bought me, I am your son by adoption, I am singing with humble heart, do not forget me '. He is always uplifted by his own singing and dancing with his drum. (See earlier references, particularly pages 167, 169 and 170.)

Despite the scar inflicted by one of his colonial master's denying his innate joy in traditional dancing, George Ambo has passed largely unscathed through the Colonial Age. Influenced in the most significant and positive way by his other white teachers, he has learnt greatly from them but never imitated them. He has always retained his Papuan identity and dignity. The following example illustrates the attitude which he had to accept before becoming a bishop:

> In those early days, white missionaries treated Papuan people very differently. My consecration made the biggest difference in the world. Before that, at meetings or at the diocesan conferences, we did not eat together. When I came to be interviewed by Bishop Philip shortly before my consecration in 1960, he asked me to have a cup of tea with the European staff. I said, 'Father Bishop, I never had a cup of tea with Europeans in my life, so I am not coming'. At that time, some of the Europeans were not ready to eat with Papuans. So I always stayed away. The second time I came to see him, he told me about his vision for me. Then he asked me for lunch with the white staff. I did not go but had lunch with my uncle Roland Somboba. After my consecration, I had no fear. During conference time both my clergymen and I had our meals with the white people. I felt they were my brothers and sisters.

Still reflecting on the regrets in his life, Bishop George said,

> The thing that comes to my mind, and which I feel in my heart, is that I was not educated with a university degree. When Bishop Philip asked me to be an assistant bishop, the first thing I said was that I only reached Grade 5 in my school education. I did not study

the English language but just picked it up as I heard people speak. As a bishop, when I was asked to preach in the big cathedrals in Sydney or overseas, oh!…I wished I had learnt English properly so that I could express clearly what I thought and felt about my work.

One of the great worries now is that he is running out of time to help his countrymen to accept Jesus Christ as being Papua New Guinean. From the early days of his episcopate, he has been concerned with the localisation of his Church, but he feels there is still a long way to go before this can be achieved.

Most of our clergymen do not believe in and are not in favour of a liturgy, prayer book and other theologian thoughts being produced in the local languages.

As we have seen, in his retirement Bishop George himself is engaged in producing a prayer book in *Ewa-ge* and *Binandere*, but he would like to see many more such translations into local languages. Although he himself made a significant start on localisation of the Church, he regrets not having pushed hard enough for it while there still was time.

Yet, despite his feelings of regret, he has in fact been recognised as the most influential person in creating an indigenous Papua New Guinean Church. His greatest achievement has been to marry the English religious culture with that of his own country. He is accepted as the first indigenous Church leader to introduce many aspects of Papuan culture on the imported Anglican form of worship, making it more meaningful for the indigenous people. As described earlier, using traditional elements, he created *The Gona Mass*, the first liturgy of indigenous character to be adopted as a model by local Churches. Thus he has had great influence in the development of a truly Papua New Guinean Church.

Many people have admired Bishop George's capacity for hard work and self-discipline. Having been under the rule of discipline, first in his childhood in the traditional society, later at mission school and colleges, he has come to expect a strictly disciplined life, not just for himself but for others who work for the Church. His aim has been to impose on himself and his clergy a disciplined leadership and a way of life according to the standard expected of Church leaders. It is obvious to all who know him that he has been a fine example for others to follow, both in his official life and in his home, which he and Marcella have made into a place of Christian love.

Bishop George's own words on the last pages of the story of his life express his heartfelt gratitude to the (Anglican) Christians in the UK and in Australia for their support:

We are very, very thankful to the Anglican Christians in both countries for their prayers, respect, love and Chrtistian charity over the past years.

Thinking especially of the time of his retirement, he continues,

When we received invitations from ABM (Australian Board of Mission) and from the PNGCP (Papua New Guinea Church Partnership) in the UK for both of us to visit, we were thankful from the bottom of our hearts. We never thought that our Christian brothers and sisters would do so much for us. Our stay in England was well organised by our PNGCP. In every home we visited, we were received with great joy and gratitude of hearts. To the Christians in Australia, both of us express our thankfulness for their help over the years. As we travelled round these countries, my wife realised that it had not been easy for missionaries to offer for service in PNG. She realised it was a very great sacrifice for them—leaving parents, friends, beautiful homes and the comfort of a higher standard of living. We will never forget how much we owe to the Anglican Church overseas for their devoted support. Because of this, we were able to do our Lord's work with which we had been entrusted.

Despite this deep feeling of gratitude, Bishop George fears for the future of the Anglican Church in his country. Since his retirement he has seen the discipline, which he so keenly sought to uphold in the Church, gradually slacken. Such problems as misappropriation of funds and the need to close for some time the diocesan office in Popondetta owing to lack of responsible staff, have reinforced his view that Independence came too early to his Church. Realising that it will still be a long time before most of his people are fully ready to stand on their own without support, he sees no other way but to ask most forcefully for help from overseas. Feeling quite desperate about the situation at the time of this interview recorded just over a year ago, and still today being deeply troubled and disillusioned with Independence which he fought so hard to delay, he sent this impassioned plea for expatriate helpers.

Anglican Christians, this is my concern: Discipline is slack amongst our Church leaders, our people are divided by incoming sects and our faith is generally weak. If you believe that the Anglican Church should continue in Papua New Guinea, you must pray for us and produce people and money to help us. Are you Australians so blind that you do not see the hard work done in the past by those who gave their lives for the Anglican Church of my country? Were their efforts all for nothing? Are you not sad about the present state of our Church in this Province? I fought for a European bishop in Port Moresby. Another one is urgently needed here in Popondota.

(To Bishop George's great joy, since recording this, two bishops from England have been consecrated: Bishop Peter Fox for Port Moresby and Bishop Roger Jupp—for two years principal of Newton Theological College—for Popondota.)

Furthermore, I would like to see an expatriate administrator, who can train Papua New Guineans to cope with the administrative work of the Diocese. For many of our people money is still a new thing which they do not know how to handle correctly. Expatriate archdeacons and priests are also needed to work with and teach our clergy. If Anglicans in Australia believe in my concern, they must take action now! If they take the easy line, they are largely the ones to blame for the failure of our Church to survive.

Perhaps the most remarkable thing to note about George Ambo, a transitional man passing through an incredibly difficult period from Stone Age to Space Age, was his ability to make the mental leap from a Papuan traditional culture to that of our modern Western world. Going through the slow pace of the colonial prewar years, he adjusted with faith and courage to the fast-changing environment and turmoil surrounding Independence. Having travelled widely overseas, attending Lambeth Conferences in England and meetings with bishops and primates of the Anglican Communion in many different countries, he made a deep impact on people wherever he went. Highly respected everywhere for his spiritual strength and warmth, for his powerful preaching and yet great simplicity, his humour and humility, he has been equally close to people at home and abroad. Remarkable for his talents as a poet, musician, composer, teacher, linguist and performer of traditional dancing, he has had the most profound influence on the development of his own indigenous Church.

Above all, the depth of his Christian faith has marked him as one of the most outstanding indigenous leaders of his Church. His main purpose being to proclaim the Christian message of God's universal Love, he says, 'My guiding principle has always been for all men and women to come to know Christ'. At the height of his career as Archbishop, he preached a sermon which holds the essence of his teaching and hopes for the future. It expresses his belief in the universality and ancient authority of the Catholic Church. Conscious of the different ways and divisions of the two worlds of which he is part, he states that the need for all people, whether of 'the highly civilised lands' or of 'the primitive world,' is a simple faith to live by. For him that faith is 'not anything new but of the ancient "Catholick and Apostolick Church", handed down from the Apostles and Martyrs through 2,000 years'.[356]

Bishop George's Message to His Own Church of PNG and All Other Christians

There are two main pictures of this present world...in the primitive world most people live simple lives in villages, but they live in fear of sickness, sorcery and witchcraft...in civilised lands, scientists are inventing frightening things which could destroy the world. Both civilised and primitive nations are living in fear because they trust in themselves and their own power. But how clever and how powerful is man? He cannot save himself or even master himself. Men have always been tempted to worship mere power...but power in the hands of a sinful man is a very great evil. Are we trusting man's power to satisfy all our needs and make us happy?...I strongly believe our only hope is in having power over ourselves, that power which God gives to us through our living in Christ. In a world gone astray, it is the Love of God that both your people and my people need now. I may go out to proclaim God's Love, travelling by canoe, or wading through deep swamps, or climbing over mountains, while you jump into your car or plane. But it is the same Christ we preach.

With eyes twinkling and his smile radiating warmth and joy, George Ambo sends us his message of Christian Love. A simple man of two worlds, he truly has an all-embracing breadth of mind, marking him as an outstanding Church leader of his time.

Design by Roger Tigari

Appendix 1

According to clan history, passed on by mouth from father to son for several generations, Bishop Ambo's people originally came from the inland area of Asigi. That was in the Togaho District in the land of the Orokaiva. At that time, three clans had come together: Somboundi (or Somboba) to which the Ambos belong, Bougaundi and Dunemba. These three clans formed one big clan called 'Popoda Barida'. Leaving the land of the Orokaiva, this big clan group followed the Bewa River, today the Barida and Kaimo Rivers, down to the coast where they settled in the areas stretching from the vicinity of Gona to Garara, now Killerton.

According to oral history there were no records of tribal fighting or cannibalism amongst the coastal people at that time. The most powerful tribal groups in the area were the Yega-Bapa and the Sebaga-Andere. ('Bapa' was the nickname for the group of smaller clans, to which the Ambos' Somboba people belonged.) It was between these two major groups that a serious conflict was to occur which caused significant changes in their way of life.

Beginning of Tribal War and Cannibalism

The early peace which existed amongst the coastal people themselves, was eventually shattered by a fight over fish. Seemingly a trivial incident, the event has been remembered widely in oral histories of the areas around Gona and Buna. The basic story seems clear and simple. Some Bapa boys were trying to catch fish in the Garara (Killerton) Lagoon, but did not have a net. A chief of the Sebaga-Andere Clan, Opeba Jeburu, lived in a village amongst the *pandanus* palms near the lagoon. (Garara means *pandanus*.) Seeing the boys, he ordered one of his men to bring a big fishing net for them to use, as they were the first to see the fish. Having caught the fish, the Bapa youngsters set off for home, taking with them the folded net with all the fish inside. Seeing this, some of the chief's men angrily chased the boys. Grabbing the end of the net, they shouted abuses at the Bapas for not having offered to share their catch. A fight began, at first with sticks and driftwood, but soon escalating into a major battle between the Yega-Bapas and the Sebaga-Anderes. The battlefield was Garara Lagoon. A man named Derariba, fighting with the Sebaga-Andere, killed one of the six brothers during the battle. In the words of a tribal elder: 'Derariba...speared Somboba's son. He died at the end of the spear!' 'Somboba's son' was Gounde.

In George Ambo's words,

> My great grandfather was Gounde. I came from Gounde. He was killed at Garara Lagoon. Yega-Bapa Clans fought against Sebaga-Andere Clans over fish. Gounde was killed during that fight.

244

The Elders tell us, that after his death, the Sebaga-Andere were 'confused'. While they '...sat idle, not knowing what to do...', their ally, Derariba, the murderer of Gounde, went away to his food garden. At the end of the day, as he was returning to his village, he saw in the distance some men blocking the road. In the darkness, Derariba escaped to the sea. Holding on to some driftwood, he began floating towards his home. The Bapa people, seeing the ripples on the water, discovered it was a man. One of them called out, 'It's not *wo* (fish) but *embo* (man). Who is he? They have killed Embawo [a name for Somboba's son] and we have been staying [at home], so why can't someone go down and kill him!' So they killed Derariba and placed him on the beach, where his own people found the dead body. They brought it home and buried it.

From this time, the era of friendship between the two major clan groups of the coast had ended; a new period of warfare to kill for revenge had been ushered in by events at Garara. A consequence of this was the introduction of cannibalism. Having moved further east along the seashore, the Sebaga-Andere began organising war-parties against their enemies. Cannibalism became a feature of the fighting.

Until then it had been the custom to leave behind the dead bodies of the enemy, to be picked up by their relatives for burial in their own lands. Now, the winning warriors carried away with them their victims, to be cooked and eaten in the villages of the victors. Eventually, as the white government came into the area and the fighting stopped, many Sebaga-Andere people settled at Buna and Sanananda. But their part of the beautiful Garara Lagoon, they never won back. Bishop George explained that this was '...because it was won over the losing of one of the leaders of our clan, my great grandfather, Gounde'.

The descendants of Gounde settled at Kurou, near Gona, whereas Gounde's brother Jumaba's descendants lived with most of the Somboba Clan at Garara.

(From information provided by Bishop George Ambo to Elin Johnston at Keoje in 1998, and from the Rev'd Richard Bowie in Canberra, also in 1998)

All Souls School
Gona
St. 25-9-41.

Dear Mans Eather.

I will write a letter to you to tell you about the sickness at Gona. Sickness is not on the Station, but is in the village. On that time eight Christian people and seven heathen people died in Gona village. That is why, doctor Wright said to the people on the Gona bay; "I want you all to go out in the gardens and build a little house and live there, and after the sickness is finished, you can go back to your villages." And all the people in Buna to Bakumbari are out in the gardens; except my fathers and sisters and Mono - Peter and his wife, they have stayed in the village. The sickness is nearly finished, Will you pray for us in our sickness?

And I will tell you, how the school is going on. We

began our work at six oclock and finished it about
eight oclock. Then halfpast-eight we went-down to
dispensary for our siro.. At halfpast-eight we went
to the Church to say our mattins.. After mattins is
founded Father James Benson take gin, and we go
out to begin our school work.. And we begun our
school.. about-nine oclock to halfpast-twelve, and
we sang our angelus prayer then we went to the village.
In January 9 and bylaramus are going to College and
Arnold Paulos, Sinihon and Skato are going to Dogura
or about-the end of October..

Will you pray for ous every day and we will pray
for you every day.. Please give my love to the
children in your school "Godwill bless you in your
father and mother your brothers..

Good Bye,

I am your friend

George Honawa.

Appendix 3
Newton College, log-book kept by Fr Eric Cassidy

The following extracts from diary notes made by Fr Cassidy in the Newton College log-book give some idea of the conditions under which the three northern students, George Ambo, Simon Peter Awoda and Albert Maclaren Ririka, had to cope with their theological studies. Some five months before their arrival at Ganuganuana (Dogura), a start had been made on the humble beginnings of the college:

12th February [1952]: Romney and 2 assistants [presumably local men] began to collect material for building 3 native houses and a chapel. On various occasions odd workers were enlisted to clear some ground (mission girls, relatives of hospital patients etc.) and two rows of bananas were planted — one row given by Wamira, plus 20 pineapples, and the 2nd row given by Mukawa, and the planting of the latter was done by Wedau.

July: Wedau gave 3 *bendoro* [hardwood bush tree] logs for the altar, and Gordon and his uncle [presumably local villagers] gave 1 hen...Two students of St Aidan's College (Nicodemus and Byron) worked on *bendoro* logs in preparation for the altar ...A work bench was constructed by Henry late of Doubena.
[During June schoolboys from Dogura had roofed the 3 houses and chapel with grass, this forestalling the use of *sago*-leaf which the Principal brought back with him from Eroro for roofing the chapel ...]

Residence at College:
On Saturday morning (26th July) I moved into residence. About 30-odd students from College (St Aidan's) came as a 'working-bee' and toiled from 10am till 1pm, cutting a drain, digging ground for gardens (for students and Principal) cutting grass and clearing up.

Arrival of Students:
On Monday 28th July [1952], the 3 students (Simon Peter Ambo, Albert Maclaren Ririka and George Ambo) arrived by the 'M-K' [*Maclaren King*, the mission boat] in the afternoon, together with their wives and children.
The next morning they marked their arrival by killing a black snake about 5 ft long, near one of their houses. They went to mass at St Aidan's and later set out for a supply of firewood.
On Tuesday [and subsequently] Mass was celebrated at a temporary altar erected in one of the upstairs rooms of the Principal's Cottage. Some posts

were obtained for making kitchens and a further supply also on Wednesday. Thursday and Friday were given to the erection of kitchens. Simon Peter having a swollen ankle was detained in Dogura Hospital.
On Friday one of the recently purchased hens graciously laid an egg — apparently without any cackling! We trust the laying of the egg was not due to mere absent-mindedness.

7th August. George Ambo and Albert Maclaren began work on wall in Chapel behind the Altar (*sago* ribs).

25th August. The College began its regular life of devotion and study according to a time-table for services, lectures and College jobs...

24th September. First clutch of chickens hatched out (6 from 10 eggs).

26th September. Second clutch out (7 from 9 eggs). The mother hen was dead in the box next morning. Both of the hens and their boxes were abounding in lice...

6th October. Students began examination tests on past 2 months' work.

6th November Bought some sugar-cane and *tapioca* 'seed' for 2 sticks of tobacco.
Two chickens (6 weeks old) disappeared... Simon Peter (yesterday) was greatly distressed over his difficulty of expressing his thoughts in English in his exam-test papers.

1953:

13th January. The bishop blessed the houses (of Warden and Students), Gardens and College, in the presence of most of Dogura's white staff, St Aidan's College, St Paul's boys and girls, medical workers etc. (8am)

22nd February. On past few days Evensong was said on the lawn outside the Chapel because of the heat.

8th March. Began to dig 'moat' to form a fence for a pig expected to arrive in a few days from Bunting's farm at Samarai.

11th March. Some Students (about 6 or 7) from St Aidan's helped to dig 'moat' for piggery...

29th April. A son born to George Ambo and Marcella.

12th May. Calicoes issued (1 white and 2 blue) to each student...

5th August. High wind blew Simon Peter's house sideways.

6th August. Students went to the bush to cut and dress posts for corners of house.

7thAugust. Students brought remainder of timber from bush and helped by about 40 students from St. Aidan's College restored the house and added support ...

7th Sept. Warden left for Samarai to visit dentist, due there on 8th but who arrived there a fortnight after the due date! (ie on 22nd) ...

30th November. Simon Peter to hospital.

9th December. Simon Peter returned to College.

25th December. Holidays till 4th January.

28th December. George, Marcella, Oliver, Alban ... to Hospital with 'Flu.

1954:

4th January. [Actually a week or so before Christmas] Discovered that Students' Small-house was nearly full-up—began digging a new one.

8th January. George and the other patients ('flu) returned from hospital. [Query this apparently duplicated entry] Began digging new Small-house for Students. Albert to Hospital with 'Flu.

4th February. Bishop David visited the College to talk with the Students in Orokaivan language and see if they were actually learning what they were taught. He thought they seemed to be doing so.

1st March. Albert to Hospital with boils ...

3rd July. Women made *Tapa*-cloth Frontals for Altar.

24th July. New 'Small-house' for Students completed (commenced on 4th January)

17th December. Roof (grass) removed from Chapel.

27th December. Holiday ...

1955:

On lst January St Aidan's Students finished the ridge cap on Chapel roof.

17th January. Exams began (Human Behaviour, Doctrine, St Mark)

26th January to 30th—Warden in hospital with poisoned foot—exams went on.

24March. Four men from Gona (per 'St Laurence' [Gona mission boat]) to build houses. Also supply of mangrove (Gona) and iron (for roofing) (Eroro)…

28th March: Unloaded posts, rafters, *kipa, sago* leaves and black iron from 'Mac'—sent from Gona, Eroro, Wanigela and Menapi (about 2pm - 5.30).

2nd June. Remaining Workboys from Gona (2) and Eroro (3) returned home. Houses (6) almost completed.

12th June (Trinity I) Ordination at Cathedral—Deacons Simon Peter (for Gona), Albert Maclaren (for Agenehambo) and George Ambo (for Dogura).

14th June. Two Deacons for North—left by 'St Laurence'...

24th June. New Students (6) with wives and Children arrived by 'Mac' from North.

25th June. (Saturday 6.30am) The Bishop dedicated the Chapel under the patronage of St Athanasius and in memory of the late bishop—Henry Newton.
Mass followed and then the 6 new houses were blessed ...

1958:

19th January. 3 Deacons ordained to Priesthood (at Conference): Simon Peter, Albert M., Geo. A.

(Fr Cassidy's log-book was made available by Fr Roger Jupp, Principal of Newton Theological College, Popondetta.)

Appendix 4

Papuan Priests ordained by Bishop George

There may be omissions and inaccuracies in this list, compiled from the material which has been available to the author; she regrets any inconsistencies or errors.

Names provided by Martin Gardham, Provincial Secretary of the Anglican Church of Papua New Guinea:

Endose, Fr llford Newman
Ewada (Kairembora), Fr Elliot
Jimboro, Fr Matthew
Jofo, Fr Cornelius
Kogora, Fr Charles Wesley

Savate, Fr Jeffrey Martin
Seia, Fr Laban
Sinoba, Fr Sergius
Soare, Fr George
Tariambari, Bp Reuben

Names provided by Fr Tom Williams, former Diocesan Secretary of Popondota:

Agapie, Fr Winterbourne
Banaga, Fr Eijah
Baupo, Fr lrenaeus
Bareo, Fr Roger Dasiga
Bejigi, Fr Lucas
Dogi, Fr Harold
Ganeba, Fr Samuel
Gaso, Fr Warrington
Guka, Archdeacon Denny Bray
Isari, Fr Warrington
Jega, Fr Samson
Br Joseph, SSF
Kopada, Fr Edison

Moi, Fr Paulus
Orosa, Fr Gideon
Orowari, Fr Jasper
Peuba, Fr Robin
Piriri, Fr Patrick
Poho, Fr Ezekiel
Poraripa, Fr Winterford
Soare, Fr Augustus
Ta'ani, Fr Barnabas
Talanoa, Bp Tevita
Tura, Fr Johnsford
Waimi, Fr Klower

NOTES

Chapter 1

1 Article by Fr James Benson in *The Anglican*, 18 March 1955. In this article Fr Benson states he arrived back at Gona on Boxing Day, 1946, whereas in his book, *Prisoner's Base And Home Again*, pub 1957, the date for his return to Gona is given as 23 August 1946 (p 192)

Chapter 2

2 Bishop George Ambo, message, Toumo Waragi, Keoje near Popondetta, 1998, pp 1–3

Interviews with Bishop George Ambo, Oro Guest House, Popondetta, 3 September 1997, Newton College, 26 October 1998, Tape 1B, pp1-8; and Tape 2A, 27 October 1998, p 11

3 CAW Monckton: *Some Experiences of a New Guinea Resident Magistrate*, pub Lane and Co, London, England, 1920, pp 54, 154

4 Article by Canon James Benson, *The Anglican*, March 11, 1955

5 Interviews with Bishop George Ambo, Newton College, 26 October 1998, p 2, and 4 November 1998, pp 1–2

6 Interview with the Rev'd Denys Ririka, Newton College, 3 November 1998, pp 7–9

Chapter 3

7 Bishop George Ambo, Personal writings, Keoje near Popondetta, 1998, pp 3–4

Interview with Bishop George Ambo, Keoje, 3 September 1997

8 Interview with Bishop GeorgeAmbo, Newton College, Popondetta, 27 October 1998, pp 11–12

9 Interview with Helen Ambo, Newton College, 4 November 1998, pp 7–8

10 Interview with Bishop George Ambo, Newton College, 26 October 1998, p 12

11 Mavis Eather, *Early Gona, Revealing Bishop Ambo's Background*, p 1

12 David Wetherell, *Reluctant Mission: The Anglican Church in Papua New Guinea, 1891–1942*, University of Queensland Press, Queensland 1977, pp 152, 288, 339

13 Interview with Bishop George Ambo, Keoje, 3 September 1997

Letter from Mavis Eather to friends, Gona 1936, in possession of Mrs Patricia Hyde; also Mavis Eather, *Early Gona, Revealing Bishop Ambo's Background*, in the possession of Mrs Patricia Hyde

14 Mavis Eather, *Early Gona, Revealing Bishop Ambo's Background*, pp 2–3

15 Letter from Mavis Eather to friends, Gona, 26 September 1940

16 Message from Bishop GeorgeAmbo, Keoje, 1998, pp 3–4

17 Interview with Mrs Patricia Hyde, Sydney, 1998

18 Thomas Inglis, Inspector of Schools, *Reports of Inspection for the Anglican Mission School at Gona*, inspected 31 August and 1 September 1939, 6 July 1940

19 Mavis Eather, *Early Gona: Revealing Bishop Ambo's Background*, pp 3–4

20 Interview with Bishop George Ambo, Newton College, 4 November 1998, p 1

21 Mavis Eather, *Early Gona: Revealing Bishop Ambo's Background*, pp 3–4

Chapter 4

22 James Benson, *Prisoner's Base and Home Again*, Robert Hale Ltd, London, 1957

23 Philip Nigel Strong, in New Guinea Mission (PNGCP) Occasional Paper, Christmas 1956, pp 3, 5, 6

24 RB Dakeyne, *Village and Town in New Guinea*, University of Sydney, Longman, p 13
    Timothy Kinahan, *A Church is Born, The Anglican Church in PNG, 1891–1991*, 1983

25 Interview with Bishop George Ambo, Newton College, 26 October 1998

26 Mavis Eather, *Early Gona: Revealing Bishop Ambo's Background*

27 Interview with Bishop George Ambo, Newton College, 26 October 1998

28 Interview with Bishop George Ambo, Newton College, 27 October 1998

29 David Wetherell, *ABM Review of Mission*, 1977, pp 11–12.

30 *The Bush Brother*, Vol 50, No 3, 30 November 1955, pp 10–13
    The Anglican, 14 October 1955, Obituary
    Church Times, London, October 14, 55, In Memoriam—James Benson
    Letter to Richard Bowie, unsigned, from Philip Lodge, 236, Kilvinton Village K1, Castle Hill, 25 March 1975
    Letter to Richard Bowie from Warren Hall, 492, Napier Street, Bendigo, Victoria, 19 March 75
    James Benson, Form of Profession

31 Mavis Eather, Second Journal, Gona, 1938–9

32 Mavis Eather, *Early Gona, Revealing Bishop Ambo's Background*

33 Letter from Sarah Jenkins to Richard Bowie, 15 January 1974

34 Interview with Bishop George Ambo, Newton College, 26 October 1998

35 Letter from James Benson to Philip Strong, 1938

36 Mavis Eather, *Early Gona, Revealing Bishop Ambo's Background*

37 Interviews with Stephen Tago and Maureen Ambo, Popondetta, November 1998

Chapter 5

38 Letter from James Benson to Philip Strong, Gona, 1937
    Letter from James Benson to Philip Strong, Ambasi, 10 August 1938

39 Anne Chittleborough, *The Anglican Church in Papua New Guinea*, pub NG Mission London, 1976, p 8
    NG Mission (PNGCP), UK, Occasional Paper, no 95, January 1933, p 5

40 Letter from James Benson to Philip Strong, Ambasi, 10 August 1938

41 David Wetherell, *Reluctant Mission, The Anglican Church in Papua New Guinea 1891–1942*, pub University of Queensland Press, 1977, pp 37, 42, 78, 81, 84, 186, 241

42 Anne Chittleborough, *The Anglican Church in Papua New Guinea*, pub NG Mission London, 1976, p 8
    Anne Chittleborough, *The Anglican Church in PNG for Primary Schools*, small edition printed locally for use in the author's school class

43 Letter from James Benson to Philip Strong, Ambasi, 30 August 1938

44 Mavis Eather, *Early Gona: Revealing Bishop Ambo's Background*

45 Letter from Mavis Eather to friends, Gona, 6 December 1939

46 Thomas Inglis, Inspector of Schools, *Reports of Inspection for the Anglican School at Gona.* Inspected 31 August and 1 September 1939, and 6 July 1940

47 Interview with Bishop George Ambo, Popondetta, September 1997

48   Mavis Eather, Personal Journal, Gona, March 1939

49   Bishop George Ambo, Personal Writings, Keoje, 1998

50   Letter from Philip Strong to Mr Benson (father of James), Port Moresby, 22 October 1942

Chapter 6

51   Dorothea Tomkins and Brian Hughes, *The Road from Gona*, pub Angus and Robertson Ltd, Great Britain, 1970, pp 26–30

52   Letter from Mavis Parkinson to Avis, Gona 12 June 1942

53   Personal Writings, Bishop George Ambo, Keoje 1998, p 5

54   *ibid*   pp 6–8

55   Information provided by Dr David Wetherell

56   David Wetherell, *Reluctant Mission, The Anglican Church in Papua New Guinea 1891–1942*, pub University of Queensland Press, 1977, p 313

57   *ibid*   pp 113, 312
     Also information provided by Amy Paisawa, widow of Fabian Paisawa

58   According to Dr David Wetherell, Reuben Mark was a descendant of Harry Mark, one of the first two South Sea Islands teachers who arrived at the Anglican Mission Headquarters at Dogura in 1893. Also, according to Bishop George, Fr A P Jennings left the College soon after George's arrival, to train ordinands at Dogura for the deaconate and priesthood.

59   Interview with Bishop George Ambo, Popondetta, 27 October 1998

60   According to Dr David Wetherell, AH Buckland, Missionary 1935-42, became a supervisor of labour camps run by ANGAU after 1942. Later, he was a teacher at Sogeri School.

61   Letter from James Benson to George and Rosie, undated
     See also, Personal Writings from Bishop George Ambo, 1998, p 8

62   Letter from Mavis Parkinson to Avis, Gona June 1942

63   Bishop George Ambo, Personal Writings, 1998, pp 9, 10

64   James Benson, *Prisoner's Base and Home Again*, Robert Hale Ltd, London,   1957, pp 20, 28–32

65   Dorothea Tomkins and Brian Hughes, *The Road from Gona*, pub Angus & Robertson Ltd, Great Britain, 1970, pp 39, 41–45
     Also *Komboro*, St Aidan's College Magazine, September 1962

66   Dorothea Tomkins and Brian Hughes, *The Road from Gona*, pub Angus & Robertson Ltd, Great Britain, 1970, pp 59–62

67   Information given to the author in 1988 by local people of the Mt Lamington area. See also Hand, Bishop David, KBE, MA, ThD, *Modawa, Papua New Guinea and Me 1946–2002*, pub privately and printed Sal Press, Port Moresby, PNG, 2002, p 118

68   Bishop Philip Strong, Obituary, *The Anglican* 14 October 1955

69   Letter from the Bishop of New Guinea to the father and relatives of the Rev'd James Benson, Port Moresby 22 October 1942

Chapter 7

70   Interview with Bishop Oliver Heyward, Melbourne, 28 October 1999

71   Bishop Philip Strong, panegyric at the funeral of the Late Canon Oliver Brady, January 1972

72   Charles Smyth, *The Church and the Nation*, pub Hodder and Stoughton, Great Britain, 1962, pp 157, 158, 162, 163, 169, 172

73 David Wetherell, *Reluctant Mission, The Anglican Church in Papua New Guinea 1891–1942*, pub University of Queensland Press, 1977, pp 43, 53, 54

74 *Komboro*, St Aidan's College Magazine, No 13, May 1960

75 Dorothea Tomkins and Brian Hughes, *The Road from Gona*, pub Angus and Robertson Ltd, Great Britain, 1970, pp 82, 83

76 Bishop George Ambo, Personal Writings, Keoje 1998, pp 8, 9, 10

77 *ibid*

78 *Weekend Australian*, 29 and 30 August 1992, p 58ff

79 Bishop George Ambo, Personal Writings, Keoje 1998, pp 8, 9, 10

80 Dr Blanche Biggs, Note for Oliver

81 Interview with Bishop George Ambo, Newton College, Popondetta, 28 October 1998
Interview at Oro Guesthouse, Popondetta, September 1997

82 Interview with Bishop George Ambo, Popondetta, 28 October 1998; also comments by Dr Blanche Biggs

83 Interview with Bishop George Ambo, Popondetta, 4 November 1998; also interview with Bishop Oliver Heyward, Melbourne October 1999

84 Mavis Eather, *Early Gona, Revealing Bishop George Ambo's Background*, p 8

85 Interview with Bishop George Ambo, Popondetta, 9 November 1997

86 Dr Blanche Biggs, Note for Oliver

Chapter 8

87 Warrington Yaruso Manubada, *A Story of the Anglican Mission*, printed at the Holy Cross Press, Gona, Papua 1960, pp 4, 5, 6

88 Letter from the Bishop of New Guinea to Fellow Workers, Members of the Family and Friends, Cathedral of St Peter and St Paul, June 26th 1943, pp 3, 4

89 Padre Bell, *Among the Ruins*, ABM, New Edition 1946, pp 9, 10

90 Warrington Yaruso Manubada, *A Story of the Anglican Mission*, printed at the Holy Cross Press, Gona, Papua 1960, pp 5, 6

91 Bishop George Ambo, Personal Writings, Keoje, 1998, p 13

92 Letter from George Ambo to Mavis Eather, Gomberu near Gona, 19 May 1946

93 David Wetherell and Charlotte Carr-Gregg, *Camilla: CH Wedgwood 1901–1955, A Life*, NSW University Press, 1990, pp 198–210

94 *ibid*   pp 199–200

95 *ibid*   pp 168–169

96 Interview with Bishop George Ambo, Popondetta, 3 November 2000

97 Bishop G. Ambo, Personal Writings, Keoje 1998, p 13
Also, Bishop George Ambo, Writings on a Sorcerer, Keoje January 1999

98 Interview with Bishop George Ambo, Newton College, Popondetta 26 October 1998, pp 5, 8, 9, 10

99 Bishop George Ambo, Personal Writings, Keoje 1998, p 14

100 Interview with Stephen Tago, Tape 6, Newton College, Popondetta, 2 November 1998

101 Letter from Mavis Eather to Friends, Gona September 1940

Chapter 9

102 Bishop George Ambo, Personal Writings, Keoje 2000, p 6
Interview with Bishop George Ambo, Newton College, Popondetta, 4 November 1998, pp 4, 5

103 Interview with Bishop George Ambo, Popondetta, 4 November 1997, p 4

104 *ibid*

105 Bishop George Ambo, Personal Writings, Keoje 1998, pp 14, 15

106 Interview with Bishop George Ambo, Newton College, 26 October 1998, p 8

107 Letter from Bishop George Ambo to Mavis Eather, 19 May 1946, All Souls' School, Gona

108 Letter from Marcella Karau to Mavis Eather, 19 May 1946

109 Letter from Bishop George Ambo to Mavis Eather, All Souls' School, Gona, 2 August 1946

110 Interview with Bishop George Ambo, Popondetta, 3 November 2000

111 Bishop George Ambo, Personal Writings, 1998, p 15

112 Bishop George Ambo, Personal Writings, Keoje, 2000, p 6

113 Canon James Benson, *Prisoner's Base and Home Again,* Robert Hale Ltd, London, 1957, p 192

114 Bishop Philip Strong, Obituary for Canon James Benson, *The Anglican*, Friday 14 October 1955

115 Information from Nancy White to Dr Blanche Biggs in undated note
In 1954, Fr Benson, ill at Dogura hospital, permitted Nancy White to copy two poems, written by him in prison in Rabaul. Nancy sent copies of the poems to Blanche Biggs, who later gave them to the author in Brisbane, 1998

116 Information given to the author by Fr John Wardman, Fr Edward Kelly and Miss Elsie Manley

117 Interview with Bishop George Ambo, Popondetta, 3 November 2000

118 Information supplied by Elsie Manley

119 Message from Bishop George Ambo, 1998, p 15 (There seems to be some discrepancy regarding the date for the dedication of Gona as Holy Cross. Dr Blanche Biggs, at Gona for the occasion, wrote in her diary entry for 14 May 1949: 'Holy Cross Day, and Gona's dedication as Holy Cross.')

120 NG Mission (PNGCP), UK, Occasional Paper, No 134, Christmas 1956, p 18

121 NG Mission (PNGCP), UK, Occasional Paper, No 129, February 1952, p 31

122 *ibid*

123 Article by Fr James Benson, *The Anglican*, 11 March, 1955

124 Interview with Bishop George Ambo, Popondetta, 3 November 2000

125 Bishop George Ambo, Personal Writings, 1998, p 14

Chapter 10

126 Nancy White, original MS, *Sangara,* 1951, p 11 (for *Sharing the Climb*, Oxford University Press, Australia, 1991)

127 Letter from Nancy White to her mother, original MS, *Sangara,* 1951, p 34 (for *Sharing the Climb*, Oxford University Press, Australia, 1991)

128 Bishop George Ambo, Personal Writings, 1998, Keoje, 1998, p 16

129 Interview, Bishop George Ambo, Tape 1, Oro Guesthouse, Popondetta, 4 September 1997

130 *ibid*

131 Nancy White, original MS, *Sangara,* 1951, p 60 (for *Sharing the Climb*, Oxford University Press, Australia, 1991)

132 Bishop George Ambo, Personal Writings, 1998, p16

133 Nancy White, original MS, *Sangara,* 1951, p 61 (for *Sharing the Climb*, Oxford University Press, Australia, 1991)

134 Interview with Bishop George Ambo, Newton College, 28 October 1998

135 Interview with Bishop George Ambo, Oro Guesthouse, Popondetta, 4 September 1997

136 Interview with Bishop George Ambo, 26 October 1998, Newton College

137 Interview with Bishop George Ambo, Tape 1, 4 September 1997
     Also, Bishop George Ambo, Personal Writings, Keoje, 1998, pp 16, 17, 18

138 Nancy White, original MS, *Sangara,* 1951, pp 78, 79, 81–83 (for *Sharing the Climb*, Oxford University Press, Australia, 1991)

139 Interview with Bishop George Ambo, Popondetta, 3 November 2000.

140 Text given to the author by the Rev'd Denys Ririka, son of Albert Maclaren Ririka, Newton College, November 1998

141 Interview with Bishop George Ambo, Newton College, 27 October 1998, pp 3, 4

142 Elin Johnston, *Dodoima – Tales of Oro*, 1995, p 93
     Also, Nancy White, original MS, *Sangara,* 1951, p 83 (for *Sharing the Climb*, Oxford University Press, Australia, 1991)

143 Interview with George Ambo, Newton College, 27 October 1998, pp 3, 4

144 Timothy Kinahan, *A Church is Born, 1983, The Anglican Church in Papua New Guinea.* Printed by PNGCP, UK

145 Nancy White, original MS, *Sangara,* 1951, pp 87, 88 (for *Sharing the Climb*, Oxford University Press, Australia, 1991)

146 Interview with George Ambo, 4 September 1997
     Also Bishop George Ambo, Writings, November 2000

147 Interview with George Ambo, Newton College, 27 October 1998

148 *ibid*
     Also, Nancy White, original MS, *Sangara,* 1951, pp 99–102 (for *Sharing the Climb*, Oxford University Press, Australia, 1991

149 Fr James Benson, article in *The Anglican*, 4 March 1955

150 Interview with Bishop George Ambo, 4 September 1997, p 8
     Also Bishop George Ambo, Writings, November 2000

151 NG Mission Society (PNGCP) UK Occasional Paper No 129, February 1952, pp 33–37

152 Nancy White, original MS, *Sangara,* 1951, pp 119, 200 (for *Sharing the Climb*, Oxford University Press, Australia, 1991)

153 George Ambo, letter to Nancy White, Newton College, Ganuganuana, Milne Bay, 7 September 1952

154 Interview with Bishop George Ambo, 4 September 1997, p 9

Chapter 11

155 NG Mission (PNGCP), UK, Occasional Paper, No 130, December 1952, p 9

156 NG Mission (PNGCP), UK, Occasional Paper, No 146, Summer 1967, pp 14, 15
Bishop John Chisholm, *Clergy Training in NG*
David Wetherell, *Reluctant Mission, The Anglican Church in Papua New Guinea 1891–1942*,
pub University of Queensland Press, 1977, p 273

157 *ibid* pp 53, 280, 283, 303

158 *ibid* pp 273, 275

159 *ibid* p 339

160 Right Rev'd Philip Nigel Strong, MA, Bishop of NG, *Out of Great Tribulation*, written for
his Diocesan Conference at Dogura, Papua, 30 June 1947, pp 72, 73

161 Bishop George Ambo, Personal Communications, Keoje, Gona, pp 7, 8, 9

162 Interview with Rev'd Douglas Jones, York, 2 June 2000, pp 2, 3, 7

163 Bishop George Ambo, Personal Communications, Keoje, pp 9, 10

164 Interview with Rev'd Charles Helms, Melbourne, January 2000, pp 2, 6

165 Interview with Bishop George Ambo, Tape 1a, Popondetta, 4 September 1997, p 9

166 Interview with Bishop George Ambo, Tape 3, Newton College, Popondetta,
28 October 1998, pp 2, 3

167 Letter from Bishop George Ambo to Mavis Eather, Newton College, 5 April 1954 (in the
possession of Mrs P Hyde)

168 Interview with Oliver Ambo, Port Moresby 3 November 1998, Tape 7, p 5

169 Interview with Helen Ambo, Newton College 4 November 1998, Tape 8

170 Interviews with Sr Jean Henderson, Melbourne, 2000, p 6; Rev'd D Jones, York, 2000, p 2;
Rev'd Charles Helms, Melbourne, 2000, pp 2, 4, 5, 6, 7

171 Interview with Bishop George Ambo, Tape 3, Newton College, 28 October 1998, p 2

172 Interview with Sr Jean Henderson, 12 July 2000, p 6

173 Rev'd Eric Cassidy, in *ABM Review*, November 1960, *The Papuan Ministry*

174 Bishop John Chisholm, in NG Mission Society (PNGCP), UK, Occasional Paper, No 146,
Summer 1967, *Clergy Training in NG*, pp 14, 15

175 Interview with Bishop George Ambo, Tape 8, Newton College, 4 November 1998, pp 2, 3

176 Interview with Dr Blanche Biggs, Brisbane, 9 November 1998

177 Interview with Rev'd C Helms, January 2000, p 3

178 Bishop George Ambo, Personal Communications, Keoje, 2000, p 10ff

179 Dr Blanche Biggs, Note from Diary, June 1958

180 Bishop George Ambo, Personal Communications, Keoje, 2000, p 12

181 Interview with Bishop George Ambo, Tape 8, Newton College, 4 November 1998, p 4

182 NG Mission (PNGCP), UK, Occasional Paper, No. 133, May 1956, pp 8, 9

183 NG Mission (PNGCP), UK, Occasional Paper, No. 134, Christmas 1956, Extract
from the Bishop of New Guinea's Address at Conference, January, 1956

184 NG Mission (PNGCP), UK, Occasional Paper, No 146, Summer 1967,
Bishop John Chisholm, *Clergy Training*, p 16

185 NG Mission (PNGCP), UK, Occasional Paper, Article by Rev'd GE Reindorp,
Vicar of St Stephen with St John, Westminster, printed in year book for the parish,
November 1951, pp 50–52

186 NG Mission (PNGCP), UK, Occasional Paper, No. 134, Christmas 1956, pp 34, 35
     NG Mission (PNGCP), UK, Occasional Paper, No. 131, December 1953, p 3

187 Bishop George Ambo, Personal Communications, Keoje, 2000, p 12

188 The Rev'd Peter Robin, Communication to the author, 30 March 2001

189 George Ambo, Personal Communications, Keoje, 2000, p 12

190 Interview with Rev'd D Jones, York 2000
     NG Mission (PNGCP), UK, Occasional Paper, No 136, August, 1958, Articles by
     Bishop P Strong and Rev'd Norman Cruttwell, pp 3, 10–13

191 Dr Blanche Biggs, Note from Diary

192 Bishop George Ambo, Personal Communications, p 14
     Interview with Bishop George Ambo, Tape 2, Popondetta, 1997

193 Interview with Oliver Ambo, Tape 3, Port Moresby, 1997, p 8

194 Interview, Bishop George Ambo, Tape 8, Newton College, 4 November 1998, p 3

195 Bishop George Ambo, Personal Communications, Keoje, 2000, p 15

Chapter 12

196 NG Mission (PNGCP), UK, Occasional Paper No 130, December 1952, Letter
     from the Bishop of New Guinea (Bishop Philip Strong), p 5

197 Bishop George Ambo, Personal Writings, Keoje 2000, p 13

198 *Komboro*, St Aidan's College Magazine, No 6, December 1958, pp 8, 9

199 *ibid*

200 George Ambo, Personal Writings, Keoje 2000, pp 16, 17

201 NG Mission (PNGCP), UK, Occasional Paper No 129, February 1952, pp 29, 30

202 *Komboro,* No 1, January 1958, p 5

203 NG Mission (PNGCP), UK, Occasional Paper No 136, August 1958, pp 12, 13

204 Fr Oliver Brady, letter to Dr Blanche Biggs, Garogarona 26 February 1956, in the
     possession of Bishop Oliver Heyward

205 Interview with Stephen Tago, Popondetta, 2 November 98, Tape 6, pp 5, 6, 12, 13

206 Fr Oliver Brady, letter to Dr Blanche Biggs, St Aidan's College, 26 September 1957

207 Bishop George Ambo, Personal Writings, Keoje, 2000, p 17

208 *Komboro* No 6, December 1958, p 6

209 Fr Oliver Brady, letter to Dr Blanche Biggs, Hobart 23 March 1959

210 *Komboro* No 6, December 1958, pp 4, 5, 6

211 Bishop George Ambo, Personal Writings, Keoje, 2000, p 17

212 *Komboro* No 12, December 1959, p 2

213 Christopher Garland, *Romney Gill, Missionary 'Genius' and Craftsman*, pub Christians
     Aware, Leicester, England, 2000, pp 57, 58, 129

214 David Wetherell, *Reluctant Mission: The Anglican Church in Papua New Guinea (1891–1942)*,
     pub University of Queensland Press, 1977, p 315

215 Bishop George Ambo, Personal Writings, Keoje 2000, pp 18–21

216 Bishop George Ambo, letter to Mavis Eather, Boianai, 7 December 1959, in the
     possession of Mrs P Hyde

217 Bishop George Ambo, letter to Mavis Eather, All Saints' Church, Boianai, 25 February
     1960

218 George Ambo, Personal Writings, Keoje 2000, pp 23, 24, 27

219 Bishop of New Guinea, letter to the staff, Dogura 10 August 1960, pp 7, 8, 35, 36
     Philip Strong's Diary, 8th May and 9th May 1960, courtesy of Elsie Manley
     Bishop George Ambo, Personal Writings, Popondetta September 2001

220 Bishop George Ambo, Personal Writings, pp 24–27

221 *ibid*

222 *ibid*

Chapter 13

223 Interview with Dr Blanche Biggs, Brisbane, 9 November 1998, p 10

224 Letter from the Bishop of New Guinea to the Staff, Dogura, 10 August 1960, pp 7, 8, 35, 36, in the possession of Elsie Manley

225 Bishop George Ambo, Personal Writings, Keoje, 2000, pp 25–27

226 Interview with Oliver Ambo, Port Moresby, 1997, Tape 3 p 10

227 Holy Name Secondary High School for Girls had been established at Dogura by 1960.

228 Interview with Stephen Tago, former Minister for Defence in the PNG Government, and friend of Bishop George Ambo, Newton College, 2 November 1990

229 Interview with Bishop George Ambo, Popondetta, 1997, Tape 2 pp 7, 8

230 George Ambo, Personal Writings, Keoje 2000, pp 28–35.
     Also, in 1958, Henry Kendall, a priest from England, had been appointed Mission Secretary and Rector of Samarai. He was later consecrated Bishop of the Milne Bay District. See *Not Forever in Green Pastures, the Personal Memoirs of the Rt Revd HTA Kendall, MA*, pub by the Diocese of Queensland, pp 169, 170, 239

231 Fr Lashford was an Australian priest in Port Moresby. The Franciscan Friars had come to Koki, Port Moresby, in 1958–59, according to Bishop David Hand.

232 Information from Sr Jean Henderson

233 Interview with Oliver Ambo, Port Moresby 1997, Tape 3 pp 7, 8

234 Rev'd Eric Hawkey, Provincial Chaplain for the Province of Queensland and Organising Secretary for ABM

235 Canon Oliver Brady, letter to Dr Blanche Biggs, Yarrabah, 11 November 1960, in the possession of Bishop Oliver Heyward, Melbourne

236 Bishop George Ambo, Personal Writings, Keoje, 2000, p 35

237 Bishop George Ambo, Description of Consecration, Keoje, 2000, pp 1–7

238 Canon Oliver Brady, letter to Dr Blanche Biggs, Yarrabah, 11 November 1960

Chapter 14

239 Letter from Dr Blanche Biggs, St. Luke's Tuberculosis Hospital, Embi, Papua, 13 November 1960

240 In *Papuan Pastor, The Story of George Ambo, Auxiliary Bishop of NG,* p 16
     Bishop George Ambo, Personal Writings, November 2000, p 6

241 Bishop George Ambo, Personal Writings, November 2000, p1

242 Canon Oliver Brady, letter, Yarrabah, No 11, 1960

243 Dr Blanche Biggs, letter, Embi, 27 November, 1960

244 Bishop GeorgeAmbo, Personal Writings, November 2000, p 5

245 Dr Blanche Biggs, letter, Embi, 27 November, 1960

246 Bishop George Ambo, Personal Writings, November 2000, pp 1–4

247 *ibid*

248 Bishop GeorgeAmbo, Personal Writings, September 2001, pp 2–8

249 *Family, News of the Anglican Church in PNG*, December 1989, p 2

250 Interview with Bishop George Ambo, Newton College, Popondetta, 28 October 1998, Tape 3, p 3

251 Dr Blanche Biggs, letter, Embi, 11 March 1961

252 Interview with Fr Edward Kelly, Winchester, 10 June 2000, pp 3, 4

253 Bishop GeorgeAmbo, Personal Writings, September 2001, pp 1–5

254 *ibid*

255 NG Mission (PNGCP), UK, Occasional Paper, No 139, January 1963, pp 1, 3, 4

256 *ibid* pp 1, 2, 8–12

257 Interview with Bishop GeorgeAmbo, Newton College, 28 October 1998, Tape 3, pp 3, 4

258 Graham Hume Hassall, PhD, *Religion and Nation-State Formation in Melanesia: 1945 to Independence*, pub Australian National University, 1990, printed in 1992 by UMI, University Microfilms International, Bell and Howell Information Company, Michigan, Ch 6, pp 131–134

259 NG Mission (PNGCP), UK, Occasional Paper, No 141, Lent 1964, pp 1, 8–12

260 Dr Blanche Biggs, letters, Embi, 13 July 1963 and 9 February, 1964

Chapter 15

261 Henry Kendall, *Not Forever in Green Pastures, The Personal Memoirs of The Rt Revd HTA Kendall, MA,* pub Diocese of North Queensland, pp 148, 192, 193

262 *ibid* p 138

263 *ibid* p 143

264 Bishop George Ambo, Personal Writings, Popondetta, 2001, pp 2, 3

265 Interview with Ray Kendall, Brisbane, November 1998, pp 10, 11

266 Interview with Bishop George Ambo, Popondetta, 1998, Tape 4B, p 5

267 Interview with Bishop David Hand, Port Moresby, 2000

268 Interview with Edward and Ruth Kelly, Winchester, June 2000

269 Interview with Stephen Tago, Tape 4, November 1998, Popondetta, p 4
     Interview with Bishop George Ambo, Tape 2A, Popondetta, 1997, pp 10, 11

270 Interview with Bishop George Ambo, Tape 1B, October 1998, Popondetta, p 6
     Interview with Bishop George Ambo, Tape 2a, October 1998, pp 1, 2, 3

271 Recommended by the late Archbishop Sir Frank Woods, for trial in Melbourne in the late 1960s. First published in 1964 by SPCK, London. Made and printed in Great Britain by Camelot Press Ltd, London

272 Edward Stourton, *Absolute Truth*, first pub in 1998 by Penguin Books Ltd, Harmondsworth, Middlesex, England, pp 187-196

273 Interview with Bishop George Ambo, Tape 2a, October 1998, pp 1, 2, 3

274 Interview with Bishop George Ambo, Tape 1b, October 1998, pp 5, 6

275 David Wetherell, *Reluctant Mission: The Anglican Church in Papua New Guinea (1891–1942)*, pub University of Queensland Press, Queensland, 1977, p 65

276 Christopher Garland, *Romney Gill, Missionary 'Genius' and Craftsman*, first pub Christians Aware, Leicester, UK, 2000, pp .224, 225, 226

277 Henry Kendall, *Not Forever in Green Pastures, The Personal Memoirs of The Rt Revd HTA Kendall, MA,* pub Diocese of Queensland, pp 144, 197, 198

278 Letter from Nancy White, Manau via Popondetta and Ioma, 12 December, 1956, to The British & Foreign Bible Society, Sydney

279 Interview with Denys Ririka, Newton College, Popondetta, November 1998, Tape 4a, p 12, and Tape 7, pp 1, 2

280 Interview with Stephen Tago, Newton College, Popondetta, 1998

Chapter 16

281 Diocese of PNG Newsletter, Easter 1974, pp 11–16

282 Dr David Wetherell suggests that Bishop George may have been thinking of Bishop M Stone-Wigg's booklet: *The Papuans: A People of the South Pacific*, edited by HH Montgomery, London 1907. See David Wetherell, *Reluctant Mission: The Anglican Church in Papua New Guinea (1891–1942)*, pub University of Queensland Press, 1977, pp 135, 136, 361

283 Ganga Powell, compiler, *Through Melanesian Eyes. An Anthology of PNG Writing*, pub The Macmillan Company of Australia Pty Ltd, 1987, p 190

Also, John D Waiko, *A Short History of PNG*, pub Oxford University Press, 1993, p 267

284 Ulli Beier, ed *Black Writing from New Guinea*, published by University of Queensland Press, 1973, pp xii, xiii

285 John Kasaipwalova, *Reluctant Flame*,1987, in *Through Melanesian Eyes* (see note 283 above), pp 144, 145

286 John D Waiko, *A Short History of PNG*, pub Oxford University Press, 1993, pp153–193

287 *Diocese of PNG Newsletter*, August 1971, pp 4, 5, 10

NG Mission (PNGCP), UK, Occasional Paper, September 1971, pp 4, 7

288 Arthur Jawodimbari, *Politics of Confusion and Religion*, article in *Prelude to Self-Government, Electoral Politics in PNG 1972*, Editor David Stone, pub Research School of Pacific Studies and University of PNG at the Australian National University, Canberra, ACT, 1976, pp 492–503

289 Elin Johnston, *Dodoima – Tales of Oro*, published by the author, production by Pacifika Press, Auckland, 1995, pp 1–5

290 *Post Courier*, 14 April 1972, pp 24, 25, 29

Also, *A Message to the People of the Orokaiva and the Blocks*, from MJ Denehy, ADC

291 Interview with Bishop GeorgeAmbo, Newton College, 20 May 2002, Tape 1

292 Interview with Archdeacon Martin Chittleborough, May 1998, Tape 4

293 Report by MJ Denehy, ADC, Division of District Administration, Popondetta ND, 29 February 1972

294 Interview with Bishop George Ambo, Newton College, 20 May 2002, Tape 1

295 NG Mission (PNGCP), UK, Occasional Paper, April 1975, p 4

Also, NG Mission (PNGCP), UK, Occasional Paper, August 1975, p 5

296 Interview with Bishop George, Tape 1, May 2002, 27 October 1998, Tape 2

297 Letter from Martin Chittleborough, Christian Training Centre, Popondetta, April 1975

298 Graham Hume Hassall, PhD, *Religion and Nation-State Formation in Melanesia: 1945 to Independence*, Australian National University, 1990, pp 317, 318

299 NG Mission (PNGCP), UK, Occasional Paper, April 1976, pp 3, 4

300 NG Mission (PNGCP), UK, Occasional Paper, 1973, pp 7, 10

301 NG Mission (PNGCP), UK, Occasional Paper, April 1977, pp 3, 7, 8

302 NG Mission (PNGCP), UK, Occasional Paper, April 1977, pp 8, 9

303 Bishop George Ambo, Personal Writings, Keoje, 2002

304 Letter from Martin Chittleborough to his father, CT Chittleborough, Popondetta, 28 April 1975

Chapter 17

305 Letter from Philip Strong to Bishop George Ambo, Cathedral Close, Wangaratta, 30 May 1977

306 Letter from Bishop George Ambo to Philip Strong, Popondetta, 14 June 1977

307 Letter from Bishop George Ambo to Martin Chittleborough, Popondetta, 15 June 1977

308 Bishop George Ambo, Personal Writings, Keoje, 2002

309 *Family, News of the Anglican Church in PNG*, December 1989, p 2

310 Letters from Bishop George Ambo to his daughters, Popondetta, 22 July 22 1977

311 Letter from Bishop George Ambo to Diocesan Chairman, Gloucester, UK, September 1977

312 NG Mission (PNGCP), UK, Occasional Paper, November 1978, pp 12, 13, 32, 33

313 *ibid* pp 3, 6, 7

314 *ibid* p 30
Letter from Bishop George Ambo to his sons, Popondetta, 15 June 1978
Interview Bishop Ambo, Popondetta, November 1997

315 Henry Kendall, *Not Forever in Green Pastures, Personal Memoirs of The Rt Revd HTA Kendall*, MA, pub Diocese of North Queensland

316 Personal Writings, Bishop George Ambo, Keoje, October 2001

317 Personal Writings, Bishop George Ambo, Keoje, 2002, p 9

316 Interview with Bishop George Ambo, Oro Guest House, Popondetta, November 1997

319 Interview with Bishop George Ambo, Newton College, 2002, Tape 2, pp 7, 8

320 Interview with Martin Chittleborough, Port Willunga, South Australia, May 1998

321 Interview with Bishop George Ambo, Popondetta 2001, Tape 1, p 14

Chapter 18

322 Papua New Guinea Church Partnership (PNGCP), 32 Kings Orchard, Eltham, London, SE9 5TJ, Occasional Paper, November 1983

323 Bishop George Ambo, Personal Writings, Keoje, 2002, pp 5, 6

324 Interview with Bishop George Ambo, Popondetta, 2001, Tape 1, pp 9, 10
Interview with Lancelot Sangitari, Popondetta, 2001, Tape 2, p 3
Statement by Tom Williams, August 2002

325 Papua New Guinea Church PartnershipPNGCP, UK, Occasional Paper November 1985, pp 4, 5

326 Interview with Peter Hill, Popondetta, 1986

327 Rex Kaikuyama, *Pentecostal-Charismatic Movement and the United Church*, MTh Thesis (unpublished), presented to the Faculty of the Pacific Theological College, Suva, September 2001, pp 63-64

328 *ibid* p 70
Also, Jeremy Beckett, *Torres Strait Islanders: Custom and Colonialism*, Cambridge University Press, pp 79-84

329 Interview with Bishop George Ambo, Popondetta, 2001, Tape 1
Notes from Tom Williams, August 2002

330 Interview with Bishop George Ambo, Newton College, May 2002, Tape 1, pp 4, 5
Notes from Tom Williams, August 2002

331 Interviews with Stephen Tago and Arthur Jawodimbari, Popondetta, 2001, Tape 2, pp 5, 6

332 Interview with Bishop George Ambo, Newton College, May 2002, Tape 1, pp 10, 11

333 Letter from Elin Johnston to Nancy White, Martyrs' School, 1989

334 Interview with George Ambo, Popondetta, November 2001, Tape 1 side A

335 Bishop George Ambo, Personal Writings, Keoje, 2002

336 Interview with George Ambo, Popondetta, 1997, Tape 2, pp 4, 5

337 Interview with Martin Chittleborough, Port Willunga, South Australia, May 1998, Tape 4 side B

Chapter 19

338 George Ambo, Interview Popondetta, 21 November 2002, p 10

339 Stephen Tago, Interview Popondetta, 1998, 7, 8
     Oliver Ambo, Interview Port Moresby, 1998, p 3

340 Denys Ririka, Interview Popondetta, 3 November 1998, p 6

341 George Ambo, Interview Popondetta, November 2001

342 *ibid*

343 Oliver Ambo, Interview Port Moresby, November 1998, p 3

344 Oliver Ambo, Interview Port Moresby, November 1997, pp 9, 10

345 Tom Grahamslaw, *Pacific Islands Monthly*, May 1971, pp 105–118

346 Hank Nelson, Article in *Journal of Pacific History*, Vol XIII 1978: *The Swinging Index, Capital Punishment and British and Australian Administrations in PNG, 1888–1945*, pp 148, 149

347 George Ambo, Interview Popondetta, November 2001

348 George Ambo, Interviews Popondetta November 1997 and November 2001
     Helen Ambo, Interview November 19 98, and Oliver Ambo, Interview Port Moresby, November 1998

349 Denny Bray Guka, Interview Melbourne, July 2000

Chapter 20

350 *Family, News of the Anglican Church in Papua New Guinea*, December 1989, No 34

351 George Ambo, Interview Popondetta, 1997

352 George Ambo, Interview Newton College, 21 May 2002, pp 9, 10

353 Lancelot Sangetari, Arthur Jawodimbari, Stephen Tago, Interviews Popondetta, 27 November 2001
     Martin Chittleborough, Interview Port Willunga, South Australia, May 1998
     David Hand, Interview Martyrs' School, Agenehambo, October 2000

354 Newsletter, PNGCP, UK, Summer 1996

355 George Ambo, Interview Popondetta, 2001

356 Sermon preached at Epping, Sydney, in the 1980s. See the *Creed* in the *Book of Common Prayer*.

References — Books and Other Resources

Beckett, Jeremy: *Torres Strait Islanders: Custom and Colonialism*, Cambridge University Press, UK, 1987

Beier, Ulli (editor): *Black Writing from New Guinea*, pub University of Queensland Press, 1973

Bell, Padre: *Among the Ruins*, pub ABM, 1946

Benson, Fr James: *Prisoner's Base and Home Again*, pub Robert Hale Ltd, London, 1957

Carr-Gregg, Charlotte: see Wetherell, David and Carr-Gregg, Charlotte

Cassidy, Eric: *The Papuan Ministry*, in *ABM Review*, 1960

Chisholm, John: *Clergy Training in NG*, in NG Mission (now PNGCP) Occasional Paper Nos 146, 1967

Chittleborough, Anne: *The Anglican Church in Papua New Guinea*, pub New Guinea Mission, UK, 1976

Chittleborough, Anne: *The Anglican Church in PNG for Primary Schools,* small edition printed locally for use in the author's school class

Dakeyne, RB: *Village and Town in New Guinea*, Longman Australia Pty Ltd, 1968

Eather, Mavis: *Early Gona, Revealing Bishop Ambo's Background*

Garland, Christopher: *Romney Gill, Missionary 'Genius' and Craftsman*, pub Christians Aware, Leicester, UK, 2000

Hand, (Bishop) David, KBE: *Modawa – Papua New Guinea and Me 1946–2002*, pub privately and printed at Sal Press, Port Moresby, PNG, 2002

Hassall, Graham Hume: *Religion and Nation-State Formation in Melanesia: 1945 to Independence*, pub Australian National University, 1960

Hughes, Brian: see Tomkins, Dorothea and Hughes, Brian

Inglis, Thomas: *Reports of Inspection for the Anglican Mission School at Gona*, 1939, 1940

Jawodimbari, Arthur: *Politics of Confusion and Religion* in Stone, David (editor), *Prelude to Self-Government, Electoral Politics in PNG 1972*, pub Research School of Pacific Studies and University of PNG at the Australian National University, Canberra, ACT, 1976

Johnston, *Elin: Dodoima–Tales of Oro*, privately published, 1995

Kaikuyama, Rex: *Pentecostal-Charismatic Movement and the United Church*, unpublished MTh thesis, Faculty of the Pacific Theological College, Suva, Fiji, 2001

Kasaipwalova, John: *Reluctant Flame* in Powell, Ganga (compiler), *Through Melanesian Eyes. An Anthology of PNG Writing*, pub Macmillan Company of Australia Pty Ltd, 1987

Kendall, HTA: *Not Forever in Green Pastures, the Personal Memoirs of the Rt Revd HTA Kendall, MA*, pub Diocese of Queensland

Kiki, Albert Maori: *Ten Thousand Years in a Lifetime*, pub 1968

Kinahan, Timothy: *A Church is Born, The Anglican Church in PNG, 1891-1991*, pub PNGCP, UK, 1983

Manubada, Warrington Yaruso: *A Story of the Anglican Mission*, pub Holy Cross Press, Gona, Papua, 1960

Monckton, CAW: *Some Experiences of a New Guinea Resident Magistrate*, pub Lane & Co, London, 1920

Powell, Ganga (compiler): *Through Melanesian Eyes. An Anthology of PNG Writing*, pub The Macmillan Company of Australia Pty Ltd, 1987

Reindorp, GE: article in NG Mission (now PNGCP) Occasional Paper, reprinted in *St Stephen with St Paul, Westminster, Parish Year Book*, UK, 1951

Smyth, Charles: *The Church and Nation*, pub Hodder and Stoughton, Great Britain, 1962

Stone, David (editor), *Prelude to Self-Government, Electoral Politics in PNG 1972*, pub Research School of Pacific Studies and University of PNG at the Australian National University, Canberra, ACT, 1976

Stourton, Edward: *Absolute Truth*, pub Penguin Books Ltd, Harmondsworth, UK, 1998

Strong, Philip Nigel: *Out of Great Tribulation*, address at Diocesan Conference, Dogura, 1947

Tomkins, Dorothea and Hughes, Brian: *The Road from Gona*, pub Angus and Robertson Ltd, Great Britain, 1969

Waiko, John D: *A Short History of PNG*, pub Oxford University Press, 1993

Waiko, John D: *Be Jijimo: A History According to the (Oral) Tradition of the Binandere People of Papua New Guinea* (doctoral thesis)

Wetherell, David: *Reluctant Mission: The Anglican Church in Papua New Guinea, 1891–1942*, pub University of Queensland Press, 1977

Wetherell, David: *ABM Review of Mission*, 1977

Wetherell, David and Carr-Gregg, Charlotte: *Camilla: CH Wedgwood 1901–1955, A Life*, pub NSW University Press, 1990

White, Nancy: *Sharing the Climb*, pub Oxford University Press, Australia, 1981

Newpapers, Periodicals (various issues and dates)

ABM Review

Bush Brother, The

Church Times, UK

Family, News of the Anglican Church in PNG

Komboro, St Aidan's College Magazine

Newsletter, Diocese of PNG

Occasional Papers, NG Mission (now PNGCP), UK

Papuan Pastor

Post Courier, PNG

Post Courier

Interviews (various dates and places — refer Index)

Ambo, George

Ambo, Helen

Ambo, Maureen

Ambo, Oliver

Chittleborough, Martin

Helms, Charles

Henderson, Jean

Heyward, Oliver

Hill, Peter

Hyde, Patricia

Jawodimbari, Arthur

Jones, Douglas

Kelly, Edward

Ririka, Denys

Sangitari, Lancelot

Tago, Stephen

(list of References continued overleaf)

Personal notes, messages, letters, information, journals, log-books, diaries (refer Index)

Ambo, George

Ambo (Karau), Marcella

Benson, James

Biggs, Blanche

Brady, Oliver

Cassidy, Eric

Chittleborough, Martin

Crutwell, Norman

Denehy, MJ

Eather, Mavis

Hall, Warren

Hand, David

Henderson, Jean

Jenkins, Sarah

Kelly, Edward

Kelly, Ruth

Kendall, Ray

Lodge, Philip

Manley, Elsie

Paisawa, Amy

Parkinson, Mavis

Robin, Peter

Strong, Philip

Wardman, John

Wetherell, David

White, Nancy

Williams, Tom

Mt Lamington area, various local people

Index

A

269

E

Eather, Mavis 16, 17, 18, 19, 20, 22, 24, 25, 26, 30, 31, 33, 34, 35, 52, 56, 66, 67, 75, 97, 102, 117, 233, 234

Eiwo 75, 76, 77, 79, 88, 89, 91, 94, 219 – Church of St David, *90*

Elizabeth, Queen, see Queen Elizabeth II

Elliot, Sr Nancy 71, *78*, 89, *143*

Embi 44, 138, 145

Embogi 226

Emboia 7, 9, 15

Eroro 137, 138, 196

Eupu, Edric 177

Ewa-ge

Ewa-ge language 7, 58, 66, 102, 164, 166, 168, 191, 223, 236, 240

F

Franciscan Brothers 192, 229

G

Gadebo, Fr (later Bishop) Isaac 195, 203, 216

Galilee, Lake of 160

Garara 15, 54, 62, 88, 200, 211, 214

Garogarona 50

Gatara 1, 2, 68, 101

Gaume 5

Gill, Fr Cecil 28, 30

Gill, Fr Romney 26, 28, 39, 115, 164

Ginjari 5

Gloria 117, 118, 191, 192

Glorious Ascension, Community of the 98

gold 6

Gomberu 54, 55, 57, 58, 59, 61, 64, 65, 66, 67, 69, 70, 198

Gona 1, 5, 6, 9, 15, 16, 17, 20, 21, 24, 25, 28, 33, 35, 37, 38, 39, 42, 43, **45,** 47, 48, 50, 51, 54, 55, 56, 58, 59, 61, 62, 64, 66, 67, 68, 69, 71, 75, 79, 88, 89, 94, 100, 101, 102, 109, 135, 137, 138, 139, 146, 162, 164, 168, 177, 178, 182, 194, 196, 210, 229, 234, 238 See also All Souls' Mission Station and School

Gona Mass, The 164, 168, 223, 240

Gora 197

Gough, Most Reverend HR 130

Govers, Marjorie 70, 71

Grahamslaw, Tom 226

Guise, Edward 209

Guise, John (later Sir John) 148, 151, 183, 209

Guka, Archdeacon Denny Bray 229

Gunther, Dr 88

Guy, Fr Gordon 193, 195, 196

Guy, Peggy 195, 196

H

I

J

U

V

W

Y

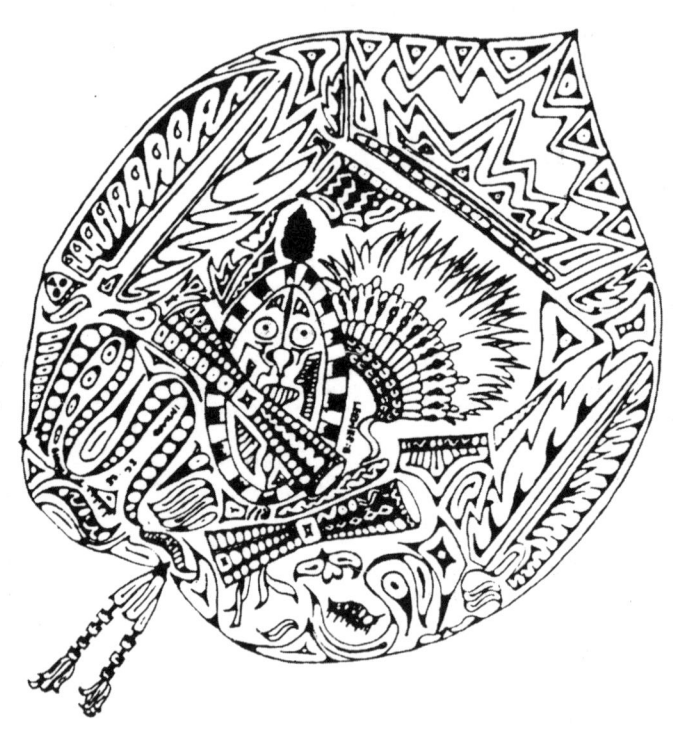